Flip the System Australia

This is a book by educators, for educators. It grapples with the complexities, the humanity and the possibilities in education. In a climate of competing accountabilities and measurement mechanisms; corporate solutions to education 'problems'; and narratives of 'failing' schools, 'underperforming' teachers and 'disengaged' students; this book asks 'What matters?' or 'What should matter?' in education.

Based in the unique Australian context, this book situates Australian education policy, research and practice within the international education narrative. It argues that professionals within schools should be supported, empowered and welcomed into policy discourse, not dictated to by top-down bureaucracy. It advocates for a flipping, flattening and democratising of the education system, in Australia and around the world.

Flip the System Australia: What matters in education brings together the voices of teachers, school leaders and scholars in order to offer diverse perspectives, important challenges and hopeful alternatives to the current education system.

Deborah M. Netolicky has almost 20 years' experience as a teacher, school leader and researcher in Australia and the UK. She is Honorary Research Associate at Murdoch University and Dean of Research and Pedagogy at Wesley College, Perth. Deborah blogs at theeduflaneuse.com and tweets as @debsnet.

Jon Andrews leads his school's staff professional development program, system of teacher coaching and feedback, beginning teacher mentoring and staff engagement with professional learning.

Cameron Paterson is responsible for the strategic leadership of learning and teaching, innovation, and promoting excellence in teaching practice at SHORE School in Sydney. He is closely connected to Harvard's Project Zero. In 2016, he received the 21st Century International Global Innovation Award for Teaching.

Flip the System Australia
What Matters in Education

Edited by Deborah M. Netolicky,
Jon Andrews and Cameron Paterson

LONDON AND NEW YORK

First published 2019
by Routledge
2 Park Square, Milton Park, Abingdon, Oxon OX14 4RN

and by Routledge
711 Third Avenue, New York, NY 10017

Routledge is an imprint of the Taylor & Francis Group, an informa business

© 2019 selection and editorial matter, Deborah M. Netolicky, Jon Andrews and Cameron Paterson; individual chapters, the contributors

The right of the Deborah M. Netolicky, Jon Andrews and Cameron Paterson to be identified as the authors of the editorial material, and of the authors for their individual chapters, has been asserted in accordance with sections 77 and 78 of the Copyright, Designs and Patents Act 1988.

All rights reserved. No part of this book may be reprinted or reproduced or utilised in any form or by any electronic, mechanical, or other means, now known or hereafter invented, including photocopying and recording, or in any information storage or retrieval system, without permission in writing from the publishers.

Trademark notice: Product or corporate names may be trademarks or registered trademarks, and are used only for identification and explanation without intent to infringe.

British Library Cataloguing-in-Publication Data
A catalogue record for this book is available from the British Library

Library of Congress Cataloging-in-Publication Data
Names: Netolicky, Deborah M., editor. | Andrews, Jon, editor. | Paterson, Cameron, editor.
Title: Flip the system Australia : what matters in education / edited by Deborah M. Netolicky, Jon Andrews and Cameron Paterson.
Description: Abingdon, Oxon ; New York, NY : Routledge, [2019]
Identifiers: LCCN 2018031596| ISBN 9781138367616 (hardback) | ISBN 9781138367869 (pbk.) | ISBN 9780429429620 (ebook)
Subjects: LCSH: Educational change--Australia.
Classification: LCC LA2102 .F55 2019 | DDC 370.994--dc23
LC record available at https://lccn.loc.gov/2018031596

ISBN: 978-1-138-36761-6 (hbk)
ISBN: 978-1-138-36786-9 (pbk)
ISBN: 978-0-429-42962-0 (ebk)

Typeset in Bembo
by Integra Software Services Pvt. Ltd.

Contents

List of figures ix
Foreword x
JELMER EVERS

Introduction: what matters in education? 1
DEBORAH M. NETOLICKY, JON ANDREWS AND CAMERON PATERSON

PART I
Teacher identity, voice and autonomy: turning the system inside out 7

1 Elevating the professional identities and voices of teachers and school leaders in educational research, practice and policymaking 9
   DEBORAH M. NETOLICKY

2 Teachers' perceptions of commercialisation in Australian public schools: implications for teacher professionalism 19
   ANNA HOGAN AND BOB LINGARD

3 Flipping the system, but in which direction? reclaiming education as a public concern 30
   GERT BIESTA

4 Podcasts: vehicles for professional growth and system flipping 39
   CAMERON MALCHER

5 Education beyond risk: vulnerability as a challenge to neoliberalism's colour-blind order 43
   BENJAMIN DOXTDATOR

PART II
Collaborative expertise: reprofessionalising the system   53

6   Flipping large-scale assessments: bringing teacher expertise to the table   55
GREG THOMPSON, DAVID RUTKOWSKI AND SAM SELLAR

7   Schools for the future: networks and innovation   64
CAMERON PATERSON AND KEREN CAPLE

8   Developing teacher leadership and collaborative professionalism to flip the system: reflections from Canada   74
CAROL CAMPBELL

9   Changing education in action: lighting the collective efficacy flame   85
GAVIN HAYS AND ADAM HENDRY

10   From weakness to strength: turning the challenge of 'out of field teaching' into a team that thrives   89
YASODAI SELVAKUMARAN

11   Flipping their lids: teachers' wellbeing in crisis   93
ANDY HARGREAVES, SHANEÉ WASHINGTON AND MICHAEL T. O'CONNOR

PART III
Social justice: democratising the system   105

12   "In 2017 we seek to be heard": de-tangling the contradictory discourses that silence Indigenous voices in education   107
MELITTA HOGARTH

13   Locked out, left out: three generations schooled and classed   115
KELLY CHEUNG

14   Learning with connection: shifting teachers' practice through authentic engagement with Aboriginal and Torres Strait Islander communities   124
KEVIN LOWE

15	Empowering Aboriginal and Torres Strait Islander students in schools BEN LEWIS	133
16	Reach them then teach them: engagement in alternative education settings DAN HAESLER AND MELISSA FOTEA	137
17	Makerspace as 'soul work' of public schooling TOMAZ LASIC	145
18	Equitable education in Australia: empowering schools to lead the way PASI SAHLBERG	149

PART IV
Professional learning for a flipped system — 161

19	Coaching for agency: the power of professionally respectful dialogue JON ANDREWS AND CHRIS MUNRO	163
20	Changing the landscape through professional learning RACHEL LOFTHOUSE	172
21	From silo to Study Group: subverting teacher learning RYAN GILL AND CARLA GAGLIANO	182

PART V
Leadership for a flipped system — 187

22	Empowering educators through flipped school leadership? SCOTT EACOTT	189
23	Riding two wild horses: leading Australian schools in an era of accountability REBECCA CODY	198
24	A culture of trust: key practices of compelling leadership PAUL BROWNING	204

25 Context matters: women leading in rural schools 214
    SUSAN BRADBEER

26 One school's journey to create a new education paradigm 222
    RAY TROTTER

27 Finding our roots in the leaves: an ecology of change in leading
    learning that matters 232
    FLOSSIE S. G. CHUA, DAVID N. PERKINS AND DANIEL G. WILSON

    Conclusion: speaking hope into education discourse 242
    DEBORAH M. NETOLICKY, JON ANDREWS AND CAMERON PATERSON

    List of contributors 247
    Index 253

Figures

18.1	Student academic achievement and the strength of socioeconomic gradient in OECD countries in 2015	151
18.2	Science performance score in PISA 2015 and parents' level of education in 2015	154
20.1	Metamorphosis: a practice development led model for individual professional learning and institutional growth	178
26.1	Creating a new education paradigm: the Wooranna Park Primary School journey	227
27.1	Preschoolers Amy, Cathy, Eugene, Rob, and Reena with teacher Lynette George learning to use Blackwood leaves as soap	232

Foreword

Jelmer Evers

While writing the foreword to this wonderful book, I realised that it hasn't been five years since the first book was published in what would turn out to be an international series, a movement even, for and by teachers. *The Alternative: Stop the performativity culture in education*—(it sounds better in Dutch)—was published in October 2013 (Evers and Kneyber 2013). The book was a reaction against what we, as teachers, experienced as an increased narrowing of our collective professional autonomy.

Looking back, a lot has happened in just five years. Things have changed tremendously; French historian Fernand Braudel and the historians of the Anales School argued that doing history consists of the description and understanding of the interaction between different time scales; *Le temps événementiel*, the events that people live through with the inclusion of individual agency, linked more closely to the here and now. *Le temps conjuncturel*, a more long-term history that deals with groups and more general social, political and cultural trends. And finally, *La longue durée*, the very long-term structural history, that Braudel argued was driven more by geography and even the history of ideas (Braudel 1980). Braudel's ideas can be crudely summarised in geographical time, social time and individual time. The above-mentioned historical-temporal perspectives interact with each other and allow us to understand history more clearly, with more nuance, and I would argue that they help us understand the present more clearly.

The Alternative was very much driven by the here and now. By an urgency driven by my own and René Kneyber's classroom practice. My ideas of what was good education and my professional identity clashed with real policies that increasingly promoted a culture of performativity in schools. What supposedly could be measured was supplanting my professional judgement and it was affecting my everyday work with students and colleagues. Of course, *The Alternative* focused on the deep philosophical and ethical dimensions of what it means to be a teacher and what it means to do the right thing. It also offered a broad analysis of the systemic issues plaguing education, captured in the term *Global Education Reform Movement* (GERM), ranging from the global to the national Dutch perspective. The book was situated broadly in a narrative from the 1990s to 2013. The international follow-up, *Flip the System: Changing education from the ground up*, took a more global perspective and although with a very Western bias, it did have the same temporal, social and economic scope of neoliberalism's impact on education. Although the democratic imperative in education and our profession was at the centre of the alternative we formulated—what a flipped system looks like—I don't think we fully grasped how democracy itself was under threat just a couple of years ago.

How different the world looks now came into stark focus when I recently visited the European Parliament in Strasbourg with my students. While most of the international student delegations in their speeches and interventions broadly subscribed to the liberal values underpinning the European Union, it was the student delegation from Hungary that struck a completely different tone. Other delegations differed on details and technicalities and engaged with each other from classical liberal or social-democratic viewpoints, but they all stayed clearly within a democratic and liberal paradigm. The Hungarian students, on the other hand, held the view that Europe should be defended and based on Judeo-Christian values and that individual and minority rights should be subjugated to the view of the majority. In a liberal society, this is their right, of course, but my students immediately picked up the fact that there was a more fundamental clash in worldviews at play that day.

It probably wasn't a coincidence that these students hailed from the country that in Europe has progressed the most towards authoritarianism and illiberal democracy under president Orban. In its yearly report on the state of freedom and democracies *Populists and Autocrats the dual threat to global democracy*, Freedom House writes that, "with populist and nationalist forces making significant gains in democratic states, 2016 marked the 11th consecutive year of decline in global freedom" (Puddington and Roylance 2017). Rising authoritarianism is a symptom, I think. There are many challenges that have come into focus more clearly over the last couple of years, like: rising inequality; the mainstreaming of white supremacy and misogyny; the capture of states by the happy few; the failure of globalisation for the majority of the world's population; surveillance capitalism creeping into our daily lives; deregulation and automation leading to precariousness; the use of Big Data affecting our jobs and welfare states; and Big Tech that goes unchallenged by our politicians. The list goes on and on. These factors are interrelated and profoundly impacting our liberal democracies in a negative way. These same issues are affecting our schools and our profession. Zooming out from the post-Cold War era, taking a long-term historical perspective, shows us what unique and brittle experiments democracy and free quality public education for all actually are.

Of course, these breaking points have been a long time in the making and the publication of Thomas Piketty's (2013) *Capital in the Twenty-first Century*, published in the same year in French, is a watershed moment in several respects. What was confined to the fringes, a critique of capitalism and neoliberalism, has become mainstream. Long-term simmering contradictions between capitalism and democracy have increasingly come to a head, and the long-term perspective has finally broken through again not in the least through

Piketty's own efforts. Short-termism and a very narrow disciplinary perspective have definitely been an ailment that afflicted economics, which in the post-Cold War world has come to dominate public discourse, policy and also educational policy and thinking. It is this short-termism and narrowing of the mind that has been so destructive to education and our profession.

Yet, there is a flipside to this destructive coin. Things we took for granted, have come into focus more clearly as something worth defending. This is what Flip the System to me personally is about. *The Alternative* was a book standing beside a longer line of books of the Professional Honour Foundation, starting in 2008. Over the years, I slowly regained my professional pride and dignity, and this came to be through collaboration, inquiry and reflection, with colleagues from all over the world and across professions. This is what Thijs Jansen calls neo-republican professionalism. As he puts it:

> Republicanism denotes a self-conscious involvement in the common good that we as citizens share in society. It is crucial that citizens themselves determine what should be understood by 'the common good,' … By governing themselves, citizens free themselves from the arbitrary exercise of power by others.
>
> (Jansen 2016)

There is so much strength in a shared professional identity, one that we've lost or remains largely untapped. It is a force that transcends borders and nationalities and is therefore one of the keys to answering the challenges of our time and can form the basis of reinventing democracy and our schools. As Professor Susan Robertson (2018) notes, "education – as a societal good – is both a means to participating in the public, and means of creating 'the public'".

Which brings me back to Flip the System, the series. The books and their ideas have grown out of connections and relationships with teachers from all over the world; from a collective search and need to make education better and more than it is now. In its Swedish context, it was popularised by the never-tiring Sara Hjelm. The original book was edited into a Swedish context by Per Kornhall. *Flip the System UK: A teachers' manifesto* started with two teachers, Jean-Louis Dutaut and Lucy Rycroft-Smith, who met René Kneyber at ResearchED in the UK and who I now consider to be good friends. This Australian book was started by three fellow teachers—Deborah Netolicky, Jon Andrews and Cameron Paterson—who I know, quite well it feels, through social media. Each of the books was born from its local context and propelled by teachers from within that context, but each has local and global contributions and implications. What characterises the books are the different approaches, themes and frameworks. There were gaps in the original *Flip the System*. We didn't address questions about race, gender and Indigenous people, issues that this volume addresses. Australia has its own unique history, traditions and policies. From being a federal system, the influence of NAPLAN and the struggle to implement the recommendations of the first Gonski report.

With the release of the flawed Gonski 2 report in 2018, it seems that this book is more needed than ever.

This volume has enriched my thinking again, opening up a unique Australian perspective, but it also deepens the shared professionalism we, as teachers across the world, have. For example, Melitta Hogarth's powerful testimony that Aboriginal and Torres Strait Islander peoples must have a real say in their own education has both local and universal implications. Either there is equity and equality, or there isn't. Either people have a real voice, or they don't. In the end, education is about human agency *for all*. Agency can be achieved by literally and virtually opening up our classrooms, and by teachers stepping out and being open and connected to the world. This book is yet another testament to the depth and scope of our profession. Reading the contributions gave me a sense of wonder and of possibility. We, as a profession, must extend and connect this to the wider issues facing the world, the democratic imperative. We must also take a long-term view and learn from the challenges, but also the solutions, of the past. If we can harness this energy into organising and activism, a flipped education system is within our grasp. Therefore, I would like to finish with the words from Hillel the Elder that have guided us from the very beginning:

> If I am not for myself, who will be for me?
> But if I am only for myself, who am I?
> If not now, when?

References

Braudel, F., 1980. *On history*. Chicago, IL: University of Chicago Press.
Evers, J. and Kneyber, R., 2013. *Het alternatief: Weg met de afrekencultuur in het onderwijs!* Amsterdam: Boom.
Jansen, T., 2016. Sketch of a neo-republican frame for understanding and promoting the resistance of public professionals in education and healthcare. *Workshop IISL Radical Temporality: Law, Order and Resistance*, Oñati.
Piketty, T., 2013. *Le capital au XXIe siècle*. Paris: Le Seuil.
Puddington, A. and Roylance, T., 2017. *Populists and autocrats: The dual threat to global democracy. Freedom in the world 2017*. London: Freedom House.
Robertson, S., 2018. Recovering the political in the idea of education as a public good—and why this matters. *Unite4Education*. Available from: www.unite4education.org/global-response/recovering-the-political-in-the-idea-of-education-as-a-public-good-and-why-this-matters/ [Accessed May 1 2018].

Introduction

What matters in education?

Deborah M. Netolicky, Jon Andrews and Cameron Paterson

The welcome

Welcome to *Flip the System Australia: What matters in education*. It is a book, a moment in a movement, and a collective roar into the abyss of the international education narrative. Like educational practice throughout the world, this book builds on the stories, perspectives and research of those who have come before. We are grateful to Thijs Jansen's Professional Pride series, René Kneyber and Jelmer Evers' *Het alternatief* (2014), their original Flip the System book (Evers and Kneyber 2016), and Lucy Rycroft-Smith and Jean-Louis Dutaut's *Flip the System: A Teachers' Manifesto* (2018). They and their many contributors have laid the path to which we are adding. This book is, in many ways, the third book in the Flip the System series (although we use 'series' loosely, as the publications are ones that have grown organically and wildly from grass roots). It is in one way the next part of a layered international conversation, this time bedded in an Australian context. It is also its own treasure trove of perspectives around education, a diverse jewel-like collection of teacherly and scholarly voices with an important contribution to make locally and globally. It is a platform for reclaiming education for the teaching profession in ways that focus on the multiplicities, complexities and humanity of education, as well as the role of research and data.

Australia is unique. It is a country with a national curriculum, but one implemented by disparate state education systems with different levels of autonomy. Within Australia—the world's largest island, the world's sixth-largest country and the world's second most sparsely-populated continent—contexts are manifold. Our diverse population largely clings to the coastline in cities, but we have a plethora of isolated rural towns. Our schools are public and independent, primary and secondary, co-educational and single-sex, boarding and sporting. They are funded in complex ways by federal and state governments. In 2008, the *Melbourne Declaration on Educational Goals for Young Australians* set out a vision for Australian education that persists today, and that is reflected in the contributions of this book: that

> Australia values the central role of education in building a democratic, equitable and just society—a society that is prosperous, cohesive and

> culturally diverse, and that values Australia's Indigenous cultures as a key part of the nation's history, present and future.
>
> (Barr et al. 2008, p. 4)

Of its two goals, the first was that Australian schooling promotes equity and excellence. Democracy, equity, justice and diversity are at the core of Australian education and of this book, but they are often challenged by the realities of the education system in which schools and teachers must operate. For instance, although the first Gonski review (Gonski et al. 2011) made the case for equitable school funding that was needs based and sector blind, that case was not realised thanks to various political machinations. Australia suffers from a disconnect between bureaucracy and the profession, and a tension between its vision for equitable education and the realities of competition and marketisation.

Australia, perhaps shackled to its colonial past, is inclined to follow other countries such as the UK and the US in its education policy and practice. Many of our educational tensions are well known and globally shared: top-down punitive accountability (Fullan and Quinn 2016), pedagogy debates, a climate of competition and separation between colleagues (Clarke 2018), increasing reliance on numeric data to track learning (Wood 2018), the negative effects of testing and an epidemic of anxiety (Hargreaves 2018). The Australian education system is driven in part, as other countries' education systems are, by performative measures. We have the AITSL professional standards for teachers and principals (but, oddly, not for middle leaders). We have the national testing regimes of NAPLAN and OLNA, and the international ones of TIMSS, PIRLS and PISA. We have the Australian Tertiary Admission Rank (ATAR) and its associated examinations. The wave of testing and data seems to have reached a critical mass and is eroding the richness of the school experience. While the current generation of teachers knows no other narrative in schooling (Fitzgerald 2017), we should heed warnings about the over-attribution of causality in relation to standardised tests such as PISA, the negative effects of pairing standardised testing with punitive accountability regimes, and competition between countries in the global testing race (Sellar, Thompson and Rutkowski 2017). As Wiliam (2018) notes, "looking at what other countries are doing has its place, but the solutions will have to be home grown" (p. 89).

The second Gonski review into Australian education (Gonski et al. 2018) responded with alarm to Australia's declining PISA ranking with a suite of recommended reforms around curriculum, assessment, reporting, standards and professional learning. While the review invited stakeholder submissions, including those from teachers, its deficit language of 'cruising' schools and teachers who it suggests only support students to 'attain the minimum proficiency' smacks of a distrust of the teaching profession and deficit assumptions about current education practices. It is in this environment of professional criticism, distrust, and a focus on standardised measuring of student achievement, that marketised 'what works' solutions and corporate data solutions are increasingly being peddled in the Australian context. As Elmore (2016) and Ball (2018) note, education systems, and the meaning of education itself, are being transformed and colonised by the commercial products, services, partnerships and players now operating in education. Competition has left schooling as the plaything for the highest bidders, think-tanks and ideologues. Education has become a commodity, but the teaching profession can push back against neoliberal mechanisms and advocate for a re-humanising of schooling. Yet context is the key to what *might work* in education settings. While effective education policy emanates from evidence, education evidence is diverse and complex (Fitzgerald 2017). As Wiliam (2016) notes, 'What works?' is rarely the right question in education, as "just about everything works somewhere, and nothing works everywhere" (p. 63). Rather than looking to other countries as exemplars because of their PISA ranking, or following a purist 'what works' agenda, schools and systems would benefit from asking what might work, in what contexts, and under what conditions. We propose that the question we should be asking and exploring is 'What matters?' in education.

The system

Education is a vast human and economic resource that is relentlessly changing. Schools, education departments and school districts have an insatiable appetite for signals that reassure us that progress is occurring. The future is the basis for much educational thought, enacted through policy, professional learning and practice. Schools and teachers look ahead, plan ahead and are propelled by a desire for progress. Everyone seems to want the future and we want it to be *better*. In this frame, education is viewed as a linear process—by age and by gradual mastery—in which education successively leads towards 'the future' in a sequential fashion. Schools are structured by years, weeks, timetabled lessons, modules of curriculum, consecutive assessments. There is the assumption of undeviating progression towards clear outcomes. Attendance is recorded. Tests are marked. Structured disciplinary knowledge is progressively mastered and accrued until the educated masses are released into the world beyond schooling. Professional standards are categorised by career stage and teachers are expected to march along predetermined lines of professional growth. This linear accumulation of time, experience, knowledge and school experience has optimistic intentions to prepare each student for their future, and to support each teacher through their career. We would, however, be wise to meditate on Sellar's (2016) point that the noble and optimistic aim of 'reaching all' and 'benefitting all' is strewn with complexity and politics that can hinder the promise of education. A laser-like focus on progress and on preparation for the future can lead to a simplified understanding of education and its dehumanisation, in which we value spreadsheets, numbers, box-ticking, percentages, test scores and quantitative data over the complexities of the individual, of teaching, of learning, and of schools.

This is 'the system' we are working to flip. Evers and Kneyber (2016) conceptualise the education system as a hierarchical pyramid with governments and policymakers at the apex, making decisions disconnected from those at the nadir: school leaders, teachers and students. Schools in this system are highly bureaucratic institutional settings, and teachers are increasingly undervalued, constrained individuals. The longitudinal Australian Principal Health and Wellbeing Survey (Riley 2017) reveals increasing workload, emotional labour and wellbeing issues for those working in Australian schools. Those individuals or groups that wield influence on policy and operate bureaucratically are physically removed from schools but construct narrow, publicly scrutinised measures of the success of schooling and these impact on teacher agency. Students and their thinking are often invisible or ignored in the measurement of educational impact. Rather, the representations of learning made public are marks and rankings. These neoliberal apparatuses have the regrettable effect of fuelling a culture of performativity and leading to the fabrication of inauthentic performed professional identities. One aspect of the future that creates strong debate is the suggestion that there will be an inevitable obsolescence of teachers in the educative process. While there already exists the ominous but sophisticated means to harvest psycho-behavioural data to inform interventions, and artificial intelligence promises to personalise and deliver knowledge transactions, teachers are our best chance of forecasting change and coping with the ethical and intellectual challenges of unpredictability.

The contributors

This is largely a book by educators, for educators. We three Editors are all practising teachers and school leaders, working in three schools in three different states of Australia: Western Australia, Queensland, and New South Wales. We all teach high school classes and have co-curricular responsibilities alongside our leadership roles. Our thinking for this book began when we wrote a brief contribution for *Flip the System UK* (see Netolicky et al. 2018). Our co-writing and co-editing has occurred primarily online in spaces such as Google Docs, Dropbox, email and Twitter direct messaging. Despite this being a two year project, it was only at the point of book completion that we finally met at a national conference, for the first time in the same place. The work for this book has happened in the in-between spaces in our lives; between our time teaching, leading, parenting, spouse-ing, presenting, and contributing to other education pursuits. While it has been a labour of love and of necessity—we believe deeply in the power and importance of this book —our work as Editors has been a salient reminder to us of why teacher and school leader voices are so rarely heard in system narratives: education work is busy and replete with emotional labour and a seemingly growing list of draws on our time and resources. We are first and foremost in the service of our students, and there are ethical dimensions to working in schools that mean it is often not possible to tell our stories in a manner that protects those who are vulnerable. These challenges extend to our contributors. Some of those in teaching and school leadership roles struggled with the time, the voice, or the ethical complexities, of writing publicly about their work, volunteering their voices, sharing their experiences and articulating their hopes, fears and frustrations. Flipping the system by sharing the voices of those in our schools is fraught with challenges. There are very real reasons why these voices are so hard to come by in the public sphere.

We remain, however, committed to sharing the voices of teachers and school leaders, alongside scholars. We intentionally seek to tell the stories of those who are already showing us how to flip the system within their day to day practice. We are aware of the limitations of our editorial partnership, as three high school teachers in roles which see us lead whole-school work. We are limited by our experiences and our networks but are committed to elevating the stories of those in different contexts to our own. We are deeply aware of the inequities in the Australian education system, and in education systems around the world. In education discourse some voices and groups have been privileged, while others have been marginalised, ignored or silenced. We have been deliberate in our attempts to include contributions from a balance of education sectors and from authors diverse in gender, race, role and experience. We admit that our ability to flip the system in this way may be imperfect, and perhaps even insufficient, but we hope that this book is a step in the right direction. At the heart of this book are the practising teachers and school leaders who have generously and often bravely taken the time to write their contributions, share their perspectives, and participate in research studies. We hope that this book acts as a gateway for others in the teaching profession to find their voice, and for governments, ministers and policymakers to seek out the perspectives of those working in schools.

The readers

This is a book with a wide audience. It is for teachers, would-be teachers, student teachers, veteran teachers, ex-teachers, the teachers of pre-service teachers, school leaders, professors, policymakers, politicians, researchers, education consultants, community partners and even the media. As Evers and Kneyber (2016) suggest, flipping the system is about changing education from the ground up by allowing teachers to take the lead as a trusted and meaningful part of global education conversation. Some of this book's voices are those often ignored in education reform, and yet are crucial voices to drive change in education. Here we project experiences from those across all sectors and places in and beyond our vast and diverse Australian land to propel critical education debate, build a sense of agency and celebrate the privilege it is to contribute to the educative process. This book does some talking but is ultimately about listening to the wisdom of the profession and engaging them at system level. We hope that by amplifying diverse but collective voices, this book can be part of a move to a world in which similar voices are sought out and valued by those traditionally at the decision-making peak of the education system.

References

Ball, S.J., 2018. Commercialising education: Profiting from reform! *Journal of Education Policy*, 33 (5), 587–589.

Barr, A., Gillard, J., Firth, V., Scrymgour, M., Welford, R., Lomax-Smith, J., Bartlett, D., Pike, B. and Constable, E., 2008. *Melbourne declaration on educational goals for young Australians*. Ministerial Council on Education, Employment, Training and Youth Affairs. Carlton: Australia.

Clarke, Z., 2018. Shedding our inhibitions: from external to internal accountability. In L. Rycroft-Smith and J.L. Dutaut, eds., *Flip the System UK: A teachers' manifesto*. Abingdon: Routledge, 37–41.

Elmore, R., 2016. "Getting to Scale..." it seemed like a good idea at the time, *Journal of Educational Change*, 17, 529–537.

Evers, J. and Kneyber, R. eds., 2016. *Flip the System: Changing education from the ground up*. Abingdon: Routledge.

Fitzgerald, D., 2017. Crossroads: The future of school assessment, *Journal of Professional Learning*, Semester 2. Available from: https://cpl.asn.au/journal/semester-2-2017/crossroads-the-future-of-school-assessment [Accessed 7 May 2018]

Fullan, M., and Quinn, J., 2016. *Coherence: The right drivers in action for schools, districts, and systems*. Thousand Oaks, CA: Corwin.

Gonski, D., Boston, K., Greiner, K., Lawrence, C., Scales, B. and Tannock, P., 2011. *Review of funding for schooling final report*. Canberra, Australia: Department of Education, Employment and Workplace Relations.

Gonski, D., Arous, T., Boston, K., Gould, V., Johnson, W., O'Brien, L., Perry. L. and Roberts, M., 2018. *Through growth to achievement report of the review to achieve educational excellence in Australian schools*. Canberra, Australia: Department of Education and Training.

Hargreaves, A., 2018. Time for a flipping change In L. Rycroft-Smith and J.L. Dutaut, eds., *Flip the System UK: A teachers' manifesto*. Abingdon: Routledge, 161-168.

Kneyber, R. and Evers, J., 2014. *Het alternatief: Weg met de afrekencultuur in het onderwijs!* Amsterdam: Boom.

Netolicky, D.M., Andrews, J., and Paterson, C., 2018. Flipping the system: A perspective from Down Under. In L. Rycroft-Smith and J.L. Dutaut, eds., *Flip the System UK: A teachers' manifesto*. Abingdon: Routledge.

Riley, P., 2017. *The Australian principal occupational health, safety and wellbeing survey 2017 data*. Fitzroy, Victoria: Australian Catholic University. Available from: www.principalhealth.org/au/2017_Report_AU_FINAL.pdf [Accessed 24 May 2018].

Rycroft-Smith, L. and Dutaut, J.L. eds., 2018. *Flip the System UK: A teachers' manifesto*. Abingdon: Routledge.

Sellar, S., 2016. Leaving the future behind. *Research in Education*. 96 (1), 12–18.

Sellar, S., Thompson, G., and Rutkowski, D., 2017. *The global education race: Taking the measure of PISA and international testing*. Alberta: Brush Education.

Wiliam, D., 2016. *Leadership for teacher learning*. Moorabbin, VIC: Hawker Brownlow.

Wiliam, D., 2018. *Creating the schools our children need: Why what we're doing now won't help much (and what we can do instead)*. Palm Beach, FL: Learning Sciences.

Wood, P., 2018. Lesson study: an approach to claiming slow time. In L. Rycroft-Smith and J.L. Dutaut, eds., *Flip the System UK: A teachers' manifesto*. Abingdon: Routledge, 115–122.

Part I

Teacher identity, voice and autonomy

Turning the system inside out

The absence of teachers in policy formulation, on boards of professional bodies or at the helm of critical agendas suggests a lack of trust in those who work each day with students in classrooms. There are many who purport to speak *for* teachers, and plenty of contexts in which non-teachers are invited to speak on how to improve teaching. Education is debated, reprimanded or celebrated by those who speak from a distance, away from the day-to-day realities of teaching and working in schools. The exclusion of teachers from education discourse does little for the identity and agency of the profession in broader society, let alone for the individual. The unrecorded ordinary folk who prop up the system have such richness of experience and breadth of expertise; they have voices and their voices should be heard. While there are a few practitioners who achieve exposure of their views, writing and work through mass media, questions still remain about whether they represent and characterise the system at large and indeed the considerable variability of contexts across the vast education landscape.

This section of the book assembles contributions that strongly advocate for the presence of teacher voice and expertise within discourses and decisions, which directly affect the work and purpose of schools, as well as sculpting the identity and power of the profession in resisting forces that accentuate a deficit view of education. The power to transform education is within it, not outside it.

Deborah Netolicky draws on her doctoral research to suggest that in the ever-changing policy arena of education, true and sustained improvement can come from a system that recognises and includes the experience of teachers, and that collaborative dialogue and action is central to diffusing promising ideas and practices. She points to trust as central to building the profession, one that seeks to grow and understand teachers and teaching, as opposed to the often competitive, blame-ridden portrayal.

Anna Hogan and **Bob Lingard** explore the susceptibility of education to commercial interests and influence. They contend that this phenomenon has a long history and is becoming ever more pervasive. Drawing on evidence from a commissioned survey and analysis of teachers' perceptions, they find that commercialisation generates teacher worries ranging from employment insecurity to wellbeing impact due to escalation of workload and detrimental impacts of student learning expectations. They call for urgent public debate and for a line to be drawn.

Gert Biesta explores who 'owns' education, including the roles of teachers, students and parents. He posits that policy and subsequent accountabilities have led to a transformation of the role of teacher, in which teachers are undermined by the language of learning which often defines their action, thus reinforcing a top-down logic. He contends that different generations of teachers find meaning and value in discourses of education that derive from different policy eras, resulting in varying professionalising and deprofessionalising experiences.

Cameron Malcher argues that market conditions and ever-contested funding structures have impacted the experience of teacher professional learning, resulting in the emergence of greater personal responsibility over the guidance or support of schools and systems. He suggests that a wide array of practice and research sharing methods have proliferated in Australia and served the profession well under difficult financial conditions and time constraints. Drawing on his own experience of podcasting, he illuminates the great potential it possesses to engage the profession in debate and empower teachers.

Benjamin Doxtdator challenges the risk management lens so often applied to students in schools. He takes aim at the mechanisms resulting from a risk lens such as 'what works', corporate, and technology 'solutions' that standardise education and disempower teachers. He argues for the consideration of the impact that these discourses, infrastructures and technologies have on education, and especially on those within the system who are most vulnerable.

1 Elevating the professional identities and voices of teachers and school leaders in educational research, practice and policymaking

Deborah M. Netolicky

'The System'. It sounds mechanistic and Orwellian, which is to some extent what the education system, in Australia and around the world, has become. Australia, the national context of this book and this chapter, is influenced by the globalisation and economisation of education policy, and an emphasis on performative accountabilities (Lingard, Thompson, and Sellar 2016). School leaders navigate relentless and competing pressures from governments, policy-makers, test administrators, boards, parents, communities, and the often unsupportive media. The worth of educators, and that of the schools in which they work, is constantly judged via league tables, external testing results, and visible data. Polarising media narratives seem intent on assigning blame or pitting stakeholders against one another, encouraging educators and scholars alike to bend to the will of the output-hungry machine. Education policies, which shape realities and experiences of schooling, use language to create a reality that privileges certain ideas while excluding others (Ball 2017). The ideas privileged include accountability, compliance, and numbers. Quantitative data are valued over the professionalism of teachers. Data and accountabilities become the 'truths' around which teachers and school leaders define themselves (Ball 2016). Teachers are disciplined within mechanisms of audit and accountability, impacting on the degree of professional autonomy they feel (Keddie 2017). Meanwhile, they do their best to serve their students and carve out time for what really matters: their students, their teaching, and the learning and relationships in their classrooms.

Yet when governments set education up around quotients, results, and league tables, "our worth, our humanity and our complexity are abridged" (Ball 2016, p. 1133). Educators' identities are reduced to a limited and limiting range of options, defined by a system of machinic production, ruthless competition, and unceasing surveillance. When averages are sought, or large numbers of disparate studies amalgamated, the complexity of education and of classrooms can be overlooked (Snook *et al.* 2009). Schools and educators working in schools are pressured to comply, often at the expense of the humanness that sits at the heart of the system. National and school compliance cultures stifle teacher voice (Keddie 2017). The subjective voices and intricate identities of teachers and school leaders, not to mention students, are often absent, marginalised, or simplified in educational policymaking. Not only that, but when teachers and school leaders resist policies and performative measures, they risk being censured, marginalised, or ridiculed (Ball 2016). This chapter argues that it is vital that we eke out, listen to, and elevate, the voices of those on the ground in our schools. I deliberately include in this chapter those voices often at the nadir of the system: teachers who are frequently overlooked in school reform efforts (Hargreaves 1995, Cordingley and Buckler 2012), and middle leaders who are absent from much research around school leadership.

I write this chapter as a boundary-spanning teacher, school leader, and researcher, who has taught English and Literature in high schools for almost 20 years. I continue to teach in the classroom and now act within the realm of senior leadership. Currently, I lead professional learning, research, and pedagogy, in a Pre-Kindergarten to Year 12 Australian school. I am also a research adjunct at an Australian university and continue the research and academic writing that began with my PhD. In this chapter I share partly my own perspective, informed by lived experience as an educator and qualitative researcher. I also, importantly, share the perspectives and voices of the other 13 participants of my PhD study (Netolicky 2016a): two teachers, six middle leaders, and five executive leaders from one independent Australian school. It is through offering and lifting up these voices from the field—rather than those of the Minister's office, the think tank, or the academe—that this chapter embodies system flipping. The chapter illuminates how the constantly shifting self-perceptions and self-constructions of teachers and school leaders are shaped, and in doing so shines a light on a less tangible, less measurable, messier, and more human side to teaching and leading schools.

Professional identity as a lens into education that resists performative drivers

Neoliberal and capitalist drivers in education have gone hand in hand with a global push to develop the 'quality' of teachers and teaching, and to hold teachers and schools to account over performance data through endless processes of quality assurance (Groundwater-Smith and Mockler 2009). Initiatives in Australia intended to measure achievement and drive improvement include NAPLAN (Annual National Assessment Program—Literacy and Numeracy), the National Partnership for Improving Teacher Quality, talk of performance-based pay for teachers, and the AITSL (Australian Institute for Teaching and School Leadership) National Professional Standards for Teachers and Principals. Professional standards are one of the ways teachers and principals are governed, valuing decontextualised traits and behaviours that construct a particular version of 'what works' (Niesche and Thomson 2017). As with elsewhere in the world, policy and media narratives in Australia often focus on performative data without considering human elements such as emotion, identity, and experience. Niesche and Thomson (2017) argue that "school leadership has increasingly been robbed of its educative purpose and is now ruled by school effectiveness and improvement discourses" (p. 203). There are toxic side effects to neoliberal regimes of accountability, such as teaching to the test, inequity, unrealistic measures of improvement, closing down professional judgement, and stifling the capacity to innovate (Thomson 2009).

A focus on identity can be a useful lens through which to consider education, despite being a slippery concept (Lawler 2014) that lacks a clear definition (Mockler 2011). Schools are socially and culturally constructed worlds encompassing complex relations between elements such as participant, world, act, thought, knowledge, and meaning (Lave and Wenger 1991). Examining professional identity allows for the exploration of what it is that shapes educators' development of professional identity, what shifts educator self-perceptions, and in what ways schools and systems might work with a greater understanding of educator identities when designing and implementing education reform. Beijaard, Meijer, and Verloop (2004) identified teacher professional identity as an emerging research area. Their review of literature suggests that interpreting the relationship between educators' stories and their professional identities has a sound theoretical basis, and that the literature would benefit from further attention to the role of context, including looking at relevant others as well as teachers.

While some researchers support the notion that professional identities are fixed or formed early, much research demonstrates that identities are flexible, multiple, and continually shaped by contexts and relationships. Not only do identities shift, but they are multifaceted and situation-specific. That is, each person has a fluid and ever-changing set of identities; they call into action the identity appropriate to the situation in which they are currently functioning. This chapter aligns with theorists who conceptualise identities as pluralistic, multiple, overlapping, and intersecting constructions, operated by the individual and changing over time (Breen 2014, Holland *et al.* 1998, Lawler 2014, Robertson 2017). For my purpose here, identity is the ongoing sense-making process of contextually embedded perceived-selves-in-flux. Drawing on Holland *et al.*'s (1998) description of identities as "imaginings of self in worlds of action" (p. 5), identity is the socioculturally entrenched way that we make sense of ourselves, to ourselves.

Little is understood about the ways in which teacher identity interacts with reform mandates to affect teachers' experiences of professional vulnerability (Lasky 2005). The body of scholarship on teacher professional identity is also limited to primarily traditional routes to becoming a teacher and traditional classroom experiences, leaving out those involved in alternative routes such as fast-track teacher training (Thomas and Mockler 2018). There is also limited research into the ways in which professional learning interacts with professional identities. The body of literature on educator identity is often focused on the pre-service or early career teacher, sometimes on the principal, and rarely on the middle leader or mid-career teacher. Stories of identity are a lens through which to view how people grow, change, and develop their ways of being in, and interacting with, their worlds. Paramount to understanding the importance of teacher and school leader identities is the way that experiences are described and constructed. Rich stories that reveal educators' senses of professional identity and perceptions of their own living, learning, teaching, and growth, add a new dimension to current data that drive education reforms such as teacher quality initiatives, professional standards for teachers, and performance pay schemes. Sharing of teachers' and school leaders' stories facilitates education interventions more readily integrated with educators' identities and practices than initiatives driven primarily by the strategic aims of schools or systems, and analyses of student data.

Questions about professional identity emerge. In what contexts are professional selves fluid or fixed? How and when is professional identity shaped and in what ways does it interact with educators' learning and experiences across their work and lives? What internal and external factors might facilitate either malleability of identity or resistance to identity change? The area of contextually based educator identity, in combination with lived experiences of professional learning and school reform, is a valuable one ripe for further exploration. Examining educators' identity transformations as a result of school-based professional learning and participation can illuminate how identities and practices might be shaped.

Professional identities in one Australian school

This chapter looks to my PhD participants to describe their lived experiences of their contextually embedded perceived-selves-in-flux, accepting Mockler's (2011) argument that the storied nature of identity lends itself to description, rather than definition. In this chapter I share data from my PhD study for which the research site was an Australian, non-selective, independent, Pre-Kindergarten to Year 12 school, with about 1500 students from metropolitan, rural, and international backgrounds. My PhD study was situated within a social constructionist paradigm. Interviews and storying were qualitative methodologies used to illicit multi-voiced descriptions of the lived experiences of teachers and school leaders. It assumed that identities are enmeshed with the worlds they inhabit (Holland *et al.* 1998, Rodgers and Scott 2008); that people can best be understood through their situated experiences and the retelling of those experiences; and that as professionals we are always becoming (Dunne, Pryor, and Yates 2005).

The study was set against the background of a professional learning intervention. At the time (2013 to 2014), this was a new intervention that used a combination of Cognitive Coaching and the Danielson Framework for Teaching[1] as a model of professional conversation and formalised reflection on teaching practice. The intervention was not a stand-alone reform but was introduced alongside already-existing work such as professional learning community teams and the work of external pedagogical consultants with classroom teachers. The Danielson Framework and Cognitive Coaching were already embedded in parts of this particular school, and therefore were seen by the school as contextually appropriate tools to support teacher growth.

PhD participants were drawn from a pool of those involved in the observation-and-coaching intervention. They were: two teachers from the intervention, six middle leaders, and five executive leaders, and myself as the researcher (also at the time a teacher at the school, the leader of the intervention, and a participating coach and coachee). Four of the 11 teachers involved in the first-pilot-year of the intervention volunteered to participate, although two later withdrew (perhaps indicative of the vulnerability of teachers in sharing their experiences). All 20 academic leaders at the school were invited to participate; five executive leaders and six middle leaders agreed. The four teachers and I (the immersed participant–researcher) were interviewed twice in 2013, while the 11 school leaders were interviewed once in 2014. A number of stringent ethical measures were put in place in order to address risks to participants and the complexity of my embeddedness in the research context (Netolicky and Barnes, 2017). For the purpose of this chapter, the framework of analysis is the lens of lived experiences of, and perceptions around, professional identity, of these 14 participants. What follows is a summary of data and findings around the identities of these teachers and school leaders.

What shapes teacher and school leader identities: findings from my PhD

Professional identities, for the participants of my PhD, were fluid, shaped by their whole lives, and tied to belief, purpose, and context. They confirm that personal and professional identities are interwoven (Robertson 2017). My study found that lifelong learning and capacity for professional transformation were fundamental parts of participant identities. Teachers and school leaders in the study viewed themselves and each other as continuous learners with a capacity for deep reflection and growth. Their learning occurred, not necessarily through opportunities badged as professional development, but through experiences that were professional and personal, formal and informal, in and out of educational contexts, and singular and collaborative (Netolicky 2016b).

Life experiences, not just education ones, shaped teacher and leader identities, beliefs and behaviours. One leader summarised this when they said, "My whole life has probably shaped who I've become". One leader talked about the "huge influence" of their grandmother; "a very very strong woman and a very resilient woman. But always there, always on the periphery, always there if you needed her". Experiences of teachers shaped participants, including the researcher and some leaders. One leader had "vivid memories of teachers who knew their stuff" and who "went way above and beyond the call to find whatever avenue they could get to get their kids to get their stuff", including one who held seminars at her home. This leader's "memorable teachers" were those who revealed themselves "as people", revealing who they were within and beyond the classroom and showing an interest in students within and beyond the classroom.

All three participant groups (teachers, leaders, researcher) discussed the importance of their experience of role models and anti-models in teaching and school leadership. Role models included those who were seen as successful, or who noticed, empowered, and encouraged participants. Two school leaders used the metaphor of the bowerbird to explain how they picked and chose aspects from other leaders with whom they had worked, in order to build their own "nest" of leadership attributes, strategies, and vision. "We watch", one said, "and we take from each other. ... we collect the skills that we see". Anti-models were just as important, with one teacher noting, "I don't want to become one of those old jaded teachers". Another leader described a negative experience in which a member of school management "used to write down all the things I wasn't doing right and then hand them to me on a Friday ... she never gave me any positives, and I need praise". As a result of this continuous "overwhelming" and "basically negative" feedback, which was given without discussion, this leader "almost stopped" teaching, but now sees "a direct correlation" between that experience and the way they operate as a leader. Participants strove to be different to those who had made them feel small, or who they had perceived as being ineffective.

For one teacher, one leader, and me, travel emerged as a transformative experience that impacted on professional identity. For one teacher, volunteering in an out-of-school mentoring program with disadvantaged youth was a "leveller" that stopped them "from taking things for granted and makes me realise that this little bubble isn't reality". One leader had been shaped through working with teachers in a third world orphanage. It changed their perspective and helped them to realise the privileged position of those in their own country and school. "We take for granted what we see as hardships, which are actually to them privileges." This leader knew that "those kids and those teachers would give anything for the difficulties we face in life". So when school leadership becomes stressful, "I put myself back on the balcony in 45 degrees, no running water, no power, cold potato curry for dinner. It's actually alright". In this case, travel and service influenced professional identity, beliefs, and behaviour.

Becoming a parent was a catalytic professional identity shaping experience shared by myself as researcher-insider participant, and one teacher. For the teacher, this life milestone meant a "shift in work/life balance" and the realisation that constantly working "doesn't necessarily make you a better teacher". Parenting allowed the teacher to understand, empathise with, and resist blaming parents for their children's behaviours.

Beliefs underpinning teacher and school leader identities

Central to participants' discussion of their professional selves was the foundational beliefs that underpin their actions and enactment of their identities. One leader described this as their "core" self. Across the participants emerged the shared the notion of "making a difference" and "lifelong learning". These were acknowledged as concepts that were ubiquitous and seemed clichéd, but which were nonetheless a driving factor for these educators. Common to many participants was the central focus on the student. About relationships with members of the school community, including students, parents and colleagues, one teacher said, "I think if any teacher has not got that right then it almost doesn't matter what they do in the classroom because if they have not got that trust and respect then it is not going to work anyway". Relationships were an innate, intrinsic part of teacher professional identity. Teachers and leaders spoke of a deep sense of purpose, with one leader expressing their realisation that teaching can empower those "excluded" or "different" or whom the "education system had failed".

Leaders in this study were concerned with empowerment and advocacy, and constantly navigated identity tensions. One leader explained that they "try and build leadership in every single teacher so every teacher is a leader, every student is a leader. We're all leaders and can lead others and ourselves to get better at what we do". This leader didn't think of themselves as "top of the pyramid" but as "part of a team".

School culture has been found to impact teachers' professional identities, satisfaction, commitment, and motivation (Day *et al.* 2006). My PhD study found that teachers and leaders feel the need to align with the school context, to feel that their individual self aligns with the organisation. Alignment with context led to feelings of authenticity and belonging. For the studied teachers, this need for alignment manifested in their sense of authentic connection with the school and their leaders. For leader participants, alignment meant a personal resonance as well as sensitivity to individual, departmental and organisational contexts and identities in terms of how they approach relationships and change.

In weaving together the perspectives of teachers, middle leaders, and executive leaders, my PhD study found that professional identities are entwined with school context and personal life. The participants desired alignment of their personal vision with the organisational vision, as well as that organisational vision would be mirrored in organisational action or "walking the talk".

Shifting selves, vulnerable voices

Professional identity is rich, socioculturally grounded, complex, and dynamic. Teachers' and leaders' senses of themselves are inextricably wound up in their work. This chapter accepts the complexity of teaching and the vulnerability that comes from teachers' and leaders' highly personal investment in their professional practice. This chapter embodies eking out, listening to, and elevating the voices of those on the ground in our schools. The voices I have shared here are only a few that emerge from one particular school context. More voices from more contexts are needed. Teachers, school leaders, schools, and national education systems, are not the sum of their students' test scores. It is worth seeking to understand how teachers, and those school leaders charged with supporting the work of teachers and schools, perceive and enact their professional selves, and experience professional life and education reform.

The participants in the study discussed here reveal the idiosyncrasies of teachers as individuals with their own stories and their own journeys of professional identity, learning, and growth. While there were elements of themselves that some educators saw as foundational, such as beliefs, even these were shown to be shapeable through lived experiences. The perceived-as-important notion of "being authentically oneself", as expressed by participants, was not fixed. Rather, it was combined with the notion of "*becoming* oneself". While the sense of being oneself was valuable to participants, their professional selves evolved and shifted over time due to experience; the authentic self was not static. This suggests that while educators feel connected to a sense of a core professional self at any given point, over time their identity evolves as a result of life and work experiences. Policy and research would benefit from honouring teachers' and leaders' voices, addressing the multidimensionality of work in schools, and acknowledging its situatedness and complexity. Education reforms would benefit from engaging with how teachers and school leaders perceive and describe themselves, their lives, and their work.

The system has the potential to be an inclusive and collaborative crucible in which those working in schools are given platforms to speak, in which teacher and school leader experience and professionalism is trusted, and in which we seek to understand and grow, rather than to blame. Of course, teaching should not be a profession without accountabilities and we should seek ways to understand how to best serve our students and communities. Education is, however, not an algorithm but a human endeavour, and one that can be improved through attention to the intricacies of the people operating within the system.

Note

1 The Danielson Framework for Teaching is a framework that identifies a comprehensive range of teacher responsibilities and what these might look like in action. The Framework clusters its 22 components of teaching into four domains of teacher responsibility: Planning and Preparation, The Classroom Environment, Instruction, and Professional Responsibilities. The Framework is used in many North American States for teacher evaluation but was used in this instance as a tool for professional conversation and reflection on practice, complementary to the AITSL Professional Standards for Teachers.

References

Ball, S.J., 2016. Subjectivity as a site of struggle: Refusing neoliberalism? *British Journal of Sociology of Education*, 37 (8), 1129–1146.

Ball, S.J., 2017. *The education debate*. 3rd ed. Bristol: Policy Press.

Beijaard, D., Meijer, P.C., and Verloop, N., 2004. Reconsidering research on teachers' professional identity. *Teaching and Teacher Education*, 20 (2), 107–128.

Breen, M. C., 2014. Teacher identity and intersubjective experience. In: P.M. Jenlink, eds. *Teacher identity and the struggle for recognition: Meeting the challenges of a diverse society*. Lanham, MD: Rowman & Littlefield Education, 27–36.

Cordingley, P., and Buckler, N., 2012. Mentoring and coaching for teachers' continuing professional development. In: S.J. Fletcher and C.A. Mullen, eds. *The Sage handbook of mentoring and coaching in education*. London: Sage, 215–227.

Day, C., Kington, A., Stobart, G., and Sammons, P., 2006. The personal and professional selves of teachers: Stable and unstable identities. *British Educational Research Journal*, 32 (4), 601–616.

Dunne, M., Pryor, J., and Yates, P., 2005. *Becoming a researcher: A companion to the research process*. New York: Open University Press.

Groundwater-Smith, S. and Mockler, N., 2009. *Teacher professional learning in an age of compliance: Mind the gap*. Dordrecht: Springer.

Hargreaves, A., 1995. Development and desire: A postmodern perspective. In: T.R. Guskey and M. Huberman, eds. *Professional development in education: New paradigms and practices*. New York: Teachers College, 9–34.

Holland, D., Lachicotte, W., Skinner, D., and Cain, C., 1998. *Identity and agency in cultural worlds*. Cambridge, MA: Harvard University.

Keddie, A., 2017. School autonomy reform and public education in Australia: Implications for social justice. *The Australian Educational Researcher*, 44 (4–5), 373–390.

Lasky, S., 2005. A sociocultural approach to understanding teacher identity, agency, and professional vulnerability in a context of secondary school reform. *Teaching and Teacher Education*, 21, 899–916.

Lave, J. and Wenger, E., 1991. *Situated learning: Legitimate peripheral participation*. London: Cambridge University.

Lawler, S., 2014. *Identity: Sociological perspectives*. 2nd ed. Cambridge: Polity.

Lingard, B., Thompson, G., and Sellar, S., 2016. National testing from an Australian perspective. In: B. Lingard, G. Thomson and S. Sellar, eds. *National testing in schools: An Australian assessment*. Abingdon: Routledge, 1–17.

Mockler, N., 2011. Becoming and 'being' a teacher: Understanding teacher professional identity. In: N. Mockler and J. Sachs, eds. *Rethinking educational practice through reflexive inquiry*. Dordrecht: Springer, 123–138.

Netolicky, D.M., 2016a. *Down the rabbit hole: Professional identities, professional learning, and change in one Australian school*. Thesis (PhD). Murdoch University.

Netolicky, D.M., 2016b. Rethinking professional learning for teachers and school leaders. *Journal of Professional Capital and Community*, 1 (4), 270–285.

Netolicky, D.M. and Barnes, N., 2017. Method as a journey: A narrative dialogic partnership illuminating decision-making in qualitative educational research. *International Journal of Research & Method in Education*, 1–14.

Niesche, R., and Thomson, P., 2017. Freedom to what ends? School autonomy in neoliberal times. In: D. Waite and I. Bogotch, eds. *The Wiley international handbook of educational leadership*. Hoboken, NJ: Wiley, 193–206.

Robertson, S. 2017. Transformation of professional identity in an experienced primary school principal: A New Zealand case study. *Educational Management, Administration & Leadership*, 45 (5), 774–789.

Rodgers, C.R., and Scott, K. H., 2008. The development of the personal self and professional identity in learning to teach. In: M. Cochran-Smith, S. Feiman-Nemser, D. J. McIntyre, and K. E. Demers, eds. *Handbook of research on teacher education*. 3rd ed. New York: Macmillan, 732–755.

Snook, I., O'Neill, J., Clark, J., O'Neill, A.M. and Openshaw, R., 2009. Invisible learnings? A commentary on John Hattie's book: Visible learning: a synthesis of over 800 meta-analyses relating to achievement. *New Zealand Journal of Educational Studies*, 44 (1), 93–106.

Thomas, M.A.M., and Mockler, N., 2018. Alternative routes to teacher professional identity: Exploring the conflated sub-identities of Teach For America corps members. *Education Policy Analysis Archives*, 26 (6), 1–21.

Thomson, P., 2009. *School Leadership-Heads on the Block?* Abingdon: Routledge.

2 Teachers' perceptions of commercialisation in Australian public schools
Implications for teacher professionalism

Anna Hogan and Bob Lingard

Introduction

This chapter reports on a survey conducted with Australian Education Union (AEU) members that sought to investigate the extent of commercialisation in Australian public schooling. Commercialisation is the creation, marketing and sale of education goods and services to schools and school systems by private providers. Commercial services commonly include the provision of curriculum content, assessment services, data infrastructures, digital learning, professional development for staff, supply of contract and replacement teachers and school administration support. Our data suggest that commercialisation is now commonplace in Australian public schools.

Commercialisation has had a long history in schools, beginning with commercially produced textbooks that have been around since the early twentieth century. Similarly, teachers in our survey reported that resources and curriculum materials that supported their development of innovative learning experiences were still important (Lingard *et al.* 2017). However, teachers expressed concern that increasing commercialisation would lead to an intensification of the de-professionalisation of teaching. This chapter explores these concerns, and focuses on teachers' perceptions of how commercialisation is impacting their work, their students' learning and their personal wellbeing and what the implications are for teacher professionalism and for the democratic and social justice purposes of public schooling.

In what follows, we provide some backdrop to issues of teacher professionalism in contemporary education systems and explore the paradoxes between highly regulated professional standards and the more individual professional aspirations of teachers. We then briefly outline the research we are drawing on and document how commercialisation provides both affordances and challenges to teachers' work and professionalism. In the conclusion, we draw out how teachers perceive commercialisation as potentially de-professionalising and argue that there is a need for enhanced public debate about commercialisation in schools and the extent to which public schools should become commercialised.

Background: teacher professionalism and system restructuring

Since the end of the Cold War, there has been the restructuring of schooling systems in the Anglo-American nations, including Australia, which has witnessed these systems granting more autonomy to schools, at the same time as schools face tighter top-down, test-based accountability pressures (Lingard et al. 2016). New technologies of governance structure the ways schooling systems now work (Ball 2017). These technologies include marketisation, which has seen the creation of quasi-markets in schooling that emphasise parental school choice agendas, a new managerialism that sees systems steered at a distance through test results and other large data sets, and a narrowing curriculum focus linked to influential census literacy and numeracy tests (such as NAPLAN in Australia). The education state running public schooling has been restructured through new public management and more recently through what has been called network governance, with much state activity outsourced to the private sector, public–private partnerships becoming common, and private sector actors now constituting part of policy networks setting policy agendas and being more systematically involved in testing and curriculum work. Global edu-businesses find this a conducive and facilitative context for their profit-based involvements in public schooling. Commercialisation in schooling is at one with these developments. Teaching and teachers' work have been affected by these system restructurings with implications for teacher professionalism.

Unfortunately, teacher voices have been absent from these restructurings. As such, teachers have been the objects of these policy developments, rather the subjects of them. This chapter challenges this absence and argues the necessity of teacher voices to effective educational change and to reform content and processes, including consideration of the impact of restructuring on teacher professionalism. Bottom-up, backward mapping to policy from the requirements for the most effective pedagogical classroom practices is essential to effective and progressive school reform. This would see, as this collection argues, a flipping of the system.

Teaching, as public service work in state bureaucracies, has long been a state-managed profession. In comparison with the more 'independent' professionals of say medicine and law, teachers' professional autonomy is highly regulated and controlled by state-sanctioned standards (Goodson 2002). This state-mediated professionalism links to the great significance of schooling (and thus, teachers' work) to the nation, given its role in producing socially and economically prosperous future citizens. For these reasons, Hargreaves and Goodson (2002, p. 1) argue there is "enormous interest, politically and administratively in identifying, codifying and applying professional standards of practice to the teaching force". In Australia, for example, the Australian Institute for Teaching and School Leadership Limited (AITSL), a federal government body, in conjunction with the various state level teacher registration authorities, provides national standards for teaching and initial teacher education programs.

As AITSL (2017) suggests, the standards let teachers know what they should be aiming to achieve at every stage of their career, so their practice can be improved inside and outside of the classroom. In reality, particularly with these standards governing accreditation of initial teacher education programs at universities, as well as teacher registration and promotion, these are the 'steering mechanisms' the state uses to regulate teaching and teaching practices (Hargreaves and Goodson 2002).

Many social commentators argue that highly prescriptive standards work to both professionalise (in terms of the broader tasks, greater complexity and more sophisticated judgements required by teachers) and de-professionalise teachers (more pragmatic training, reduced discretion over goals and purposes and increased dependence on learning outcomes prescribed by others) (Biesta 2015, Sachs 2016). The paradoxical characteristics of teacher professional standards are further complicated in Australia by the governing board of AITSL that has no representation from currently practising teachers or from the teacher unions, the largest omnibus organisations representing teacher interests. A characteristic of the traditional professions such as law and medicine is the importance of professional self-governance. Teaching, in contrast, is managed by a national state authority, here AITSL, with no teacher voices represented. Given the absence of teacher voice, teacher unions across Australia have withdrawn involvement and support from AITSL. In this context, it seems teacher unions have important industrial and professional work to do. Moreover, the restructured state, with openings for privatisation and commercialisation and with new test-based modes of educational accountability, carries real implications for the state-managed profession of teaching and for aspirations to a more traditional model of a profession. Here, the state mandates what teachers need to do regarding curriculum and assessment and manages and regulates the profession, at the same time further authority regarding teachers' work is being usurped by the intervention of commercial providers and their products. This chapter argues for teacher voices to be brought back in to policy processes and decision-making.

Methods

Data for this chapter were collected as part of a survey of Australian teachers and school leaders. All 2193 voluntary participants were current members of the Australian Education Union (AEU) and/or AEU-affiliated state organisations[1] that represent teachers and principals working in Australian public schools. The study was commissioned by the New South Wales Teachers Federation (NSWTF) to chart the extent, and perceptions, of commercialisation in public education (Lingard, Sellar, Hogan, & Thompson, 2017). The majority of the respondents were from NSW (53.6%) and Qld (25.9%) respectively. 54.6% of respondents worked in urban communities with other participants working in regional centres (24.1%), rural (18.1%) and remote (3.2%) communities. Respondents identified the socioeconomic status of their school communities as very advantaged/advantaged (20.2%), average (33.8%) and disadvantaged/very disadvantaged (46%). The majority of teachers were working in primary schools (42.6%) and high schools (41.5%). In total, 57.9% were classroom teachers, while principals and deputy principals made up 7.3% and 7.4% of the respondents respectively. A comprehensive overview has been published elsewhere (Lingard et al. 2017).

Participant responses were coded by the demographic information collected as part of the survey. These include the participants' gender, years' experience, role within the school (for example, whether they were a principal or classroom teacher), socioeconomic status (SES) of the school community and geolocation (remote, rural, urban) of the school. This information was collected, and is provided here, because we have significant evidence that these factors can matter in the experience of education in specific contexts. These are represented in the following order in brackets after each quote: (Gender, Years' Experience, School Role, SES, Geolocation) so that the following qualifier (Female, 7, Teacher, Avg, Rural) indicates that this opinion was voiced by a female teacher with seven years' experience who worked in a school in an average SES community in a rural community.

Results

One key theme that emerged from the survey concerned a strong perception that public school commercialisation was impacting teachers' work and lives. Over 40% of the responses expressed concern that commercialisation was working to change what teachers teach and how they teach it, with consequential negative effects on teacher professionalism, including deprofessionalisation and diminished wellbeing. However, as we will detail below, commercialisation is complex with both affordances and challenges. Indeed, many teachers and school leaders viewed some commercial resources as beneficial to schooling in the twenty-first century, as long as they are able to maintain control over who delivers these services and the extent to which their classrooms become commercialised.

Affordances of commercialisation

The most commonly referred to benefit of commercialisation was that commercial products are useful resources for teaching and learning. In particular, teachers perceived that commercial resources were necessary for their day-to-day practice and an important component to adequately resource public schools. Many participants reported that commercial products were helping "time poor" teachers design "high quality learning experiences" and assisting them to "differentiate learning" for their students. As one response highlighted:

> I find that teachers (including myself) are purchasing lesson plans and units of work as they don't have the time to do it themselves anymore. Being

an English teacher and having to teach a new curriculum and teach new HSC texts and a new area of study, it has become impossible to keep up with the work load and we feel forced to purchase these ready-made units of work.

(Female, 10, Teacher, Disadv, Rural)

Some responses argued that when "commercial businesses provide high quality, well-written and presented products that abide by teaching guidelines, these are not a problem" and are actually "advantageous to support the delivery of curriculum based on the needs of individuals and groups within a school context" (Female, 39, Other (Recently Retired), Adv, Urban). Moreover, when teachers lack a particular skill or area of expertise, it is best to "outsource". For example, one response indicated that their school purchased the Jellybeans music program because their teachers "do not have the skillset, equipment or musical expertise to implement these learning programs" (Female, 26, Teacher, Adv, Urban). In fact, over 25% of survey participants agreed that commercial products help "provide teachers with a wide range of resources to support a well-structured learning program" (Male, 40, Teacher, Disadv, Urban).

However, in reporting the benefits of commercial resources, most responses also included a warning or caveat to their usefulness. Concern was expressed about the "lazy approach to teaching" in which teachers might adopt a "one size fits all approach where the textbook (usually commercially produced) becomes the *de facto* curriculum" (Male, 13, Teacher, Disadv, Urban). Others noted that while commercial companies can provide resources at a "reasonable price" not all schools can afford to purchase this type of support and thus equity issues exist and the "gap between the haves and have nots continues to grow" (Female, 29, Teacher, Disadv, Rural). Similarly, there was some apprehension about the "hidden agendas" of commercial organisations and how they might be "driving curriculum and assessment to take over publicly devised aspects of education" on a for-profit basis (Male, 35, Teacher, Adv, Urban). For example, one respondent observed: "Commercial producers have a place in the resource market for teachers but must never be considered as a substitute for quality teaching—this is what we are trained to do and we must remain the experts in this regard" (Male, 36, Principal, Disadv, Urban).

Challenges of commercialisation

Respondents went beyond describing the positives and potential pitfalls of commercial products to also explain how these products impacted on their work as teachers, including their influence on curriculum, pedagogy and assessment in their classrooms. For example, while responses referenced the fact that commercial resources can be "extremely helpful", teachers were concerned these were becoming overly relied upon, with consequential effects that work to narrow the curriculum to what is contained within the textbook.

There was a general consensus amongst participants that this reliance was dangerous, given that some commercial products do not align appropriately with the Australian curriculum: "I feel these publishers, as multi-national companies, show little regard for producing quality materials that relate to the Australian Curriculum and simply provide a generic product composed from materials prepared for education systems in other countries" (*Male, 42, Teacher, Adv, Urban*). Moreover, there was a sense that some commercially available resources "are revamped versions of past products with pretty packaging" (*Female, 24, Teacher, Adv, Urban*), and that commercial providers capitalise on "learning fads which seem to go out of fashion quite quickly when the next 'you beaut' program emerges" (*Female, 32, Student Support Teacher, Adv, Urban*). Overall, teachers felt that commercial providers were focused on generating "attractive" products to generate sales and were not being held "accountable for their materials having a positive impact on student learning outcomes" (*Male, 27, Head of Learning Area, Disadv, Urban*).

Interestingly, teachers argued they had limited control over how commercial products were being enacted in their schools and classrooms. For example, teachers felt unease when "forced" to implement commercial programs that school leaders mandated as aligning with the broader strategic objectives of the school. Of particular concern was the use of commercial assessment materials to prepare students for NAPLAN tests. Numerous responses highlighted that schools often purchase standardised tests like the Australian Council for Educational Research's (ACER) Progressive Achievement Tests (PAT) in Mathematics, Reading, SPG (Spelling, Punctuation and Grammar) and Science to better prepare students for NAPLAN. Responses suggested that teachers view the focus on NAPLAN as creating an "overreliance on data" with many feeling like they are "teaching to the test" and sacrificing the "creativity and higher order thinking" skills of their students. In fact, one participant argued that "work done which is not measurable by some standardised test—e.g. behaviour, emotional intelligence, personal and social skills—is ignored" (*Female, 35, Principal, Disadv, Urban*). There was frustration amongst participants that schooling had shifted in its focus and that there was a desire to return to the more holistic notion of what it means to receive an education:

> Education is more than tests. When has a student ever said "that test changed my life"? Never. There needs to be less focus on standardised testing, which is being promoted by private education corporations, and a greater focus on enjoyment of learning and teaching skills that students can utilise in the twenty-first century.
>
> (*Female, 9, Teacher, Adv, Urban*)

The effect of mandated use of commercial resources is that teachers cannot grow as "effective and reflective teachers". They are constrained in what they can teach, how they can teach it, and even how this learning is assessed. Instead of students participating in rich learning experiences, commercial resources and programs have "resulted in classrooms full of students doing 'busy work'... [which] has resulted in a whole body of students and parents who think that if students haven't been completing worksheets they haven't been doing any work" *(Female, 40, Head of Learning Area, Disadv, Urban)*. There was a consensus amongst survey participants that teaching is increasingly adopting a "one size fits all approach" that "isn't necessarily reflective of what's best for students in your/my class" *(Female, 35, Teacher, Disadv, Urban)*.

Implications: teacher deprofessionalisation and diminished wellbeing

When considering how commercialisation impacted on teaching, many participants commented that they felt "unhappy", "exhausted", "alienated", "disillusioned", "demoralised", "lacking in confidence" and "unrewarded". A common theme emerged amongst participants that teachers were concerned about a loss of teacher professionalism and personal wellbeing in the commercialised school environment. For example, responses argued that teachers no longer had the opportunity to enact their own professional judgement. As one respondent explained:

> My school has mandated that we must all use WORDS THEIR WAY which is a Pearson spelling program. All classes [from] K-6 are now teaching spelling using this solely. We used to use Jolly Phonics in K. This has narrowed the opportunity for teachers to use their own skills and professional judgement in developing and creating a spelling program which best suits the learning styles of their students.
>
> *(Female, 25, Teacher, Adv, Urban)*

As another teacher summarised: "Teachers everywhere should be screaming about the loss of autonomy and personal/professional efficacy" because "the message comes across loud and clear; teachers are not to be trusted and the only thing that matters is academic achievement" *(Female, 35, Principal, Disadv, Urban)*. These feelings mirror research by Ryan and Bourke (2013), who argue that teachers have been discursively positioned as 'non-experts' and the last in line of a management hierarchy in which educational decisions made elsewhere (central office, regional office, school leadership) must be adopted and worked with in a standardised, accountable environment. According to Bloomfield (2006), diminished teacher autonomy has resulted from a political perception that teachers should not be viewed as professionals whose opinion should be valued, but as underperforming obstacles to change. Indeed, Thrupp (2009) observes that teachers and teaching quality have been positioned as a 'handy scapegoat' in schooling reform agendas in which associated rhetoric promoted by politicians, media, commercial interests and much of popular culture seems to suggest that if only there were better teachers in schools, there would be greater improvements in student outcomes regardless of socioeconomic disadvantage.

One particular concern amongst a number of participants was not only that this environment was leading to a loss of autonomy, but potentially the loss of teaching jobs. Health and Physical Education teachers seemed particularly perceptive to this risk as their subject is already being delivered by external private providers and not registered teachers in some schools:

> As a PDHPE teacher in a NSW primary school I am very concerned about PE and sport being outsourced to private companies who are often less qualified than PDHPE teachers. It not only makes redundant highly trained teachers who know their students well and can develop a school specific program following through from year to year, but it also de-skills classroom teachers by abdicating their responsibility for PE and sport.
> (*Female, 25, Primary School Subject Specialist, Adv, Urban*)

A plethora of research supports the notion that outsourcing learning to commercial providers displaces both the pedagogical expertise of teachers and the value of curriculum (Penney, Petrie, and Fellows 2015, Powell 2015). However, the pragmatic 'solution' that ready-made commercial programs can deliver in terms of time and investment (e.g. the economic viability of hiring an HPE teacher for a year versus the much cheaper alternative of sourcing a commercial sports program) means that schools are increasingly accepting these services in uncritical ways (Powell 2015). Structurally and in policy terms, this is linked to the devolution to schools of one-line budgets and the granting to government schools of more autonomy within tighter accountability frameworks often focused on test scores in literacy and numeracy.

A concerning number of responses suggested that circulating discourses of distrust and devaluation were making them consider leaving the profession. Various facets of commercialisation "are creating stress and anxiety for staff, and impinging on the effectiveness of teachers to deliver quality education as a result of flagging morale" (*Male, 23, Teacher, Avg, Urban*). Indeed, as one person argued: "My school has already had young teachers resign because they have become disillusioned and dispirited by the hijacking of their teaching. More are planning to follow" (*Female, 20, Head of Learning Area, Avg, Urban*). Similarly, another respondent summarised the frustration they had experienced across their career as commercialisation had become more mainstream:

> When I began teaching in 1977, primary teachers had skills; we played musical instruments, coached sports, taught art and craft, taught PE and looked after our students' welfare. We treated children with respect and considered our part in shaping their futures. I am pleased that I am approaching retirement because it is increasingly difficult for me to accept the notion that commercial providers, consultants, motivational speakers and their ilk, know more about the craft of teaching than we

do. Even more distressing to me is the easy willingness that educational administrators squander our money and time boosting the coffers of commercial interests.

(Male, 40, Teacher, Avg, Regional)

These responses clearly articulate a concern amongst teachers that it is difficult to work in a system that does not value or support teacher professionalism. Thus, there is a clear sense that while commercialisation is necessary and valuable in supporting teachers to do their job effectively, there is a point at which commercialisation becomes dangerous. For example, when teachers are forced to use a particular commercial product or service that they feel is not supporting their students' best interests, their classroom has become commercialised and the teacher de-professionalised as the focus is on the product itself, and not on the potential of the product to help the teacher (Hogan *et al.* 2017).

Conclusion

Teachers in Australian public schools have a diverse range of opinions regarding the commercialisation of schooling. Many teachers do see the need for some degree of commercial support and want the autonomy to choose commercial products and services that support their work. However, despite some perceived benefits, respondents also described many negative effects and concerns about the long-term implications of this trend. For example, concerns were expressed about the re-positioning of assessment, and more specifically standardised testing, as the cornerstone of schooling, creating new markets for test-driven products and the associated risk of teacher deprofessionalisation, when autonomy to decide what and how to teach is diminished. There is also concern that private providers and products may increasingly replace publicly-employed teachers; first in learning areas like HPE and music, but perhaps over the longer term through software and algorithms that provide personalised learning for students.

Growing commercialisation in Australian public schools clearly requires an ethical debate that schools, education professionals, policymakers and interested publics are yet to have. Teacher voices and those of their representatives need to be to the fore in those debates. This debate concerns the points at which commercial activity in school undermines the basic purposes of public schooling, such as the free, universal and secular provision of education for all, as well as its democratic citizenship functions and provision of equal opportunities (Reid 2017). As the teachers in our survey warned, increasing engagement with commercial providers, due to standardisation, technological advances and policies that drive marketisation, decentralisation and school autonomy, must be balanced against concerns that commercialisation can threaten the holistic development of students and what it means to receive a rounded education and at the same time threaten the democratic and opportunity structure purposes of public schooling.

Responding to these implications must sit within a policy context of ongoing debate concerning the appropriate intensity of commercialisation in schools, the regulatory environment that surrounds the development and sale of commercial products, the potential equity issues that influence the ability of all schools and teachers to access these commercial services, and the enhancement rather than diminishment of teachers' professional capacities, particularly through critical understanding and engagement about commercialisation. Policies emerging from these debates may further protect schools, teachers and students from being enmeshed in a web of commercial activities, which at times, involve ethically questionable practices undertaken by global corporate entities at a considerable remove from local classrooms (Hogan, Sellar, and Lingard 2016, Verger, Lubienski, and Steiner-Khamsi 2016, Reckhow 2012). As we have noted, teaching is a state-managed profession and teacher voice is absent from AITSL. The effects of the restructured education state and related enhanced commercialisation that we have addressed in this chapter have witnessed additional negative de-professionalising pressures on teachers and their work. It is time to flip the system and place teacher voices at the centre of policy debates and developments, along with the voices of parents and community. Education policy should not be determined by those with commercial for-profit interests.

Note

1 The AEU affiliated State unions include, Queensland Teachers' Union, New South Wales Teachers Federation, State School Teachers Union of Western Australia as well as the AEU Victorian Branch, Australia Capital Territory Branch, South Australian Branch, Tasmanian Branch and Northern Territory Branch.

References

Australian Institute for Teaching and School Leadership (AITSL), 2017. Australian Professional Standards for Teachers. Available from: www.aitsl.edu.au/teach/standards [Accessed 16 May 2018].
Ball, S.J., 2017. *The education debate*. 3rd ed. Bristol: The Policy Press.
Biesta, G., 2015. What is education for? On good education, teacher judgement, and educational professionalism. *European Journal of Education*, 50 (1), 75–87.
Bloomfield, D., 2006. A new discourse for teacher professionalism: Ramsey, standards and accountability. *Curriculum Leadership*, 5 (9), 27–44.
Goodson, I., 2002. *Teachers' professional lives*. London: Routledge.
Hargreaves, A. and Goodson, I., 2002. Teachers' professional lives: Aspirations and actualities. In: I. Goodson, *Teachers' Professional Lives*. London: Routledge, 1–27.
Hogan, A., Enright, E., Stylianou, M. and McCuaig, L., 2017. Nuancing the critique of commercialisation in schools: Recognising teacher agency. *Journal of Education Policy*, 1–15.
Hogan, A., Sellar, S., and Lingard, B., 2016. Commercialising comparison: Pearson puts the TLC in soft capitalism. *Journal of Education Policy*, 31 (3), 243–258.

Lingard, B., Rezai-Rashti, G., Martino, W. and Sellar, S., 2016. *Globalising educational accountability*. New York: Routledge.

Lingard, B., Sellar, S., Hogan, A. and Thompson, G., 2017. *Commercialisation in Public Schooling*. Sydney: New South Wales Teachers Federation.

Penney, D., Petrie, K., and Fellows, S., 2015. HPE in Aotearoa New Zealand: the reconfiguration of policy and pedagogigc relations and privatisation of curriculum and pedagogy. *Sport, Education and Society*, 20 (1), 42–56.

Powell, D., 2015. Assembling the privatisation of physical education and the 'inexpert' teacher. *Sport, Education and Society*, 20 (1), 73–88.

Reckhow, S., 2012. *Follow the money: How foundation dollars change public school politics*. New York: Oxford University Press.

Reid, A., 2017. Public and proud: Reclaiming the essence of public schooling in Australia. *Journal of Professional Learning*, Semester 1, 2017. Available at: https://cpl.asn.au/sites/default/files/journal/Alan%20Reid%20-%20For%20Your%20Future.pdf [Accessed 16 May 2018].

Ryan, M. and Bourke, T., 2013. The teacher as reflexive professional: Making visible the excluded discourse in teacher standards. *Discourse: Studies in the cultural politics of education*, 34 (3), 411–423.

Sachs, J., 2016. Teacher professionalism: Why are we still talking about it? *Teachers and Teaching*, 22 (4), 413–425.

Thrupp, M., 2009. Teachers, social contexts and the politics of blame. *Queensland Teacher's Union Professional Magazine*, 6–12.

Verger, A., Lubienski, C., and Steiner-Khamsi, G., eds., 2016. *World yearbook of education 2016: The global education industry*. London: Routledge.

3 Flipping the system, but in which direction?

Reclaiming education as a public concern

Gert Biesta

Flip the system!

The idea that the contemporary education system should be flipped, is difficult to contest. School education has, of course, always had a complex and multi-layered relationship with the state, the economy and the public sphere, and has never been truly a 'free space' (see, for example, Green 1990, Popkewitz 2000). Yet, the unprecedented rise of the micro-management of schools and of the life, the work and even of the soul of teachers (Ball 2003) that has taken place in many countries over the past two or three decades, has created a situation that is totally out of balance. The obsession with measurable learning outcomes in a small number of academic subjects has not just narrowed the educational 'offer,' but has also led to a high degree of cynicism, where raising test scores has become an aim in itself, irrespective of whether it has anything to do with the quality and significance of the education children and young people receive (see particularly Ravitch 2011).

The education system is not just out of balance but is also seriously out of control. The rise of a 'global education measurement industry' (Biesta 2015a) seems to have handed over the definition of what counts as good education to technocrats who provide seductive statistics and glossy league tables but operate beyond democratic accountability. At a global scale, therefore, we seem to have ended up in a situation where governments and the public often value what is being measured, rather than that attempts are made to measure what is considered valuable. Rather than putting hope in minor readjustments, the situation has run so out of hand that a total 'flip' of the system seems to be the only viable option. And given that teachers have suffered and are still suffering significantly from the top-down micro-management of their work (see Jeffrey and Woods 1998, Gewirtz 2002), it could be argued that they are the legitimate 'owners' of education and that the system should therefore be flipped in their direction. This has indeed been a major thrust of the case for flipping the system (Evers and Kneyber 2016).

Although I wholeheartedly share the concerns about the status and position of teachers—see, for example, my work on teacher agency (Priestley, Biesta and Robinson 2015) and my case for a 'rediscovery' of teaching (Biesta 2017)—I am, however, not entirely convinced that the ills of contemporary education are *automatically* solved when we give education back to teachers (bearing in mind that the question who 'we' are and in whose power it lies to give anything to anyone is important here). The emphasis here lies on the word 'automatically'. While I do not wish to contest that teachers have a crucial 'stake' in education, the purpose of this chapter is to raise some critical, and perhaps uncomfortable questions about who actually 'owns' education and where teachers stand in relation to this. This will hopefully help to state with more clarity and precision in which direction the education system should be flipped, and which directions are less desirable or actually problematic.

The social justice argument

While it is important to remain critical about the micro-management of education, it is important not to conflate good intentions with problematic consequences. Much of what is currently going on with regard to measuring and managing of education emerged out of real concerns about inequality and the ways in which school systems were reproducing rather than overcoming economic and social disadvantage. Somewhere down the line of the current culture of managing and measuring there is a social justice argument that is as difficult to contest as the current case for flipping the system (see also Stein 2016).

The social justice argument holds that every child and young person, irrespective of *who* they are, *where* they are, or where they are *from*, should have access to good education. This raises the question how we can make sure that education is everywhere of the same quality. One question this then raises, is how we can *judge* the quality of education, which can be rephrased as the question of how we can *assess* the quality of education, which then easily turns into the question how we can *measure* the quality of education. Although one could argue that even the latter version of the question should focus on education as a whole, measuring the quality of education has quickly become operationalised in terms of measuring the *outcomes* of education, and it is perhaps with the introduction of the word 'outcomes' that something started to go wrong. From the question 'Which outcomes *should* be measured?', the discussion shifted rather rapidly to the question 'Which outcomes *can* be measured?' and here the social justice argument ended up in the hands of statisticians and technocrats and became an entirely different discourse, leading to the situation where, as mentioned, policymakers and the public began to value what is being measured, often 'supported' by strong rhetorical arguments about the alleged 'basics' of education (see Biesta 2015b).

So, while we shouldn't forget the good intentions out of which the current situation arose, we also should see that these intentions can no longer be used as a justification for the current state of affairs. After all, the balance between costs and benefits has decisively shifted in the direction of the formed, and teachers, but also students, are paying a high price for this.

Parent power?

One direction in which the education system might be flipped is towards those for whom education is intended to be: children and young people and, depending on age, also their parents. The idea that parents should have a voice in the education of their children—and according to some: a *decisive* voice—has a long history, particularly in relation to discussions about religion and religious education, but also more generally with regard to the relationship between the duties of the state and the rights of its citizens, including parents (see, for some historical examples, Manning 1872, Friedman 1916, and for a recent discussion Fives 2017).

While the question of the rights of parents remains a complicated one, also because it is connected to their duty to care for their offspring, the rise of neo-liberal views and practices of governing have added a whole new dimension to this discussion, by positioning parents as customers on an education market; a market, moreover, that should provide parents with choices with regard to the education of their children (for a relatively early analysis see Gewirtz, Ball and Bowe 1995).

The main problem with markets is that they focus on the most (cost-) effective and efficient ways to service the needs of customers, but never ask the question whether what customers *say* they want is what they *should be* wanting. When you go to a shop to buy a television, the sales assistant will be happy to provide you with information about all the different options and about the latest available models, but will probably never ask whether you actually need a (new) television, let alone suggesting that rather than watching television you should get out more, join a club or sign up for voluntary work in the community. If markets do anything with the 'wants' of their customers, it is most likely an attempt to let them want *more*, as in "Customers who bought this item, also bought that item, so perhaps you should do so too".

This reveals the fundamental difference between markets and democracies. In a democratic society the fundamental question that the democratic process needs to engage with, is how to accommodate the needs, wants and desires of all individuals and groups. It is a mistake to suggest that democracy is the situation where the needs, wants and desires of those who can gain a majority become the rule, because one 'demand' of the democratic process is that such needs, wants and desires are considered in light of the key democratic values of equality, liberty and solidarity. (Without those values, democracy turns into populism where a majority could simply overturn the values that constitute the democratic space itself.)

Democracy, to put it differently, is not a *quantitative* matter of counting preferences and giving (absolute) power to the majority. Democracy, rather, is a *qualitative* matter that focuses on the far more difficult question whether what individuals and groups say they want—both in terms of material goods and immaterial desires—can be 'carried' and 'supported' by society as a whole. This is, first of all, a matter of liberty, that is, of how the desires of one group or individual impact on the liberty of other groups or individuals. But it is also a matter of equality and, hence, of social justice, that is, of just ways of giving everyone their share. These are highly complex questions, but nonetheless they are key in the democratic process—a process where, as the Rolling Stones have put it so aptly, 'you can't always get what you want'.

Although, at first sight, the idea of parent power may seem a plausible antidote for the micro-management of education, there are at least two problems with this suggestion. One is that we cannot assume that all parents will have the same preferences for their children (although we have to bear in mind that the league table industry is strongly influencing and 'channelling' common perceptions of what good schools are), so in a democratic society such preferences have to be mediated. The second problem is that, particularly under neo-liberal frames of governance, parents may be inclined to promote their private interest (including the interests of 'their' group or class) rather than keeping an orientation on the greater public good (see for a critical discussion Reay *et al.* 2008). The democratic values of values of liberty, equality and solidarity are precisely meant to provide such an orientation (which is not to suggest, of course, that answers are simple).

Pupil power?

There are similar concerns with the idea that rather than parents it's pupils themselves or, depending on age, students who should be those towards whom the education system should be flipped, because if anyone has an interest in education it must be them. We see versions of this argument popping up throughout the history of education, for example in the form of child- or student-centred education or (radical) democratic schools. And again, neo-liberalism has a voice in this as well, for example in the idea—heavily promoted in higher education in Britain—that the first duty of higher education is to generate 'student satisfaction,' which some, without much hesitation, seem to equate with customer satisfaction (see, for example, Aldridge and Rowley 1998).

Is the main duty of higher education lecturers to satisfy their students? Perhaps it is, perhaps it is not, because everything depends on the desires that students bring to the educational situation. If such desires are for education that takes them beyond where they are, that challenges them, that offers them new perspectives, that gives them desires that they could never have imagined would be worthwhile, then there is a case to be made. But in most cases the discourse about student satisfaction is about giving students what they say they want, rather than to engage them in the difficult—but hopefully in the longer term more significant—process of examining, questioning and rearranging their desires. (For the idea that education is a 'non-coercive rearrangement of desires' see Spivak 2004.)

The educational question, to put it differently, is the question whether what you desire or what you find in yourself as a desire,[1] is what you should be desiring in light of you own life and your life with others on a vulnerable planet with limited capacity for just fulfilling all our desires. And the educational work of educators, if this slightly strange formulation is permitted, is precisely to raise this question, which always implies an interruption of desires (see Biesta 2017, particularly Chapter 1). Education, in other words, has a 'duty to resist' (Meirieu 2007), not in order to suppress desires—desires are after all important to give energy and direction—and also not in order to tell children and young people what they should desire and what they shouldn't desire—which is the 'mode' of moralising authoritarian education—but in order to encourage children and young people to come into a relationship with their desires, rather than just run behind their desires and be totally determined by them.

If the latter can be characterised as an 'infantile' way of being in the world, then the former can perhaps be termed a 'grown-up' way of being in the world (see, again, Meirieu 2007), bearing in mind that we shouldn't assume that adults are automatically able to be in the world in a grown-up way, just as we shouldn't think that children are by definition not able to exist in such a way.

Although children and young people, pupils and students, have a crucial 'stake' in education, there is a limit to the idea of 'pupil power.' This limit is first and foremost an *educational* limit, in that education—if it is education and not learning (on the crucial importance of this distinction see Biesta 2013)—must bring something *to* students, must give them something, and, to be more precise, must give them 'more than they contain' (Todd 2010), more than they could ever have imagined they would want. And precisely for that reason education can never just be concerned with giving students what they want.

Teacher power?

The third group to consider are teachers and, as I have already mentioned, they play a prominent role in the current case for flipping the educational system, arguing that they want to reclaim their profession from top-down, micro-managed state control. I have already mentioned my agreement with the suggestion that the education system needs to be flipped urgently, and I have also indicated that teachers are paying a high price in the current set up, particularly because the micro-management of their practice minimizes opportunities for professional judgement and professional agency. But does all that mean that teachers are the 'natural' and uncontested category towards which the education system should be flipped? I am not entirely sure.

The first thing to note is that teachers are not a homogenous group. There are teachers who believe in control and there are teachers who believe in freedom. There are teachers who teach their subject and there are teachers who teach children. There are teachers who have a secular worldview and teachers who have a non-secular worldview. There are teachers who have the space to act, and there are teachers who don't have this space. There are teachers who want to flip the system, and there are teachers who are happy with things as they are. More importantly, how teachers are is to a significant degree also the result of the systems they work in and the systems that educated them, as teachers and, before that, as pupils. Teachers are, to put it differently, not immune for the effects of the very system that needs flipping, and, to some degree, they are a product of it (which is not to suggest, of course, that teachers would lack agency).

In my own work as a teacher I never tend to accuse my students of a lack of capacity, but always turn to the question of resources. To put it differently, I never question their ability to think but always ask the question what I, and others, have given them to think *with*. This is where I see some problems with the turn towards teachers, because I encounter a significant number of teachers who—willingly or unwillingly—seem to have adopted discourses that, in my view, run the risk of perpetuating the situation rather than leading to change. One issue I have in mind—about which I have written extensively elsewhere (see particularly Biesta 2006, 2012)—is the impact of the language of learning on education and the more general turn towards learning. While there are good reasons for paying more attention to learning, the almost total 'learnification' of education, expressed in the idea that education is 'all about learning' and that the main task of teachers is to facilitate the learning of students, has really decentred the teacher and has even raised the question whether teachers are actually still needed for the learning of the future.

If education is all about learning, then one can imagine that artificial intelligence can take over the facilitation of learning fairly soon. But if the dynamics of education are different, such as along the lines suggested in the previous paragraph, where the whole point of education is not just to fulfil the desires of students, but to put something in the way of such desires, to open up avenues for different, perhaps more meaningful or more important or more sustainable desires, and to create time and space to explore and examine desires, then we have an educational situation in which teachers play a crucial role. While adopting the language of learning may sound progressive and liberating, which may be a reason for explaining the enthusiasm amongst (some? many?) teachers, I am concerned that it has undermined the teaching profession rather than that it has enhanced the work of the teacher.

There is a similar problem with the way in which a significant number of teachers have turned towards 'evidence' and 'evidence-based research' (an expression I still don't entirely understand; isn't the point of research here to generate evidence rather than be based upon evidence?) in an attempt to regain their profession and enhance their professional agency. What is ironic, however, is that the turn towards evidence, and particularly the underlying paradigm of teaching as an intervention that is supposed to generate effects, is actually based on a misunderstanding of what teaching is and how the interaction between teachers and students should be understood. The idea of teaching as an effective intervention runs the risk, to put it mildly, of turning students into objects to be intervened upon rather than engaging with them as human beings who are trying to figure out who they are and what this world is they are finding themselves in (which is not meant to suggest that knowledge and understanding play no role in this; on the contrary). The 'logic' of teaching, in other words, is one of communication and interpretation, not of intervention and effect (see Biesta 2007, 2010, 2016, see also Davis 2017).

The issue here is not whether teaching should be evidence-*based*—which seems to suggest that evidence dictates what should happen—or evidence-*informed*—which seems to suggest that teachers have discretion in judging how to use evidence. The problem lies in the idea of evidence itself, if, that is, evidence is understood as having to do with the alleged effectiveness of interventions. And perhaps the biggest irony here is that teachers, in an attempt to liberate themselves from micro-management and top-down control, turn to an approach that makes their students into micro-manageable objects of control, rather than seeing them as human subjects whose own agency is at stake.

This means that in terms of the question in which direction the education system should be flipped, it is not enough to just say 'teachers,' because what matters is whether teachers see education as a matter of control, for example in the service of the effective production of measurable learning outcomes, or whether they see education as a public concern that always takes the question how we can encourager children and young people to want to exist in the world in a grown-up way as their orientation and frame of reference.

One direction?

To sum up: yes, the education system needs to be flipped, not just for the sake of teachers, but also for the sake of students, and for the sake of its own sanity. There is, however, not one 'natural' party that can or should lay a claim to education, because what really matters is what this claim is *about* and what this claim is *orientated* towards. It is, in other words, not parent power, pupil power or teacher power *per se* that we should be after, but the question whether parents, pupils and teachers are committed to keeping education orientated towards peaceful, sustainable and democratic ways of living-together-in-plurality—*education as a public concern*—or whether they are willing to give up on this ambition for the sake of their own interests.

Note

1 I use this formulation because many of 'our' desires are actually not our desires but are planted there, for example, by the advertising industry.

References

Aldridge, S. and Rowley, J., 1998. Measuring customer satisfaction in higher education. *Quality Assurance in Education*, 6 (4), 197–204.

Ball, S.J., 2003. The teacher's soul and the terrors of performativity. *Journal of Education Policy*, 18 (2), 215–228.
Biesta, G.J.J., 2006. *Beyond learning. Democratic education for a human future*. London/New York: Routledge.
Biesta, G.J.J., 2007. Why 'what works' won't work. Evidence-based practice and the democratic deficit of educational research. *Educational Theory*, 57 (1), 1–22.
Biesta, G.J.J., 2010. Why 'what works' still won't work. From evidence-based education to value-based education. *Studies in Philosophy and Education*, 29 (5), 491–503.
Biesta, G.J.J., 2012. Giving teaching back to education. Responding to the disappearance of the teacher. *Phenomenology and Practice*, 6 (2), 35–49.
Biesta, G.J.J., 2013. Interrupting the politics of learning. *Power and Education*, 5 (1), 4–15.
Biesta, G.J.J., 2015a. Resisting the seduction of the global education measurement industry: Notes on the social psychology of PISA. *Ethics and Education*, 10 (3), 348–360.
Biesta, G.J.J., 2015b. The duty to resist: Redefining the basics for today's schools. *Research on Steiner Education*, 6 (Special issue), 1–11.
Biesta, G.J.J., 2016. Improving education through research? From effectiveness, causality and technology, to purpose, complexity and culture. *Policy Futures in Education*, 14 (2), 194–210.
Biesta, G.J.J., 2017. *The rediscovery of teaching*. London/New York: Routledge.
Davis, A., 2017. It worked there. Will it work here? Researching teaching methods. *Ethics and Education*, 23 (3), 289–303.
Fives, A., 2017. *Evaluating parental power: An exercise in pluralist political theory*. Manchester: Manchester University Press.
Friedman, L.M., 1916. The parental right to control the religious education of the child. *Harvard Law Review*, 29 (5), 485–500.
Gewirtz, S., 2002. *The managerial school: Post-welfarism and social justice in education*. London: Routledge.
Gewirtz, S., Ball, S. and Bowe, R., 1995. *Markets, choice and equity in education*. Milton Keynes: Open University Press.
Green, A., 1990. *Education and state formation. The rise of education systems in England, France and the USA*. London: Macmillan.
Jeffrey, B. and Woods, P., 1998. *Testing teachers: The effects of school inspections on primary teachers*. London: Falmer Press.
Evers, J. and Kneyber, R., eds., 2016. *Flip the system: Changing education from the ground up*. London: Routledge.
Manning, H.E., 1872. *National education and parental rights*. London: Burns, Oats and Company.
Meirieu, P., 2007. *Pédagogie: Le devoir de résister. [Education: The duty to resist.]* Issy-les-Moulineaux: ESF éditeur.
Popkewitz, T.S., ed., 2000. *Educational knowledge: Changing relationships between the state, civil society, and the educational community*. Albany: SUNY Press.
Priestley, M., Biesta, G.J.J. and Robinson, S., 2015. *Teacher agency: An ecological approach*. London: Bloomsbury.
Ravitch, D., 2011. *The death and life of the great American school system: How testing and choice are undermining education*. New York: Basic Books.
Reay, D., Crozier, G., James, D., Hollingworth, S., Williams, K., Jamieson, F. and Beedell, P., 2008. Re-invigorating democracy? White middle class identities and comprehensive schooling. *Sociological Review*, 56 (2), 238–256.

Spivak, G.C., 2004. Righting the wrongs. *South Atlantic Quarterly*, 103 (2/3), 523–581.
Stein, Z., 2016. *Social justice and educational measurement. John Rawls, the history of testing, and the future of education*. London/New York: Routledge.
Todd, S., 2010. 'Bringing more than I contain': Ethics, curriculum and the pedagogical demand for altered egos. *Journal of Curriculum Studies*, 33 (4), 431–450.

4 Podcasts

Vehicles for professional growth and system flipping

Cameron Malcher

Since July 2013—and in partnership for much of that time with fellow New South Wales educator Corinne Campbell—I have produced the Teachers' Education Review Podcast, which focuses on education in Australia and aims to provide a professional learning resource for teachers by providing access to academics, researchers, experienced teachers, system leaders and other people of professional interest to teachers.

The story of the TER podcast is one of responding to context and circumstance, and a bit of frustrated idealism in the face of increased commodification of education and teacher professional learning. It also highlights the ease and efficacy of podcasting as a medium for teachers to flip the education system by sharing practice and insights beyond their school or local network and benefiting from the experience of others to whom they might otherwise not have access. Below I explain my own context, and the emergence of the TER podcast as a grassroots vehicle for authentic teacher learning.

The state of professional learning for teachers in New South Wales

I began teaching in NSW in 2005, the first year of new accreditation processes under the then NSW Institute of Teachers. One of the challenges of the transition was the need for mandatory professional development hours, and for some of those hours to be 'registered'. While the Department of Education provided some professional learning, in following years there was a notable growth of private providers offering registered courses and using the new professional learning accountabilities as a marketing tool.

Many of these providers offered excellent professional learning—course content itself was usually developed and delivered by experienced teachers—however, over time there was a noteworthy variation in the quality of some providers, and some courses facilitated by the same provider. Anecdotally, the seams were showing due to the tension between the Teacher Professional Learning business model and the need to provide quality content to ensure repeat business. Colleagues at work and on social media would comment and complain about courses not delivering what they felt was promised, and a degree of cynicism was evident in the discussion about non-teachers delivering professional learning programs.

The business model also loomed large over the access to professional learning available to all teachers. While the Department of Education provided services to teachers across the state, commercial providers concentrated in areas where the larger population made breadth and frequency of courses possible. But for the young teacher who had chosen rural service as a start to their career, choices would always be more limited.

Then, after winning the state election in 2011, the new conservative NSW government announced a restructure of the Department of Education that included the removal of all regional syllabus-specific consultants, maintaining only a handful based in Sydney, and also reducing the number of other administrative and support positions; this represented the second large-scale reduction in the overall number of non-school based positions in a decade, meaning a reduction in systemic support and provision of professional learning for teachers. This restructure came as part of the "Local Schools, Local Decisions" policy, which embodied the neoliberal ideology of marketised individuality being valued higher than social or systemic supports. This appeared to be the NSW education policy manifestation of the kind of deregulation agenda evident in education systems of other developed countries like the UK and USA. Where NSW schools had previously enjoyed much greater systemic support, allowing principals and school leaders to still be primarily educational leaders, this policy championed 'school autonomy' and local decision making. This meant additional administrative and managerial responsibilities, once completed by now-redundant non-school-based positions, were shifted to principals. This policy also accompanied an approximately $1.7 billion reduction in the NSW education budget over four years.

During this time the then-Labor federal government had commissioned the 'Gonski' review into school funding, which was delivered in 2012 and codified in a legislated funding model in 2012/13. It was largest reform of education funding in Australia in decades and was based on the principles of equitable, needs-based funding. NSW had been the first state to sign on to the model in April of 2013, with the governments of the ACT, South Australia and Tasmania signing up shortly afterwards, as well as the Catholic systemic schools and the Independent Schools Council of Australia, all by July 10 of 2013.

For the NSW government, this plan to increase funding represented a reversal of its planned budget cuts, however instead of returning non-school based positions, funding was delivered 'inside the school gate', with money going directly to schools. These increases in school budgets were funded, in part, by the reduction of non-school-based positions.

This decrease in state-wide provision of support, combined with an increase both in school funding and the number of teachers needing to meet accreditation requirements created further growth opportunities for private providers of registered professional learning.

It was in this context that the Teachers' Education Review podcast was created in 2013.

Talking back: a podcast is born

At a time when the direction of professional learning appeared to be increasingly commodified, the initial motivation to create a podcast – as well as identifying an absence of teacher-produced educational content in Australian podcasting – was to build a platform that elevated teachers' voices and practice and provided teachers' perspectives on topical issues in education. Planning initially for a panel discussion format, I reached out to several teachers who were already active online content producers and invited them to collaborate on the podcast. From those conversations, I ultimately formed a partnership with Corinne Campbell, then a NSW assistant principal in a public school, and together we devised a format that would become the TER Podcast.

Our first episode was just the two of us discussing issues of teaching and educational policy. We reviewed news stories related to education, Corinne provided an outline of her school's approach to developing homework policy, and we discussed PISA data and the way it had been reported in the media to focus on teachers while excluding data on systemic issues. It was a two-person attempt at the panel discussion format, and we intended to release monthly episodes. Publishing that first episode was exciting. It felt like a bit of a risk putting our opinions out there in a relatively unused format for Australian teachers, and the small-yet-positive reaction to the first episode was exhilarating.

With so much happening in education at the time and prompted by the positive experience of the first episode, Corinne and I decided to do a fortnightly episode to cover more topical content. We also thought that to discuss the Gonski funding reforms, we should take a chance and seek an interview with someone directly involved. We emailed the office of then-NSW Education Minister Adrian Piccoli and were surprised by a quick response with an agreement to be interviewed. In our minds, this provided a sense of legitimacy to the podcast and cemented the decision to commit to fortnightly episodes, as well as building our confidence in addressing system and policy issues early on.

The growth of the podcast proceeded from there. There was an interview guest on almost every episode from that point on, and we were continually surprised by the willingness of people working in education to be part of what was, effectively, an amateur hobbyist production by a couple of teachers. While producing the podcast was empowering for us and allowed for the voicing of opinions and experiences that often ran contrary to dominant media and policy narratives, it was also a method of professional learning that further empowered the listener. Audience feedback, both that which we sought directly and that provided by variations in download numbers, indicated that the variety of guests and topics was one of the primary benefits of the podcast, but also, like blogs and online videos and even plain old books, the podcast put the listener in control of the time, pace and depth of their engagement.

And so the TER podcast has continued since July 2013 as a voluntary exercise, clinging to that earlier mentioned frustrated idealism and the belief that teachers should have the greatest control over their own professional learning needs. The goal of the podcast remains to provide a resource that helps teachers set the course and pace of their learning, and in doing so, maintain greater control over and within the profession in a time of continuing, and often aggressive attempts at deregulation.

Since 2013 there has been a significant growth in the number Australian-education podcasts, with some produced by organisations, both not-for-profit and commercial entities, as well as the number of podcasts produced by educators for educators. In late 2017 several podcast producers banded together to form the Australian Educators' Online Network—providing a central point of access to podcast content at AEON.net.au, while trying to build a supportive network for teachers using this format to share their experiences and provide resources for others. The TER podcast is now one in a burgeoning arena of online content, by teachers, for teachers, that works to flip the system by reclaiming the airwaves for teacher voices, and by empowering teachers to control their narratives as well as how and when they learn.

5 Education beyond risk

Vulnerability as a challenge to neoliberalism's colour-blind order

Benjamin Doxtdator

Risk: the reliable scientist vs the rebel start-up

Education is a risky business. Or, at least it is a business where profit can be made from policies and platforms that seek to make education risk-free through evidence-based interventions. In *The Beautiful Risk of Education*, Gert Biesta (2015) charts the push to make education "strong, secure, [and] predictable", and argues that education cannot be made risk-free because "education is not an interaction between robots but an encounter between human beings" (pp. 1–2). We should take the analogy with robots seriously as platforms developed by software companies increasingly drive education. In fact, the Silicon Valley approach to flipping the education system embraces risk as part of its start-up culture and entrepreneurial ideology. We are encouraged to *move fast and break things* and to *stay foolish* (Blodget 2009, Jobs 2005). We are promised empowerment through disruptive innovation, a kind of social justice through neoliberal capitalism. Part of embracing the risk of education, according to Pearson and the World Economic Forum, means turning students into creative producers rather than passive consumers, suggesting that technology is the key to liberation (Stepner 2014, Mulgan 2015).

Obviously, the Silicon Valley approach to education is not the kind of 'beautiful' risk that Biesta has in mind since he opposes the move to make education only about preparation for participation in the economy. Biesta connects politics with pedagogy in his criticism of the learnification of education. In political discourse, *lifelong learning* replaced *lifelong education* and in pedagogical discourse, *students* have become *learners* and *teachers* turned into *facilitators*. Learnification makes it difficult to ask questions about the purpose of education and it also places a strong burden on the individual to constantly remain competitive as human capital (Biesta 2015). What should we learn and why? Often the implied answer is: whatever the future economy demands. However, that move forecloses a democratic discussion about the aims of education.

Instead of embracing the risk of education, I propose we give more careful consideration to vulnerability, something the human capital narrative leaves no room for. The term 'risk' certainly captures the anxieties of late capitalism and the heavily nationalistic tone of many reform policies (Beck 1992, A Nation at Risk 1983). But does 'risk' capture the experience of marginalised students who live the "age-old American saga of being asked to lose their heritage and community ways with language, literacy, and culture in order to achieve in U.S. schools" (Paris 2012, p. 96)? Could such a risk here be 'beautiful'? Or, are we better to consider the vulnerability of students, globally, in education systems that are increasingly shaped by corporate profit motives? While Gert Biesta's arguments offer valuable criticism of attempts to standardise education, I share Darren Chetty's concern that Biesta's discussion of Otherness falls into abstractions rather than resisting colonialism and racial injustice head on (2017, p. 477). Vulnerability, an inescapable fact of technological cultures, also gives us a language to talk about marginalisation, oppression, and precarity. Flipping the education system to embrace risk will keep us enmeshed in a neoliberal colour-blind narrative, one that pretends to not see race, impairing our ability to mount a more substantial resistance to the systems that marginalise so many students (Bonilla-Silva 2006).

From risk to vulnerability

A risk analysis of socio-technical systems aims to quantify problems, calculate probabilities, regulate, and ensure against future costs. However, risk management does not necessarily lead to reducing vulnerability. Managers can decide to "redistribute the costs of the [risk] events" and raise insurance premiums rather than address vulnerabilities up front. Through the lens of risk, "quantification becomes a value in itself that constricts both policy options and the potential for achieving public benefits through diverse means" (Sarewitz, Pielke, and Keykhah 2003, p. 810).

Education has been placed firmly within a risk lens in the national policy arena, where those students who are 'at risk' are often also seen as *a risk* (Brown 2016). As human capital, students are a risk to themselves if they do not become lifelong learners: "If you can't invent (and reinvent) your own job and distinctive competencies, you risk chronic underemployment" (Wagner and Dintersmith 2015, p. 62). Beyond the individualised risk to themselves, students constitute a risk to the GDP amidst a "rising tide of mediocrity" in the education system (A Nation at Risk 1983). McKinsey (2009) calculated the cost to the US GDP of two 'achievement gaps' over the decade from 1998 to 2008: the achievement gap between the US compared to other education systems supposedly cost up to $2.3 trillion USD, and the achievement gap between Black and Hispanic students compared to white students on standardised tests supposedly cost $525 billion USD. This latter racialised 'gap' constitutes a rising risk according to McKinsey (2009): "Left unchecked, the magnitude of such disparities will rise in coming years as blacks and Hispanics account for a larger share of the US population." Leave it to McKinsey to embody deficit thinking in the most literal, and financial, way possible.

Switching lenses from risk to vulnerability can help us avoid privatising suffering. In the context of public policy, vulnerability has been defined as the "inherent characteristics of a system that create the potential for harm" irrespective of any calculations about the 'risk' of specific events (Sarewitz, Pielke, and Keykhah 2003, p. 805). Where risk discourses emphasise *security, control, closure, legality*, and *institutions*, vulnerability discourses emphasise *solidarity, opening up, dissent, justice,* and *community* (Bijker, Hommels, and Mesman 2014). To make this shift from risk to vulnerability concrete, consider how each lens might frame an assignment where students blog publicly. A risk analysis might consider which websites the institution should block, what control the teacher has over the platform students publish on, and the legal consequences should any harm come to students. However, through the lens of vulnerability, a different set of important questions emerge: What solidarity and support do institutions "owe those who venture into public waters" (McMillan Cottom 2015)? Who do we make vulnerable by asking everyone to open up? How might an Indigenous woman expressing dissent and calling for justice be differently vulnerable than other members of the community?

Most importantly from the perspective of critical pedagogy and social justice, shifting from risk to vulnerability fits comfortably into Gloria Ladson-Billings' work about culturally relevant pedagogy which confronts deficit models of thinking by asking educators to "bring an appreciation of their students' assets to their work" (2014, p. 74). Beyond being culturally relevant, pedagogies need to be culturally *sustaining* (Paris 2012), working to "ensure that consistently marginalised students are repositioned into a place of normativity – that is, that they become subjects in the instructional process, not mere objects" (Ladson-Billings 2014, p. 76).

In her ethnographic study of vulnerability in a neonatal intensive care unit (ICU), Jessica Mesman finds the "incessant relocation of vulnerability" because "rather than diminishing vulnerability, actors merely move it from one place to another" (2014, p. 72). Any intervention carries unintended consequences, and creates a new situation with emergent and multiple vulnerabilities. New technology must be carefully integrated: "the older models are not replaced immediately when new models arrive. Initially, both models are used simultaneously to corroborate and stabilise the new device" (2014, p. 77). In the case of the ICU, it is up to the professional judgment of the nurses to decide that a new device is working properly. When we are presented with analogies between education and medicine, we must keep in mind that the nurses in Mesman's study were not asked to passively accept something that someone else told them works.

What's the effect size of culturally sustaining pedagogy?

Educators are increasingly encouraged to swallow the 'what works' pill and become 'evidenced-based' practitioners like doctors. Robert Marzano presents us with a "rank ordering" of what should work anywhere and everywhere, noting that the most effective schools "provide interventions that are designed to overcome student background characteristics that might impede learning". With the right strategies in hand, schools can "enter an era of unprecedented effectiveness", but only "if they follow the direction provided by the research" (2003, pp. 1–8).

In contrast with the agency nurses exercised in the ICU that Mesman studied, Marzano does not present teachers with a rich kind of agency that's worth wanting. Clear directions and rank orders of interventions are supposed to eliminate the need for the judgement of teachers, and thus reduce the within-school variability of student performance. Marzano's approach embodies an obvious kind of deficit thinking when he talks about students 'overcoming' their background, but a similar logic underlies John Hattie's (2015) argument that schools should "enable anyone to climb out" of poverty based on his own personal success, which he puts down to what he learned: "perseverance, deliberate practice and to never say no" (p. 6). Hattie locates whatever accounts for failure in the individual character and disposition of students rather in the wider systems of injustice.

In his brief for Pearson, Hattie (2015) argues that a *decrease* in the autonomy of doctors has been a *good* thing because "their decisions now are very much based on research evidence". For Hattie, the question becomes: "Under what conditions and to what extent should teachers have autonomy?" (2015, p. 24). His answer appears to be: only when teachers use an intervention with an 'effect size' of at least 0.4 (2009). When studies are made commensurable through effect sizes, not only are treatments standardised, but people are standardised also. This becomes obvious in Hattie's treatment of the push to reduce class sizes which he calls a 'distraction' and part of a strategy to "appease the parents". With an effect-size of 0.2, reducing class size falls below the threshold of meaningful change for Hattie. He argues that reducing class size makes little difference because "teachers rarely change how they teach when they move from larger to smaller classes" (2015, pp. 9–11).

However, Hattie's (2005) own examination of two large-scale studies in the United States reports *"much higher"* and *"close to double"* effect-sizes for minority and African-American students in smaller classes (2005, p. 390–392). So when Hattie (2015) presents that that one number—0.2—*as a distraction*, he standardises students to the white norm and conceals the differential impact that smaller class sizes might have on minority and African American students. When effect sizes are then brought into public debates to make decisions about education, who does that *make* vulnerable? What decisions will politicians and school boards make as they weigh Hattie's reported effect size against what historically marginalised families and communities might want—and need—for their children? The education debt owed to people of colour in the U.S. and elsewhere will continue to compound as long as narrow statistical measures displace a more democratic conversation (Ladson-Billings 2006).

Despite the need for a broader conversation, Hattie relentlessly frames the purpose education in mechanistic terms: "for every student to gain at least a year's growth for a year's input" (2015, p. 1). In her study of Maori and Pasifika students in Aotearoa New Zealand, Anne Milne argues that a narrow focus on raising achievement misses out on the real causes of marginalisation and exclusion for Maori and Pasifika students who achieve "above national norms in literacy" but are "still featured in dropout statistics by Year 10". Milne concludes: "The answer is obviously more complex than a single-minded focus on technical academic achievement" (2009, p. 7).

Milne exposes a double vulnerability of Maori students: to exclusion and being pushed out of school; and to the "whitening" of their children through colonialism (2009, p. 17). A similar logic of settler colonialism continues to shape Canada. My own family heritage is First Nations, Haudenosaunee, on my dad's side. Living in Brussels, people take my last name, Doxtdator, to be Dutch or German, which is basically right. The warrior the Oneida called Honyery Tewahangarakhen (b. 1724) was known as Honyery Doxtator to the white settlers because his father was a German colonist named Dachstätter. The British had hoped that the German settlers would intermarry with the First Nations peoples as part of what historian Ann Laura Stoler calls the "strategic tactics of conquest" (Tiro 2011, pp. 18–22).

But I was not racialised and excluded; I was praised for being intelligent and supported by all my teachers. Since I 'pass' for white and have the privilege that comes with that, I will never need to worry that people judge my intelligence based on assumptions about my race. But there is also a deep loss that follows the whitening of intelligence and the lack I experienced of any curriculum representation of First Nations people as intelligent. Milne notes that her own children, who come from a mostly Pakeha background with Maori heritage on their paternal grandfather's side, have made a "commitment to resist, reject, and reverse this process [of whitening] through their strong identification as Maori" (2009, p. 17). I'm not sure what the effect size calculation is on that kind of resistance, but I'm pretty sure that it doesn't matter.

On technological disappointment and sacrifice zones

The statistical techniques behind the 'what works' movement are thoroughly technological. As Theodore Porter argues, "the task of quantification [in the field of medicine] depended on an infrastructure of standardisation", and standardised measurements helped to deal with "distance and distrust" for the purpose of regulation (1995, p. 206). Following the rise of industrial medicine, educational administrators took up standardised psychological testing in the early twentieth century. Porter notes that in contrast to the teachers who were mainly women, most of the administrators were men, "looking for ways to distinguish themselves from people in the classroom" (1995, p. 210).

The 'what works' movement, with its roots in cognitive psychology, has found powerful corporate allies that back 'evidence-based' approaches with platforms to deliver content, data extraction to measure progress, and data visualisation to bridge "distance and distrust" by convincing publics that their brand of education is effective. In the affluent area of Palo Alto near Silicon Valley, Alt-School, a private school run by former Google executive Max Ventilla, developed a platform to 'personalise' learning. In November 2017, the company announced to the surprise of parents that it was closing schools to begin the phase of marketing its platform, which the company hopes is more profitable than running schools (Satariano 2017). While the original schools featured inviting spaces and were well-staffed with a low pupil-to-teacher ratio, we need to consider who becomes vulnerable when the platform is rolled out in public schools facing austerity and with student populations labelled 'at risk'.

In a world where we have been delivered complex platforms instead of labour-saving automation, David Graeber (2012) argues that neoliberalism's job is to convince us that "we do live in a world of wonders" in order to suppress "any idea of "redemptive future, but any radically different technological future" (para. 77). We have so many *bureaucratic technologies* that have "turned us into part- or full-time administrators", often generating *more* work, but not the *poetic technologies*, such as robots that do our laundry, which "work to realise impossible fantasies" (Graeber 2012, para. 70). While we may experience what Graeber calls 'technological disappointment' in the affluent parts of the so-called Global North, the Global South has long lived the nightmare of being what Naomi Klein (2016) calls a 'sacrifice zone' for extraction and waste. Our technologies depend on so much destruction that takes place *elsewhere*. From the mining of minerals in conflict zones to the ecological damage inflicted by fossil fuels, our technologies extract a heavy human and environmental cost.

Thus, I'm duly sceptical of apparently progressive movements that embrace the corporate logic of profit models through digital platforms. For example, beneath Michael Fullan's call to "make pedagogy the driver and technology the accelerator" lies a deep corporate infrastructure (Fullan 2015, p. 45). In the white paper *Towards a New End: New Pedagogies for Deep Learning* (NPDL), Michael Fullan and Maria Langworthy (2013) frame a global education 'crisis' in terms of two factors: boredom in school, and alluring technology outside of school. In short, they argue that the innovation of the market sector has failed to take root in education. But what would it mean for technology to be merely an accelerator and not a driver? Clearly, technology companies are financial drivers of policy. Behind the NPDL white paper are "global education stakeholders"—Intel, Pearson, Microsoft, Promethean, and Fullan's own company—"working together in partnership" along with a long list of 'contributors', including John Hattie and PISA king Andreas Schleicher (Fullan and Langworthy 2013, p.ii). While NPDL is supposed to put deeper learning ahead of technology, because "some of the project partners are technology companies", Fullan and Langworthy introduce a large role for a "scalable" "shared technology platform" that will be used for everything from data-collection to "capacity-building" (2013, p. 18).

By thinking of technologies in terms of 'acceleration', Fullan misses the role technologies play as "powerful forces acting to reshape human activities and their meanings" (Bijker 2009, p. 607). Pearson, one of NPDL partners, isn't generally known for unleashing a world of wonders, and schools that are designed to be 'scalable' often do so at the cost of students and families. Bridge International Academies (BIA), which operates mainly in Kenya and Uganda, "is pre-made for scaling up" (Riep and Machacek 2016, p. 6) and sees a "$64 billion parent paid market" in the "800 Million primary and nursery aged pupils living on less than $2 per person per day" (BIA no date). BIA achieves 'scalability' through "scripted instructions designed in Boston and recited word-for-word [from tablets] to children across sub-Saharan Africa". Despite the highly scripted instruction that relies on deprofessionalising teachers, BIA schools in Uganda are "not affordable for households with an average income" (Riep and Machacek 2016, pp. 24–26).

In contrast to Fullan's narrative about the crisis in schools being driven by boredom and the allure of technology, Anne Milne more closely zooms in on the most vulnerable students. Writing about Maori and Pasifika children, Milne (2009) says: "Disengagement and dislocation from their cultural identity begins when children enter our schools' white spaces" (p. 53). The educational crisis manufactured by corporations and the elite displaces responsibility and risk onto individuals to maintain their 'human capital', playing on precarity of those barely hanging on. It creates markets to operate in, to sell products and platforms that promise to reduce the risk of education, while at the same time leaving systemic vulnerabilities intact. But the real crisis in education differentially impacts students who are racialised and students experiencing poverty.

While moving from a risk discourse to a vulnerability discourse does not necessarily affirm the agency of students, Judith Butler (2014) argues that we do not need to hold vulnerability in binary opposition to agency. We are too used to understanding agency as a kind of invulnerability, as "sovereign defensiveness", but there are other forms of agency, "forms of non-violent resistance that mobilise vulnerability for the purpose of asserting existence" (p. 17). Far too often, the people in the sacrifice zones of our world are left to assert their existence against a neoliberal order while the rest of us benefit from our silence and complicity. We must mobilise, especially those of us who are protected with enough privilege and security to speak out, and assert our existence as professionals who are not satisfied with 'what works', with risk-free education, or with embracing risk without confronting neoliberalism's destruction. A meaningful flipping of the system would put vulnerability up front, making it central to the struggle ahead.

References

A Nation at Risk, 1983. Available at: www2.ed.gov/pubs/NatAtRisk/risk.html [Accessed 3 February 2018].

Beck, U., 1992. *Risk society: Toward a new modernity*. London: SAGE.

Bijker, W., 2009. Globalisation and vulnerability: Challenges and opportunities for SHOT around its fiftieth anniversary, *Technology and Culture*, 50 (3), 600–612.

Bijker, W., Hommels, A., and Mesman, J., 2014. Studying vulnerability in technological cultures. In: A. Hommels, J. Mesmanm and W. Nijker, eds. *Vulnerability in technological cultures: New directions in research and governance.* Cambridge: MIT.

Biesta, G., 2015. *The beautiful risk of education.* London: Paradigm.

Blodget, H., 2009. *Mark Zuckerberg on innovation.* Available from: www.businessinsider.com/mark-zuckerberg-innovation-2009-10?IR=T [Accessed 3 February 2018].

Bonilla-Silva, E., 2006. *Racism without racists: Color-blind racism and the persistence of racial inequality in the United States.* New York: Rowman & Littlefield.

Bridge International Academies, *Prospectus* (no date), [leaked document] Available from: www.longviewoneducation.org/wp-content/uploads/2018/02/BIA-Prospectus.pdf [Accessed 3 February 2018].

Brown, K., 2016. *Vulnerability and young people: Care and social control in policy and practice.* Bristol: Policy Press.

Butler, J., 2014. Rethinking vulnerability and resistance [lecture]. Available from: www.institutofranklin.net/sites/default/files/files/Rethinking%20Vulnerability%20and%20Resistance%20Judith%20Butler.pdf [Accessed 3 February 2018].

Chetty, D., 2017. Philosophy for children, learnification, intelligent adaptive systems and racism—a response to Gert Biesta, *Childhood & Philosophy*, 13 (28), 471–480.

Fullan, M., 2015., *The new meaning of educational change*, 5th ed. New York: Teachers College Press.

Fullan, M. and Langworthy, M., 2013. *Towards a new end: New pedagogies for deep learning.* Seattle: Collaborative Impact. Available from: www.newpedagogies.nl/images/towards_a_new_end.pdf [Accessed 3 February 2018].

Graeber, D., 2012. Of flying cars and the declining rate of profit, *The Baffler* (19), Available from: https://thebaffler.com/salvos/of-flying-cars-and-the-declining-rate-of-profit [Accessed 3 February 2018].

Hattie, J., 2005. The paradox of reducing class size and improved learning outcomes, *International Journal of Educational Research*, 43 (6), 387–425.

Hattie, J., 2009. *Visible learning: A synthesis of 800+ meta-analyses on achievement.* Abingdon: Routledge.

Hattie, J., 2015. *What doesn't work in education: The politics of distraction.* London: Pearson. Available from: www.pearson.com/content/dam/corporate/global/pearson-dot-com/files/hattie/150602_DistractionWEB_V2.pdf [Accessed 3 February 2018].

Jobs, S., 2005. Commencement address. Available from: https://news.stanford.edu/2005/06/14/jobs-061505/[Accessed 3 February 2018].

Klein, N., 2016. *Let them drown.* Available from: www.lrb.co.uk/v38/n11/naomi-klein/let-them-drown [Accessed 3 February 2018].

Ladson-Billings, G., 2006. From the achievement gap to the education debt: Understanding achievement in U.S. schools, *Educational Researcher*, 35 (7).

Ladson-Billings, G., 2014. Culturally relevant pedagogy 2.0: a.k.a. the remix, *Harvard Educational Review*, 84 (1).

Marzano, R., 2003. *What works in schools? Translating research into action.* Alexandria: ASCD.

McKinsey, 2009. *The economic cost of the US education gap.* Available from: www.mckinsey.com/industries/social-sector/our-insights/the-economic-cost-of-the-us-education-gap [Accessed 3 February 2018].

McMillan Cottom, T., 2015. *Everything but the burden: Publics, public scholarship, and institutions.* Available from: https://tressiemc.com/uncategorized/everything-but-the-burden-publics-public-scholarship-and-institutions/[Accessed 3 February 2018].

Mesman, J., 2014. Relocation of vulnerability in neonatal intensive care medicine. In: Hommels, A, Mesmanm, J. and Bijker, W., eds., *Vulnerability in technological cultures: New directions in research and governance*. Cambridge: MIT.

Milne, A., 2009. Colouring in the white spaces: Cultural identity and learning in school. Available from: www.appa.org.nz [Accessed 3 February 2018)].

Mulgan, G., 2015. Why evidence of 'what works' is vital for global education, *World Economic Forum*. Available from: www.weforum.org/agenda/2015/10/why-evidence-of-what-works-is-vital-for-global-education/[Accessed 3 February 2018].

Paris, D., 2012. Culturally sustaining pedagogy: a needed change in stance, terminology, and practice, *Educational Researcher*, 41 (93).

Porter, T., 1995. *Trust in numbers*. New Jersey: Princeton University Press.

Riep, C., Machacek, M., 2016. Schooling the poor profitably. (Education International) Available from: www.ei-ie.org/media_gallery/DOC_Final_28sept.pdf [Accessed 3 February 2018].

Sarewitz, D., and Pielke, R., and Keykhah, M., 2003. Vulnerability and risk: Some thoughts from a political and policy perspective, *Risk Analysis*, 23 (4).

Satariano, A., 2017. *Silicon Valley tried to reinvent schools. Now it's rebooting*. Bloomberg. Available from: www.bloomberg.com/news/articles/2017-11-01/silicon-valley-tried-to-reinvent-schools-now-it-s-rebooting [Accessed 3 February 2018].

Stepner, D., 2014. Why the future will be made by creators, not consumers. *WIRED*. Available from: www.wired.com/insights/2014/12/future-made-by-creators-not-consumers/[Accessed 3 February 2018].

Tiro, K., 2011. *The people of the Standing Stone*. Amherst: University of Massachusetts Press.

Wagner, T. and Dintersmith, T., 2015. *Most likely to succeed: Preparing our kids for the innovation era*. New York: Simon and Schuster.

Part II
Collaborative expertise
Reprofessionalising the system

Education has a magnetic attraction to continuous improvement and comparison. Perpetual advancement and reform are bolstered by public narratives that compare countries and schools, and polarise teachers against one another, against parents, and against governments. Those things that should be the property and work of the profession such as teaching, curriculum, assessment and professional development are often re-cast as objects that require treatment or fixing from external 'experts' or 'more successful' contexts.

Determining what might or might not require attention is in part the work of policy workers, industrial leaders, researchers and other interested parties. Teachers are often seen, not as agents or decision makers, but as the worker bees of the education hive. The teaching profession is a largely untapped resource, blamed for the system's failures and disempowered by system mandates. Yet teachers' collective experience and expertise is considerable. They understand better than anyone the nuances at work in their communities. This section of the book explores how education systems might harness teachers' wealth of knowledge and skills to build an appetite for collaboration aimed at system growth. It is through collaboration that the profession can resist forces that threaten to outsource or automate teachers' intellectual work and redefine professionalism.

International Large-Scale Assessments (ISLAs) have become a primary driver behind system-wide reforms and initiative cascades from classrooms to national policy agendas. **Greg Thompson, David Rutkowski** and **Sam Sellar** argue that there is an absence of teacher voice in interpreting results and as such there is a displacement between the designers, administrators and analytical arms of assessment systems and the validity of the data by those using them most intimately. They propose strategies for addressing the displacement issue and call for educators to engage in dialogue around ISLAs.

Cameron Paterson and **Keren Caple** present an intriguing perspective that challenges the assertion that all schooling is relevant. In the face of significant global financial, technological, environmental and sociocultural changes, education is often targeted in an effort to ready young people for uncertain futures. The authors advocate for networked learning. They do not suggest we replace the position of teacher but open our minds to the additional benefits of looking outwardly to the world beyond school for innovative possibilities of practice that support students to deepen knowledge and discover how to apply it across multiple possible contexts.

Drawing on research studies of teachers' professional learning and leadership experiences in Canada, **Carol Campbell** presents five points of reflection and consideration related to teacher-led educational growth. These five points are transferable to any setting where professional knowledge and skills are applied locally, across networks and within systems to improve work and build efficacy, identity and inform policy from the bottom-up.

Sydneysiders **Gavin Hays** and **Adam Hendry** capture the successive impacts of introducing, embedding and evaluating pedagogical changes. They posit that these changes have had a positive effect on teacher learning and development, and subsequently on student outcomes. Furthermore, they suggest that these positive benefits have also served to foster a motivational commitment by all members of the community to the vision and mission of their school.

Yasodai Selvakumaran focuses on the challenges of 'out of field teaching', with a personal story of being expected to teach outside of her area of expertise. Drawing on her own school's experience of responding to this problem by creating and utilising subject experts to support colleagues to build disciplinary knowledge and practice confidence, Yasodai gives a real-life example of how teachers are working collaboratively to address undesirable system realities.

Teachers struggle to collaborate effectively amidst the frenetic rate of reform in education and ever-increasing workloads and accountabilities. **Andy Hargreaves, Shaneé Washington** and **Michael T. O'Connor** flag six current threats to wellbeing emerging from their international research, which are evident in and applicable to other contexts, including Australia. Boldly claiming that "there is no student wellbeing without teacher wellbeing" they propose five ways to think about teacher wellbeing that should be food for thought (and action) for leaders on every rung of the system ladder.

6 Flipping large-scale assessments

Bringing teacher expertise to the table

Greg Thompson, David Rutkowski and Sam Sellar

Introduction: Australia versus Kazakhstan in the global education race

In 2016, there was widespread media coverage in Australia about the 2015 Trends in Mathematics and Science Study (TIMSS), because Australian students had declined from 18th to 28th place in Year 4 maths and from 12th to 18th place in Year 8 maths. What particularly concerned media commentators and politicians was that Australia had been outperformed by Kazakhstan. This prompted a number of newspaper headlines: "Poor Australia education ranking prompts soul-searching",[1] "'Wake up call': Australian students are worse at maths and science than children in KAZAKHSTAN",[2] "Australia crashing down international leaderboard for education, falling behind Kazakhstan"[3] and "Australia behind Kazakhstan in education rankings".[4] In response to these headlines, the Australian Federal Education Minister, Simon Birmingham, made the following comment:

> I don't *want* to denigrate Kazakhstan, or indeed their artistic skills with movies like Borat. I think, though, Australia should be seeking to be amongst the best in the world and declines like this are unacceptable, and that we need to be working hard to turn it around.[5]

We can certainly debate the reasonableness of Birmingham's interpretation that Kazakhstan—a country with a well-developed space program—should not have higher levels of science and mathematics achievement because of stereotypes promoted by Sascha Baron Cohen's 2006 movie, *Borat: Cultural Learnings of America for Make Benefit Glorious Nation of Kazakhstan*. However, another set of inferences made in this media debate deserve careful evaluation. The first of these is the assumption that "Australia is losing to Kazakhstan in the latest global education report card" (Conifer 2016). The second is that the "Quality of Australian education [is falling] behind Kazakhstan's" (Education Matters 2016). These related, common-sense conclusions require critical scrutiny. Is education a global race where the winners and losers can be identified? Do international assessments measure the quality of education systems?

International assessments, such as Programme for International Student Assessment (PISA) and TIMSS, are examples of large-scale assessments used to rank education systems, inform policy and drive professional decision-making. If we want to 'flip the system', we need to pay careful attention to how assessments like PISA and TIMSS have become tools to support a variety of ideological and political positions. We should draw fewer, yet more purposeful, conclusions from International Large-Scale Assessments (ILSAs). However, ILSAs remain poorly understood because the technical work to create and analyse these assessments, and the resulting limitations from those decisions, are not well understood among those who use the data. Essentially, ILSAs have become 'black boxes' where the limitations and cautions associated with their use are buried in technical reports while strong interpretations and public judgments abound. This is the problem of *displacement*: domain expertise that could inform ILSA interpretation is displaced from sites where these interpretations are made. The lack of dialogue between technical and domain expert groups can lead to incomplete information and faulty interpretation.

While the Kazakhstan example relates to Australia's TIMSS performance, similar headlines have been generated by Australia's PISA results. For example, in 2012, the Grattan Institute published a report titled *Catching Up: Learning from the Best School Systems in East Asia* (Jensen et al. 2012), which argued that Australian schools should copy aspects of schooling in Shanghai, Korea, Singapore and Hong Kong because these systems are 'top performers' based on their PISA rank. This report generated a spate of newspaper headlines celebrating performance in East Asia and a feature article in which then Prime Minister, Julia Gillard, implied that Australian schools were becoming the 'runt of the litter' in the Asia Pacific region (Franklin 2012). But is this this a reasonable interpretation?

Our aim in this chapter is to provide an easy to follow a set of steps for testing the statement, which was implied in the coverage of the PISA scores and rankings: *if* Australia is ranked below top performing countries in PISA, *then* there is a problem with the quality of education in Australia. This argument can be easily adapted to interrogate any headlines based on ILSA rankings, but we will focus specifically on PISA. This is the type of proposition that might be debated in a school staffroom or over dinner with friends and is colloquially described as a 'barbecue stopper' in Australia. We think it is a proposition that teachers should be able to confirm or challenge, and there are three simple questions that can be asked:

1   What does PISA measure?
2   What do PISA rankings tell us?
3   What is educational quality?

Let's consider each question in turn.

What does PISA measure?

PISA was established by the OECD to assess reading, science and mathematics literacy among 15-year-olds in OECD member countries. The assessment was first conducted in 2000 and has taken place every three years since then. In each triennial PISA cycle, one core content area serves as a major domain (e.g. mathematics in 2012, science in 2015, and reading in 2018) and is assessed more thoroughly than the other two areas, which serve as minor domains. Over time, PISA has also expanded to assess additional topics such as financial literacy and collaborative problem solving. In addition to the cognitive portion of PISA, students, principals, and, in some countries, parents and teachers, are administered a background questionnaire that solicits information about young people, their family, and their school contexts, with emphasis on the major domain.

The popularity of PISA has increased over time with the number of participating educational systems growing from 33 in 2000 to 72 in the 2015 cycle. The ambitious participation and assessment goals set forth by the OECD and its members requires a high degree of sophistication in both the sampling of participants and the collection of data. For example, within each country sampled students are only administered a small portion of the PISA assessment and those results are then aggregated to the population level to achieve country scores. Although the methods are well established in the assessment literature, they limit how the data should be used. Some of these challenges have been discussed in academic literature (Kreiner and Christensen 2014, Rutkowski and Rutkowski 2016) and the interested reader is encouraged to consult these resources. Here we simply want to emphasise two points. First, PISA measures what young people who are 15 years of age and who are enrolled in school know on a given day about content that the OECD has determined to be important for participation in the global economy. This means it is not a good assessment of the curriculum of a given country or jurisdiction. Second, PISA measures what 15-year-olds in schools have learnt from 15 years of life experience, not necessarily what they have learnt from their years of schooling. This is another problem for comparison, because different countries have different pathways for 15-year-olds. Further, in regard to sampling, in 2012, 16 of the participating countries in PISA, including top performing Shanghai, captured less than 80% of all 15-year-olds in their country (OECD 2014, p. 268). In some countries such as Costa Rica, Vietnam and Albania, only about half of 15-year-olds attend schools and were sampled for participation (Sellar *et al.* 2017, p. 44). Other important questions include whether all students equally motived to take the assessment, does motivation impact results and are some curricula better aligned to PISA, giving students in those countries an assessment advantage?

Certainly, PISA does attempt to assess a great deal of content. However, regardless of the claims made by the OECD or national educational policy makers, it is imperative to remember that *PISA measures what a representative sample of 15 year olds enrolled in school knew and could do on the day of testing in select topics which the OECD (an economic free market organization) deemed important to be successful in a free market economy.* Let us now turn to our second question, which focuses on national rankings, sometimes known as the global educational race.

What do the PISA rankings tell us?

All that most people hear about PISA is how their country ranks on the three major areas tested (math, science, and reading). However, these rankings are a very small part of ILSAs. A country's overall ranking is not the most important piece of information generated by the assessment. For example, PISA and other ILSAs collect a range of indicators that can be used to help contextualise achievement (e.g. school resources, student study habits, teaching practices), as well as information about bullying, students' perceptions of school, and their self-confidence in assessed subjects, to name a few. We have to be careful about interpreting any data presented from PISA, especially when countries are ranked because each country differs greatly. To that end, there are two main issues to keep in mind.

First, all reported PISA results should include a statistical measure of uncertainty, which quantifies multiple error sources in the results. This measure of uncertainty, or standard error, is normally reported in brackets directly following the PISA score. For example, the 2015 mathematics achievement of Australian 15-year-olds was estimated as 494, which meant a ranking of 25. When accounting for the standard error, we are 95% confident that Australia's score was between 491 and 497, which could improve its ranking by five spots to 20th on the high end or lower it by four spots to 29th. In fact, because there is overlap in the estimated scores, statistically Australia scored no differently than Austria, New Zealand, Vietnam, Russia, Sweden, France, United Kingdom, Czech Republic, Portugal, Italy. As such, PISA rankings are best understood as ranges and interpretations of the results need to take this into account. Standard errors remind all stakeholders that PISA scores are not exact, but rather estimations of what the OECD believes 15-year-olds know and can do.

Second, Australia oversamples participants so that there is more information about the performance of young people in different jurisdictions. For example, young people in the Australian Capital Territory tend to perform very well, while other states and territories have much lower scores. If scores are only reported in the aggregate it is possible that scores in one jurisdiction improve from one assessment to the next, while scores in another jurisdiction decline. Talking about the quality of Australian schools as a homogeneous group occludes information about performance that is readily available and may be provide better insight for designing policy. Often, PISA is of little use to teachers and principals who do not gain any information about their students. This extends to schools that sit for PISA, because scores are not interpretable at the student or school level. But regardless of how rankings are presented, those who rank highly in PISA are touted as having quality educational systems. How we define quality education, however, is often much more complex than what PISA measures.

What is educational quality?

'Quality' is a classic example of management jargon. It is generally assumed that everyone agrees about what 'quality' is, however Stake and Schwandt (2006) posited that "discerning quality is always a matter of expectation and comparison. Notions of quality ... have no meaning absent of notions of inferiority, insignificance, worthlessness, and unimportance" (p. 404). ILSAs imply that some countries' educational systems are inferior based on rankings. Using assessment data to determine quality requires a deep understanding of the technical limitations of the assessment. Further, once we have a clear idea of what is being measured and how it is being measured, we still need to determine whether changes in the measure indicate changes in quality. This requires a clear definition of quality.

In Australia, we have a document that sets out what constitutes 'high-quality' education for all Australian young people (MCEETYA 2008). The term 'high-quality' is not defined, but the characteristics of a high-quality schooling are implied across the nine points in the first goal of the Melbourne Declaration on Educational Goals for Young Australians, which is to ensure that 'Australian schooling promotes equity and excellence'. The Melbourne Declaration covers a range of issues, including: providing schooling that is free from discrimination; supporting Indigenous culture and knowledge and the learning of Indigenous young people; reducing the effects of socio-economic and other forms of disadvantage; ensuring that schools contribute to a cohesive society; encouraging high expectations and providing challenging learning; and ensuring that schooling meets the personalized needs of all young people. This document specifies agreed goals shared "by all Australian Education Ministers" (p. 2) to create quality education systems.

The Melbourne Declaration clearly spells out the complexity of quality in a national education system. Going through the voluminous list of the goals and sub-goals, it is clear that some aspects of the educational quality described are more amenable to being measured by ILSAs than others. When one highly aggregated measure, such as a PISA math score, becomes the sole or dominant measure of national educational quality, we need to be sure that it is valid to interpret PISA scores in this way. Given their vast knowledge of the national educational context, teachers and principals can and should play an active role in this validity process.

Validity: an argumentative approach

If you have considered the three questions above and our arguments in response to each, then you have just participated in a validity evaluation.

Arguably, you are already doing more than your government to validate the inferences drawn from ILSA data. While test developers such as the OECD produce technical reports that undertake validation at the international level, they do not evaluate the validity of inferences drawn at the national level. Participant countries must assume responsibility for evaluating the use and consequences of the tests in each specific context. With this in mind, we have a number of suggestions for participant countries regarding their responsibilities for validity.

First, we do not validate a test (i.e. validity is not a property of the test), we validate the interpretations made. Each use of test scores requires a new validation argument. Thus, we can see why the OECD could not possibly validate each interpretation made in each participating system. A key question for PISA—indeed for all ILSAs—is how the data produced should be used. Tests do not speak for themselves, nor do the data produced point to simple policy solutions. Individual scores, average scores, and comparative rankings do not themselves constitute meaning, rather they provide a starting point for conversation. The meaning attributed to test scores (at its most basic level, the notions of 'good' or 'bad' scores) requires a leap from the numbers to judgment about what these scores represent and, subsequently, what should be done. This leap from the psychometric to the inferential is complex and is the focus of validity theory.

We define validity "as the extent to which the proposed interpretations and uses of test scores are justified", which requires "conceptual analysis of the coherence and completeness of the claims and empirical analyses of the inferences and assumptions inherent in the claims" (Kane 2016, p. 198). The American Educational Research Association (AERA), the American Psychological Association (APA) and the National Council for Measurement in Education (NCME) have published the Standards for Educational and Psychological Testing, which focus on defining validity for large-scale standardized assessments. The Standards are regularly revised to incorporate new information, techniques and approaches and the latest version was published in 2014. While this report contains extensive technical insight and detail, there are some critical points that bear on PISA:

- test use is as much a matter of validity as (statistical) score interpretation;
- each use (inference) of the test needs to be validated; and
- all tests need to be clear about (i) how the scores are statistically validated and (ii) how the inferences or uses of the data are being evaluated for their validity.

As Cronbach (1980, p. 103) suggested: "The job of validation is not to support an interpretation, but to find out what might be wrong with it. A proposition deserves some degree of trust only when it has survived serious attempts to falsify it". For example, one current inference is that PISA measures the quality of an education system. This claim must be evaluated within each system in which it is made. As Kane (2013, p. 1) argues: "To make a positive case for the proposed interpretations and uses of scores, the validity argument needs to provide backing for all of the inferences". International large-scale assessments like PISA are rarely subjected to an examination of plausible challenge, particularly by the governments that pay to conduct them and which are often the primary interpreters of results.

It is useful at this stage to return to the questions asked at the beginning of this chapter: *If* Australia is ranked below top performing countries in PISA, *then* there is a problem with the quality of education in Australia. We can evaluate the validity of this claim based on the answers to our three questions. First, we have shown that PISA measures the performance of 15-year-olds in schools in participating countries on content that the OECD thinks they should know. Second, we have argued that the rankings tell us a lot less than is commonly assumed. In particular, we have suggested that they are among the least useful information that a test like PISA offers. We have also shown that when PISA data are appropriately reported, claims about 'losing' become problematic.

States and jurisdictions should accept that evaluating the validity of the inferences made from PISA data is their ongoing responsibility. If we think of participation in PISA in terms of opportunity costs, particularly given the way that it takes oxygen away from other education debates, it seems strange that participant countries assume little responsibility for what is done with the results. Jurisdictions should clearly define what PISA results will be used to make inferences and how the evidence that we currently have supports the use of tests in these ways. These positions should be based upon a long-term view, remembering that the students who sit the tests began their education around ten years earlier. A significant part of this evaluation should involve input from teachers and principals. Further, the evidence supporting the validity of claims must always be documented and reported.

'Flipping the system' using an argumentative approach to validity

While test developers and psychometricians may know how test data are intended to be used, they often have very little first-hand experience of the uses of these data in schools, classrooms, communities and school systems. We cannot think of a group that has better experience of the range of uses of tests scores than teachers and principals working in schools. Most professionals receive little training in understanding data, evidence and validity, despite this being crucial when using assessment data. This is important for two reasons: (1) some uses of test data can pervert the intent of the tests by altering the constructs for which the tests are designed and calibrated; and (2) the promiscuous use of test data can imply that test scores can be put to an infinite number of uses. The danger of assuming that the correlation of test scores with various other factors can support causal claims is always lurking. We propose that valid use of test scores could be improved by adopting an argumentative approach, where each intended use of tests scores must be argued for and subsequently evaluated.

Three useful things that teachers and schools can do to help validate ILSAs

1 Ask how ILSA rankings are being interpreted and what courses of action are being proposed. For example, translate headlines or reports about ILSA scores and rankings into a simple interpretation (e.g. *If* Australia is ranked below top performing countries in PISA, *then* there is a problem with the quality of education in Australia.)
2 Ask what justification is being given to support this interpretation and action. What steps, if any, have been taken to *falsify* this interpretation?
3 Judge whether or not the interpretation and use of ILSA scores and rankings is reasonable given the justifications, the evidence presented and any attempts to falsify the argument.

If we return to our example of PISA and Australia's performance in the 2012 assessment, then it is clear that rankings were interpreted as indicating quality, and that Australian education was of lower quality in other countries. Policymakers argued that Australian schools should be borrowing policies and practices from schools in these systems. However, as Jerrim (2015) and Feniger and Lefstein (2014) have shown, there are good reasons to suspect that the higher ranking of students in Shanghai, for example, is not a necessarily a result of the quality of schooling in Shanghai. Indeed, Loveless (2014) has argued that Shanghai's performance should not be interpreted as providing a reliable measure of the knowledge and skills of all 15-year-olds in the province. Australian media representation of Shanghai as an education reference society is troubling, and is another missed opportunity to use ILSAs wisely to inform Australia's education systems.

Flipping the system in relation to ILSAs can involve teachers and their various collective voices (such as professional associations, subject associations and teacher unions) playing a role in testing and improving the validity of inferences in their contexts. It is not good enough that erroneous assumptions based on a form of validity error are repeated in the media, by politicians and education commentators, and become the accepted narrative. The teaching profession, in conversation with the communities it serves, must have a greater voice in interpreting ILSA findings. This is not to argue that the teacher voice be privileged over technical expertise, but rather that more is possible when domain experts and technical experts meet and learn from each other. After all, who has a better vantage point from which to shape the public debate about quality education than the educators who are constantly striving to deliver it in our schools?

Notes

1 www.bbc.com/news/world-australia-38178763
2 www.smh.com.au/federal-politics/political-news/wakeup-call-australian-students-fall-behind-kazakhstan-in-maths-and-science-rankings-20161129-gszvt1.html

3 www.abc.net.au/news/2016-11-30/australia-declines-in-global-education-report/8077474
4 https://au.educationhq.com/news/37416/australia-behind-kazakhstan-in-education-rankings/
5 www.abc.net.au/news/2016-11-30/australia-declines-in-global-education-report/8077474

References

Conifer, D., 2016, November 30th. *Australia crashing down international leaderboard for education, falling behind Kazakhstan.* Available from: http://mobile.abc.net.au/news/2016-11-30/australia-declines-in-global-education-report/8077474 [Accessed 15 January 2018].

Cronbach, L.J., 1980. Validity on parole: How can we go straight? In: W.B. Schrader, ed., *New directions for testing and measurement: No. 5*. San Francisco: Jossey-Bass, 99–108.

Education Matters, 2016. *Quality of Australian education falls behind Kazakhstan's.* Available from: http://educationmattersmag.com.au/australian-education-falls-behind-kazakhstan/[Accessed 15 January 2018].

Feniger, Y. and Lefstein, A., 2014. How not to reason with PISA: An ironic investigation. *Journal of Education Policy*, 29 (6), 845–855.

Franklin, M., 2012. We Risk Losing Education Race, PM Warns. *The Australian*, 1, January 24.

Jensen, B., Hunter, A., Sonnemann, J., and Burns, T., 2012. *Catching Up: Learning from the Best School Systems in East Asia*. Melbourne: Grattan Institute.

Jerrim, J., 2015. Why do East Asian children perform so well in PISA? An investigation of Western-born children of East Asian descent. *Oxford Review of Education*, 41 (3), 310–333.

Loveless, T., 2014, January 8. PISA's China problem continues: A response to Schleicher, Zhang, and Tucker. Available from: www.brookings.edu/blogs/brown-center-chalkboard/posts/2014/01/08-shanghai-pisa-loveless [Accessed 1 August 2014].

Kane, M.T., 2013. Validating the interpretations and uses of test scores. *Journal of Educational Measurement*, 50 (1), 1–73.

Kane, M.T., 2016. Explicating validity. *Assessment in Education: Principles, Policy & Practice*, 23 (2), 198–211. https://doi.org/10.1080/0969594X.2015.1060192

Kreiner, S. and Christensen, K.B., 2014. Analyses of model fit and robustness. A new look at the PISA scaling model underlying ranking of countries according to reading literacy. *Psychometrika*, 79 (2), 210–231.

MCEETYA, 2008. *Melbourne Declaration on Educational Goals for Young Australians*. Melbourne: Ministerial Council on Education, Employment, Training and Youth Affairs (MCEETYA).

OECD, 2014. *PISA 2012 Results: What Students Know and Can Do Student Performance in Mathematics, Reading and Science (Volume I)*. Paris: OECD Publishing.

Rutkowski, L. and Rutkowski, D., 2016. A call for a more measured approach to reporting and interpreting PISA results. *Educational Researcher*, 45 (4), 252–257.

Sellar, S., Thompson, G., and Rutkowski, D., 2017. *The Global Education Race: Taking the Measure of PISA and International Testing*. Toronto: Brush Education

Stake, R.E. and Schwandt, T.A., 2006. On discerning quality in evaluation. *The Sage handbook of evaluation*, 404–418.

7 Schools for the future
Networks and innovation

Cameron Paterson and Keren Caple

Trust and agency

How can we generate networks of teachers across schools to learn from each other and sustain the conditions for innovation? Flipping the system is about changing the educational storyline to one of trust and agency, transforming from the grassroots up, not imposing reforms from above and starving the system of developing its own capacities. In this chapter, four case studies creatively reimagine ways of coping with an escalating rate of change. These examples show that when the grassroots of the school system are trusted and possess agency, it is possible to move towards more personalised and relevant curriculum and pedagogies, design and scale radical new practices, generate an evolving evidence base and collaboratively invent new possibilities.

Learning is messy and teachers all over the world have had to accept the compromise of focusing more on delivering the prescribed curriculum than developing understanding; test-taking rather than learning. We have "a distorted view of teaching that is self-reinforcing and divorced from what we know about effective learning" (Ritchhart *et al.* 2011, p. 25).

How would teachers teach if the exam was in 20 years' time? There is not an achievement gap, there is a relevance gap. Harvard Professor of Teaching and Learning David Perkins (personal communication, July 2013) argues that most of what is taught beyond basic literacies quickly gets forgotten and a huge information base may not be the right priority for our times. Instead of fixating on educating for the known, we need a vision of educating for the unknown, for the kinds of thinking and understanding that foster nimble adaptive insight in a complex world.

When teaching is regarded as a mechanistic and transactional function, as if it is something that somebody does to someone else, metaphors from factories and the military are adopted. Bureaucracy depends on what can be easily replicated and measured and as a result the obsession with test scores seems like an unpleasant parody of Vietnam War body counts. "NAPLAN, PISA, tertiary entrance ranks and league tables drive public discourse, propelling competition between schools, systems, and teachers" (Netolicky *et al.* 2018). The systematised, conveyor-belt and narrow, widely scrutinised measures impact on both teacher and student agency.

Schools are difficult places to enact meaningful change because they are designed to only tolerate limited individuality and they are constrained by the historical weight of standardisation. They occupy an oppressive, hierarchical role in order to protect the status quo, and are rife with mistaken assumptions about what it truly takes to move beyond a command-and-control model. Today's unprecedented centralisation is perpetuated because those who have the most to gain from the administrative structures are in the best position to challenge its inefficiencies. Accountability, standardisation, and bureaucratisation are the only means of controlling the unwieldy structure. However, when incremental top-down tweaks are insufficient, more radical change is required.

Case study: British Columbia

Educators in the driving seat

British Columbia has always been a top performer in global education system rankings. However, with research emerging about preparing young people for a rapidly changing world and local survey data showing low levels of intellectual engagement amongst B.C. students, leaders and educators reflected on ways in which an education system should and could enable radical change.

While many system leaders tackle educational transformation through an incremental and often top-down set of tweaks and changes, leaders from British Columbia decided that there needed to be a substantial overhaul of the school system that was driven by the desire and passion of educators themselves.

In 2011 they launched the British Columbia Education Plan. From its inception, this Plan was designed to serve as a bottom-up, collaborative innovation process that would draw on the insights, expertise and opinions of a wide range of stakeholders in order to generate a collective movement towards a more engaging, personalised and relevant curriculum and pedagogy.

Whilst one can look to the outcomes of this work in terms of improved student performance and an increase in financial investment in frontline services (by reducing the administrative spend), it is also important to consider a few of the critical elements in the B.C. roadmap toward change:

- Leading by example: From an early point in developing the new Education Plan, the central team at the Ministry of Education realised that they could not ask schools to innovate unless they themselves were capable of change. The Ministry took a very careful approach to its transformation agenda in order to build trust by co-constructing, across the province, a compelling case for change.
- Co-designing and co-constructing a vision: The Ministry began with collecting ideas from practitioners and the general public about their

vision for future education in British Columbia. An Advisory Group—with representation from all major stakeholders, including parents, students and representatives of Aboriginal groups—met in order to develop and continually test a new draft curriculum framework, drawing on their own experiences and the best ideas harvested from the website.
- Bottom-up, flexible innovation: The Ministry realised that its agenda would have to be driven forwards by inspired practitioners, enabling leadership and a wider infrastructure of support and incentives. As a result, an 'invitation to innovate' was issued, encouraging teachers and schools to generate new ideas about how to personalise learning in ways that would make sense given variable factors such as the students' needs and interests, the school set-up and the community context.
- Enabling conditions: The K-12 Innovation Partnership was set up 2015, with the goal of supporting educators who are interested in—or already are—pursuing innovative pedagogical methods at the classroom or school level. The Partnership aims to both reward and incentivise ambitious thinking and practice, which might include changes to teaching or new organisational forms and the system itself.

Schools are instructed from above to adopt an abundance of new programs and practices each year, with little consideration given to the behavioural shifts required of educators to embrace new ways of thinking and learning, and the organisational changes needing to occur for new approaches to successfully diffuse amongst the school community. The assumption that taking up a new practice is just an issue of instruction and information has ultimately led to surface compliance rather than a genuine effort and commitment to implementing promising new approaches (GELP 2013). With a massive oversupply of manuals, pamphlets, websites and PowerPoint presentations trickling down from above, little attention is paid to the demand side of the equation. Teachers, parents and students are rarely engaged in conversations and activities focused on enacting genuine, transformative change

Instead, norms of autonomy and privacy are entrenched among teachers and the isolation of cellular classrooms discourages professional interdependence. This professional seclusion operates as a bulwark against school improvement. Teachers cannot become better teachers in isolation from each other. Reliance on 'safe' pedagogy often goes hand in hand with a climate of competition between colleagues and departments (Clarke 2018). Rather than looking to each other, teachers have a habit of seeking out external experts to deliver seductively simple answers to complex educational questions and chase the shadows of evidence-based, 'scientific' teaching (Eacott 2017).

Professional capital is not created through the agendas of those at the apex of a top-down structure. It is enabled when leaders facilitate teacher collaboration and build the capacity of teachers to utilise their own professional judgement (Wood 2018). For a school to truly learn, teaching must become infused with a genuinely collegial, collaborative ethos. Breidenstein *et al.* (2012) state that there is,

> a substantial professional knowledge base that highlights a strong connection between student and adult learning. Student learning increases in schools where there are educator communities that are reflective, collaborative, and focused on issues of teaching and learning ... Adult learning in schools is best supported when teachers ... regularly engage in meaningful dialogue with colleagues about improving their practice.

The strongest influence on teacher professional practice is advice from colleagues, and teachers get better by working in teams on teaching issues. The most powerful source of information about teaching and learning in a school is the student and teacher work that occurs in classrooms. Building lateral capacity and expertise is the best alternative to external control.

Case study: Campbelltown Performing Arts High School

Collaborative learning by design

At Campbelltown Performing Arts High School, a public high school in south-west Sydney, teachers and leaders operate in a highly collaborative environment focused not just on adopting and scaling quality 'best' practice, but on designing, testing and scaling radical new practices of their own.

Several years ago the school began exploring design thinking approaches as a means of being more strategic and creative in how they respond to the individual needs of their learners. What started as experimentation with user research and rapid prototyping of new ideas has now become a shared language and a defined way of working amongst Campbelltown educators, and even between educators and learners themselves.

Members of the school community work in diverse teams to better understand the challenges currently being faced in teaching and learning, and co-design possible solutions to test. The process is highly collaborative and networked, requiring all team members to bring their own experiences and knowledge to the table in order to shape practices that are likely to have an impact on learning and be scalable across larger cohorts. Past prototyping at Campbelltown has led to teachers and learners co-designing a program in which learners collaborate with the local council on biodiversity research; making a positive contribution to their community whilst also putting theoretical knowledge into practice in a project-based learning environment.

Campbelltown PAHS's leaders understood that they could not demand that staff immediately take up a new way of designing learning—that, for some, adopting unfamiliar practices would involve letting go and mourning the loss of past ways of working and be an emotional process of behaviour change. The school crafted a range of ways in which teachers could engage in this new form of professional learning and professional practice—from jumping in at the deep end and joining a prototyping team, to testing out a component of one of the design team practices or just being kept informed of developments. As a result, the language and processes of design thinking have become pervasive within the school community as design teams have, gradually over time, involved more of their colleagues at a 'grassroots' level in conversations and activities focused on innovating their practice and improving learner outcomes. It is clear that networks can, very successfully, be local and locally responsive.

Teams now proliferate across domains previously dominated by commands. Edmondson (2012) argues that, "The knowledge-based, twenty-first century organisation depends on cross-disciplinary collaboration, flattened hierarchies, and continuous innovation". Generating ideas to solve problems is the currency of the future and teaming is the way to implement and improve these ideas. Edmondson (2012) emphasises speaking up, listening intensely, integrating different facts and points of view, experimenting iteratively, reflecting on ideas and actions, and the importance of psychological safety. Team members feel more comfortable suggesting alternatives when their leader has previously modelled that it is OK to make mistakes. A leader's role is to cultivate a culture that encourages risk-taking and allows teachers to question the status quo. Every school has its own nondiscussables and teachers must be able "to name, acknowledge, and address the nondiscussables – especially those that impede learning" (Barth 2002).

Educators also need to recognise the degree of their dependence on informal networks. Eighty per cent of learning is informal and incidental, and it is often left to chance (Cross 2007). "Workers learn more in the coffee room than in the classroom. They discover how to do their jobs through informal learning: talking, observing others, trial-and-error, and simply working with people in the know" (Cross 2007, p. 235). Companies like Google and Apple are masters at designing informal learning environments, with sofas strategically placed on landings, and kitchens and bubblers placed to facilitate easy conversation. Teachers know that their best professional conversations are in the staffroom at lunch, the car park after school, or the pub on a Friday. How can educators become more intentional about creating time and space for these informal conversations?

Schools were not constructed to be fast and agile, and they were not designed for an environment where change has become the norm. Kotter (2011) advocates introducing a second, more organic, agile, network-like structure that operates in concert with the hierarchy (which is still needed for reliability and efficiency) to create what he calls a "dual operating system". "The successful organization of the future will have two organizational structures: a Hierarchy, and a more teaming, egalitarian, and adaptive Network" (Kotter 2011, p. 2). This new network structure is dynamic: initiatives merge and disperse as required with contributions from all parts of the organisation, liberating information from silos and the hierarchy. A community of practice is a useful description for this sort of collaboration, a group of people who share a concern or passion and learn how to do it better as they interact.

Case study: ELEVATE

System and sector enabled Communities of Practice

In New South Wales, three communities of practice have been established by the Association of Independent Schools New South Wales (AISNSW) to better meet the needs of high potential learners. Each community brings together 10–15 schools from around the country – and from each schooling sector – to collaboratively develop practices that will provide intellectual stretch for learners not currently reaching their full potential. The program's sponsors facilitate a structured program exploring disciplined innovation methods, which brings the community together every one to two months. In between these workshops, schools collaborate on testing and refining their practices and bring their learnings to the next event where they download, analyse, modify and plan their next steps. Participants are expected to look critically and creatively upon the traditional structures and processes of their schools, such as timetables, curriculum and how they interact with their local community, to establish where the most interesting opportunities might exist for changes that could benefit learning.

Being part of the ELEVATE community of practice is supporting participating schools to generate both a compelling case for change for their wider communities, and an evolving evidence base as they test practices across a range of contexts and use a range of measures to monitor impact. Those in the community learn to be more agile and responsive to the unmet needs of learners through application of user-centred innovation methods; committing to understanding the often complex lives of learners and maintaining an open, ambitious mind when designing possible solutions. They also develop leadership skills as they seek to embed new ways of working into their school's culture and enable the adoption of new practices amongst colleagues. In this case, the communities not only influence their individual schools but also the systems in which they live: AISNSW looks to these hubs of innovation for the 'next practice' that might eventually be scaled across all schools in their system, and possibly beyond. The ELEVATE communities of practice live as distinct innovation zones alongside the much larger improvement agenda in schools, with bridges built in along the way to ensure that really powerful, high impact practice is eventually able to travel over to the 'mainstream' to have the greatest impact on the most learners.

While there is still a requirement for stability and order, schools now also need the flexibility, adaptability and innovative culture to prepare for uncertain and unpredictable futures. Elmore (2011, personal communication) comments that,

> The future of schools lies in networks rather than hierarchies, in lateral rather than vertical organisations. Most of the work gets done in networks, not hierarchies. The education system will essentially functionally be replaced by a series of networks. Networks cannot be managed the same way that hierarchies are managed. Social networking is a different way of organising.

A paradigm shift is occurring in the way in which people are connected, we are moving from hierarchically arranged groups to diverse social networks (Wellman 2001). As global interconnections and complexities increase, hierarchies are being supplanted by more lateral interactions. Hierarchies require unity and coordination, whereas networks require diversity and autonomy. Networks are not just about technology, they are about connecting and collaborating.

People who link or bridge otherwise distinct groups and those who possess the capacity to initiate and maintain "boundary-spanning relationships" have richer access to information, resources, and greater creative capability than those with a more insular network structure (Burt 2004). These 'border crossers' who can access a diversity of networks are able to introduce new ideas, knowledge, and practices that can lead change. Harvard Professor of Cognition and Education Howard Gardner (personal communication, March 2013) refers to searchlight intelligence. That is, the capacity to connect dots between people and ideas, where others see no conceivable link. Maybe intelligence is more about noticing than knowing?

Many of today's biggest challenges come from complex 'wicked problems' that are ill-defined and sometimes impossible to solve. Complicated problems require a hierarchy, whereas complex problems need a more networked response. For example, when a fire crew arrives at a house fire and they are faced with a standard fire, they use standard good practice, but when they arrive at a house fire and face a fire behaving unpredictably, in a manner they have not witnessed before, a more networked response is required (Daniel Wilson, personal communication, March 2016). Complicated problems are solved with good practice, complex problems are solved with emergent practices. Implementation and best practice is something you do when you know what to do; learning is what you do when you don't know what to do (Elmore 2016).

Case study: Learning Frontiers

Failing fast to succeed sooner

Learning Frontiers was an initiative established in 2013 by the Australian Institute for Teaching and School Leadership aimed at increasing deep engagement in learning, through the design of professional practices that promote engagement. Over a period of two years it brought together around

50 government, Catholic and independent schools in state-based 'design hubs' to re-envision learning based around four overarching design principles for engaged learning: connected, co-created, personalised and integrated. No funding was available for participation: schools applied on the basis of an unwavering belief that they needed to think differently about engagement if they were going to meet the needs of learners today and into the future, and were able to make resources available to see this belief through.

Most participating schools were unfamiliar with user-centred design, and set about learning an entirely new repertoire of skills—and indeed a new design-based language—so they could shed old assumptions about why their learners were sometimes disengaged and collaboratively invent new possibilities. Participants were asked to challenge the status quo through re-examining traditional school structures and processes, but also become adept at calculating and managing risk when planning and implementing prototypes. The systems and sectors of participating schools understood the nature of the work and were both supportive of their involvement and curious to learn more about their outputs, helping to legitimise activities that might previously have been viewed as disruptive without being practically involved in overseeing them. The mantra 'fail fast to succeed sooner' guided participants as they learned to become more comfortable in sharing and analysing their failures as well as celebrating their successes with other schools, understanding that prototyping is an iterative and often messy learning process.

Schools in hubs formed leadership structures to ensure that the collaborative could function effectively: the leadership group set the strategic direction of the hub, established touchpoints in between formal workshops and enabled the sharing of resources across schools when needed. Cross-school teams formed within each hub focused around particular challenges or opportunities, with emerging practices then able to be tested in different contexts and brought back to the group so they could learn from what worked and what didn't. Some hubs even formed partnerships with external organisations and community groups in order to accessing expert knowledge and tools and resources that might otherwise be out of reach for one individual school.

Despite the initiative officially ending in 2015, many design hub schools still continue with the application of Learning Frontiers innovation methods in their daily practice, and some continue to collaborate on designing practice within their hub and across state lines with other hub schools too.

Creative reimagining

There is strong agreement that the future emerging will be exceedingly different to the past. According to *New York Times* journalist Tom Friedman, (personal communication, March 2017), our central learning challenge is now helping people cope with a faster rate of change as digitisation and exponential acceleration fundamentally reshape the world. Elmore (2016) warns that our conceptions of what is possible are inhibited by our beliefs about what is practical in an antiquated institution that pays disproportionate attention to practices entrenched in an industrial, colonialist society. He states, "Learned helplessness in the face of this dysfunction is the disease of a dying institution" (Elmore 2016, p. 530).

Andreas Schleicher from the OECD speaks about the importance of creative reimagining and the digitalisation of education, suggesting that most school curriculums are "shallow shadows" in the very artificial world of education and the future of education is not about doing more of the same (personal communication, March 2017). The knowledge that is easiest to teach and assess is also the easiest to digitise, automate and outsource. School systems are good at ranking, not at developing human capital.

Teachers need to be released from Stockholm syndrome, the feelings of trust felt in some kidnapping cases by a victim towards a captor. The military uses the term 'Strategic Corporal', which is the notion that leadership in complex, rapidly evolving environments devolves lower and lower down the chain of command to more effectively incorporate the latest on the ground data into decision-making. Yet too much education reform remains top-down, imposed on schools without drawing on or supporting the development of capacities within the system. Flipping the system is about shifting the narrative to one of trust and agency, subverting hierarchies and reforming from the bottom up.

References

Barth, R., 2002. The culture builder. *Educational Leadership*, May, 59 (8), 6–11.
Breidenstein, A., Fahey, K., Glickman, C., and Hensley, F., 2012. *Leading for powerful learning: A guide for instructional leaders*. New York: Teachers College Press.
Burt, R., 2004. Structural holes and good ideas. *The American Journal of Sociology*, 110 (2), 349–399. Available from: www.bebr.ufl.edu/sites/default/files/Structural%20Holes%20and%20Good%20Ideas_0.pdf [Accessed 18 March 2018].
Clarke, Z., 2018. Shedding our inhibitions: from external to internal accountability. *In*: L. Rycroft-Smith and J.L. Dutaut, eds., *Flip the System UK: A teachers' manifesto*. London: Routledge, 37–41.
Cross, J., 2007. *Informal learning: Rediscovering the natural pathways that inspire innovation and performance*. San Francisco: Pfeiffer.
Eacott, S., 2017. School leadership and the cult of the guru: The neoTaylorism of Hattie. *School Leadership & Management*. Routledge.
Edmondson, A., 2012. *Teaming: How organisations, learn, innovate, and compete in the knowledge economy*. San Francisco, CA: Jossey-Bass.
Elmore, R., 2016, "Getting to scale..." it seemed like a good idea at the time. *Journal of Educational Change*, 17, 529–537.
Global Education Leaders' Program (GELP). 2013. *Redesigning education: Shaping learning systems around the globe*. Seattle, WA: Booktrope.
Kotter, J., 2011. Leadership and network: Two structures, one organization, *Harvard Business Review*, May. Available from: https://hbr.org/2011/05/two-structures-one-organizatio [Accessed 17 August 2018].

Netolicky, D.M., Andrews, J., and Paterson, C., 2018. Flipping the system: A perspective from down under. *In*: L. Rycroft-Smith and J.L. Dutaut, eds., *Flip the System UK: A teachers' manifesto*. London: Routledge, 228–232.

Ritchhart, R., Church, M., and Morrison, K., 2011. *Making thinking visible: How to promote engagement, understanding, and independence for all learners*. San Francisco, CA: Jossey-Bass.

Wellman, B., 2001. Little boxes, glocalization, and networked individualism. Available from http://calchong.tripod.com/sitebuildercontent/sitebuilderfiles/LittleBoxes.pdf [Accessed 18 March 2018].

Wood, P., 2018. Lesson study: An approach to claiming slow time. *In*: L. Rycroft-Smith and J.L. Dutaut, eds., *Flip the System UK: A teachers' manifesto*. London: Routledge, 115–122.

8 Developing teacher leadership and collaborative professionalism to flip the system
Reflections from Canada

Carol Campbell

Introduction

This chapter outlines four key reflections for teacher-led educational improvement. First, the development of humanity—the adults working in our schools and the students and communities they serve—should be the core purpose of educational improvement. This involves prioritising attention to developing and honouring people in the policies, processes and intended outcomes of schooling. Second, central to such changes is the intentional development of teachers' evidence-informed professional judgement combining and championing their knowledge, expertise, experiences and evidence. Third, enabling teachers to intentionally develop their leadership, to share their knowledge and to lead the de-privatisation of teaching practices is vital. Finally, realising educational improvement requires a new form of collaborative professionalism that values and includes the voices of all involved in the education system through new ways of working committed to genuinely developing mutual respect and reciprocal influence.

Ensuring humanity is at the core of public education

The core purpose of public education is—or should be—the betterment of humanity. It is as simple and complex as that! This may seem self-evident, but sometimes the focus on supporting and developing *people* gets lost in discussions of reforming standards, governance, structures and test scores. Influenced largely by the Program for International Student Achievement (PISA), national and international discussions of educational reforms and performance often become conflated to the phrase of 'excellence and equity' (see for example, OECD 2016). At the time of writing this chapter, the Gonski 2.0 report (Gonski *et al.* 2018), *Through Growth to Achievement: Report of the Review to Achieve Educational Excellence in Australian Schools*, was published with is central starting point being that Australia's declining performance in the PISA rankings requires major reform of Australia's education systems. The use of PISA data to justify major reforms of education systems is becoming a prevalent and problematic trend. Of course, excellence in educational performance and equities in performance for students of different socio-economic status are important. However, these can be narrow measures and narrow aspirations— that the purpose of education is about proficiency in specific domains of knowledge and closing gaps between student groups on measured test scores. What is needed—alongside concerns for ensuring students are equipped with the knowledge and skills to learn and develop to their fullest potential—is *consideration* of who our students are in their diverse experiences, identities, contexts, needs and aspirations and how best to support them as current and future citizens, contributing members of society and the economy, and stewards of the world in times of geopolitical, cultural, social, technological and environmental change (Campbell *et al.* 2018).

As we consider the humanity of our students, we need also to ensure that valuing, honouring and developing the humanity of our teachers is at the core of education too. In Canada, teaching is a profession. To become a teacher requires completing a university level degree and related practice. All teachers belong to a union and are expected to uphold collective professional responsibilities and rights. Teaching remains a desirable career.

In our study of *The State of Educators Professional Learning in Canada* (Campbell *et al.* 2016, Campbell, Osmond-Johnson *et al.* 2017), while there is extensive activity for teachers' professional learning and development, we also identified challenges for teachers to fully engage in their own and peer learning. A major finding was: "Time for sustained, cumulative professional learning integrated within educators' work lives requires attention" (Campbell, Osmond-Johnson *et al.* 2017, p. 71). Looking across a range of studies in Canada, teachers appear to be spending an average of 2 hours per week on their professional learning— but often this is time, before or after the official school day, on weekends or during vacation. In the Teaching and Learning International Survey (TALIS), teachers in Alberta (the only province in Canada to participate) reported working 48.2 hours per week, compared to an average work week of 38.44 hours across the 35 participating countries. Teachers in Australia, meanwhile, reported an average work week of 43 hours (OECD 2014). Studies within Canada suggest working hours averaging 55 hours per week and concerns about work intensification. If the purpose of education is to develop humanity—including the teachers who work in education—time for professional learning and development is essential.

Similarly, funding is also essential. Across Canada, all collective agreements include clauses to support teachers' professional development and teachers can draw on union funds to support self-directed professional development. However, while funding is available, it varies dramatically across Canada—from teachers being able to access $100 CDN for self-directed professional development in some localities to teachers in other localities having access to over $2500 CDN in funds per year. We identified particular issues for teachers in rural and remote communities, early career teachers, and for teachers who do not have a permanent contract in accessing funding and supports for self-directed professional learning opportunities. Inequitable variations in access to quality professional learning and development require urgent attention to enable all in the teaching profession to develop and grow.

A further major issue for attention in our study of professional learning in Canada was: "The appropriate balance of system-directed and self-directed professional development for teachers is complex and contested" (Campbell, Osmond-Johnson *et al.* 2017, p. 69). Who decides what professional development teachers engage in is an essential consideration in attempts to flip the system for teacher leadership, collective professional responsibility and teacher-led reform. In a pan-Canadian survey of teachers (CTF 2014): the majority of teachers (55.5%) responded that they had significant or somewhat ability to exercise professional judgement over their professional development; however, a majority of teachers (53.5%) also perceived their autonomy to have decreased somewhat or significantly. In our interviews, teachers expressed interest in having more control over their own professional development; yet, school and system leaders also expressed interest in having more control over setting the direction and priorities for professional development. The need for teacher choice and voice, within a wider system of professional development, is essential.

Strengthening teachers' evidence-informed professional judgement

A key element of advancing teacher leadership of educational change and improvement is strengthening teachers' professional judgement and capacity. Teaching is *the* knowledge profession (Campbell 2016) and valuing and advancing teachers' existing knowledge and providing opportunities to renew, expand and develop that knowledge is crucial.

A clear finding from our study of the state of educators' professional learning in Canada is that there is no one size fits all approach to teachers' professional learning and nor should there be (Campbell, Osmond-Johnson *et al.* 2017). Teachers need opportunities to identify and engage in professional learning that meets their priority needs at different stages in their career, in different contexts, when working with different students or subjects or grades, and based on professional and personal priorities, as well as the needs of their students and schools. Often, current discussions of professional learning focus on the nature of the experience—collaborative, job-embedded, active and so on—effective professional learning processes of course matter. However, to truly flip the system, teachers—all teachers in all contexts at all career stages—need access to quality evidence and content within professional learning opportunities and resources.

Concerns about ensuring a combination of subject and pedagogical knowledge in teachers' professional judgement and practice persist. Rather than professional development involving generic activities and instructional strategies disconnected from subject areas, a focus on specific subject knowledge in combination with pedagogical content knowledge is an important element of effective teacher professional learning programs (CUREE 2012, Dagen and Bean 2014, Desimone 2009, Desimone and Stuckey 2014, Evans 2014, Garet *et al.* 2001). However, specific professional development needs vary by teacher, career stage, and changing educational contexts. In our survey in New Brunswick, Canada, 36% of respondents identified "subject matter content" as the area of professional development *most* needed by teachers; whereas 34% of respondents identified subject matter content as the area of professional development *least* needed (Campbell, Osmond-Johnson *et al.* 2017).

As well as technological, curricular, and subject knowledge, a major finding from our research was that the priority need for professional development is to equip teachers to work with and support *all* students with diverse learning needs in inclusive classrooms. In our New Brunswick survey, "supporting diverse learning needs" was identified as the most needed area of professional development for teachers (56% of respondents) (Campbell, Osmond-Johnson *et al.* 2017). A survey in British Columbia, Canada, suggested that while teachers in the first five years of their experience may prioritise professional development on specific subject or pedagogical strategies, over time teachers' professional learning priorities may shift to broader concerns for students' equity, well-being, and learning (BCTF 2010). Across Canada, a Canadian Teachers' Federation (CTF) survey highlighted the importance of, and need for, appropriate professional learning to support teachers' knowledge and understanding of Aboriginal people (CTF 2015). Overall, the priority professional learning needs are knowledge, skills, and practices to support diverse learners' needs; this includes attention to developing teachers' pedagogical, subject, curricular, technological, and cultural knowledge linked to students' needs and wider educational, social, and political changes.

In considering the evidence-informed aspect of teachers' professional judgement, it is important to conceive of—and use—a broad definition of evidence. This is not being about data-driven solely by test scores. Evidence includes data, research, evaluation, as well as evidence from professional knowledge, experiences, practices, observations, conversations and documents. Judgement also requires being *informed* through a process of inquiry, reflection, discussion, analysis, critique, contextualisation, consideration and potentially adaptation of evidence. Evidence-informed professional judgement should be a complex and critical process not the technical and linear directives suggested by evidence-based or data-driven decision-making. Developing teachers' professional judgement to be critical of, and informed by, a range of evidence is crucial to creating teachers who flip the system by becoming and being the professionals who individually and collectively advocate for and take action to lead educational improvement locally and also nationally and internationally. Therefore, strengthening teachers' evidence-informed professional judgement is not only about enhancing their work as classroom teachers (although that is of course vital), but also intentionally and explicitly supporting teachers to develop as leaders within and beyond their classroom and school.

Enabling teacher-led de-privatisation of professional practices

In the first Flip the System book (Evers and Kneyber 2016), we wrote about Ontario's TLLP (Lieberman, Campbell and Yashkina 2016), as a model for teacher-led educational improvement to flip the system. Now, three years later, we have further evidence of the priority importance of enabling teacher-led educational improvement (see also Lieberman, Campbell and Yashkina 2017).

Teachers are leaders of learning. However, this is primarily—and sometimes solely—conceived of as leading the learning of students in their classroom and perhaps wider school community. In the TLLP, teachers are supported to become leaders of adults' learning too – their own learning, their peers' learning and learning with and through wider professional networks. Ontario's TLLP has three priority goals:

1. To support experienced teachers who undertake self-directed advanced professional development related to improved student learning and development.
2. To help classroom teachers develop leadership skills for sharing learning and exemplary practices on a board-wide and/or provincial basis.
3. To facilitate knowledge exchange for the spread and sustainability of effective and innovative practices.

A teacher—or more frequently group of teachers—can submit a proposal for TLLP funding. Through a competitive selection process, approximately 100 TLLP projects are funded per year through a partnership between the Ontario Ministry of Education (government) and the Ontario Teachers' Federation (overarching teachers' union organisation). For successful proposals, the teacher leaders participate in leadership training to plan for their project, receive funding, conduct their project over a full school year, are required to share their learning, and then present their findings at a culminating Sharing the Learning Summit.

Central to the TLLP and to the development of the teachers' leadership is gaining the courage and taking the risks to de-privative their knowledge and practices by sharing beyond their classroom walls. The form of sharing varies by projects and has evolved over the years with growing use of online sharing and social media. Flipping the system requires teachers sharing their knowledge, skills and practices: this involves individual reflection to identify tacit knowledge, to make this explicit to others and to commit to (co)developing and sharing knowledge for collaborative and collective work to bring about change. Key questions to consider are: What specific knowledge, skills and practices do I have that I could share with others? What do I know and do well that perhaps others don't know and do? What knowledge, skills or practices do I currently not have or that I want to develop? Who has strengths in these areas and how can I connect with them? Through starting to reach out and connect to other teachers, networks to share ideas, resources, actions and impact can form to flip the system.

Intentionally developing teachers' leadership skills through opportunities and experiences to actually lead in practice are vital. A clear finding from our TLLP research is that teacher leaders learn leadership by doing leadership! This does not mean that teachers must take on formal leadership responsibilities, rather teachers—within and beyond their classrooms—should have opportunities to lead learning, (co)development of knowledge, de-privatisation of practices, and generating networks to share ideas and practical resources to bring about change. In our research, we asked the TLLP teachers to rate their leadership confidence and skills prior to leading a TLLP project and after completion of their TLLP project. The TLLP teacher leaders reported statistically significant improvements in their leadership confidence for implementing practices, sharing practices, leading professional learning, being a teacher leader, and leading a team (Campbell, Lieberman et al. 2017). We also invited TLLP teacher leaders to write vignettes about their experiences and leadership growth. Using five seemingly simple prompts, personal and profound responses were written. The prompts were:

- What did you do?
- Who did you do it with?
- What happened as a result?
- What did you learn?
- What did you learn about leadership?

(Campbell et al. 2015, p. 18)

Indeed, these prompts could be useful for reflecting on, and writing about, Flip the System actions. For the TLLP teacher leaders, they wrote about the leadership experiences, benefits and challenges of: developing their own leadership while working with peers as partners; growing and developing shared leadership in teams of teachers; needing a combination of collaboration with colleagues, personal courage and professional support to bring about change; reaching out to learn from others; and addressing leadership challenges along the way in both working with others and also in learning about (and leading) themselves (Campbell et al. 2015). Our conclusion from teachers' vignettes was: "In the final analysis, learning leadership is personal, problematic, powerful, and potentially influential" (Campbell et al. 2015, p. 20).

Developing collaborative professionalism with, for and by the adults working in education

Developing individual and collaborative teacher leadership is essential to flip the system. The actions of individuals to have the courage and to take the risks to lead and share new ways of working is vital. This is necessary; however, it is also insufficient if wider collective challenges to, and shifts in, the culture, power and working of the education system are also not attempted. A key element of Flip the System is how to move from vertical hierarchies of power and authority to new ecosystems that value, engage and empower teacher leadership as fundamental within system reform and educational improvement.

Ontario is known internationally as being an education system that has been engaged in large-scale reform for the past 15 years (Campbell 2015). The original theory of action values shared leadership and developing the capacity of teachers, but also includes government-led and directed policies and actions. With an emphasis on increasing literacy and numeracy test scores and the high school graduation rate, improvements in professional capacity and in student achievement have occurred. However, after a decade of reforms, in the last round of collective bargaining, the teaching profession expressed serious concern about initiative overload, workload, too much government direction and challenges in the nature of working relationships between and among employees and management. As part of the labour negotiations, a commitment was made in the new collective agreements to develop a new way of working between educators locally, including unions and management, and with the government provincially.

Over a period of several months, teacher federations (unions), unions for support staff, professional associations for management and the Ministry of Education met to co-develop a new agreed way of working. The resulting Policy and Program Memorandum (PPM) 159 Collaborative Professionalism was collectively created by all groups and is co-owned. Influenced by the TLLP and other similar experiences, the vision for Collaborative Professionalism is that it:

- Values all voices and is consistent with our shared responsibility to transform culture and provide equitable access to learning for all.
- Takes place in and fosters a trusting environment that promotes professional learning.
- Involves sharing ideas to achieve a common vision of learning, development and success for all.
- Supports and recognises formal and informal leadership and learning.
- Includes opportunities for collaboration at provincial, district and school levels.
- Leverages exemplary practices through the communication and sharing of ideas to achieve a common vision.

(Ontario Ministry of Education 2016, p. 2)

Symposia for joint teams of labour (local teacher union presidents) and management (school and district leaders) are now being held across Ontario to have a shared conversation about changing the culture of working and commitment on how to actually realise collaborative professionalism in daily practices.

Collaborative professionalism is about *all* of us who are engaged in supporting children and young people working together and it is about *each* of us being enabled to experience mutual trust, reciprocal respect and constructive collaborative working relationships in our professional lives. Realising collaborative professionalism needs intentional work, it does not just happen. We have learned from other experiences of attempting to develop new collaborative working relationships to value and share multiple forms of knowledge that this takes time, resources, sustained commitment, daily attention and continued cultivating for a culture change to create and sustain trust (Briscoe *et al.* 2016, Campbell, Pollock *et al.* 2017). Similarly, the quest to flip the system will require sustained work over time with a genuine commitment to change established cultures, ways of working and ingrained habits and biases. Central to such shifts are valuing and trusting professional judgement, growing teacher leadership, de-privatising practices, (co)developing knowledge and sharing actions and commitments for change through mutual and reciprocal collaborative professionalism sustained over the long term.

Conclusions

For me, the central purpose of education is the betterment of humanity. This involves respecting, supporting, valuing, developing and championing the adults who work in schools as well as the students they serve. These goals are also central to flip the system to one which emphasises the importance of teachers individually and the teaching profession collectively. Developing teachers who can and will flip the system requires ensuring access to—and resources for—quality professional learning and development to support evidence-informed professional judgement and to grow teacher leadership. Individual teachers matter. Flipping the system, however, needs to go beyond important but sometimes isolated individual actions to enabling collaborative action between and among teachers and for the collective responsibility of the teaching profession. Flipping the system needs also to take account of—and to work with—the wider existing system of professionals working in education and policy-makers in government. Collaborative professionalism is about valuing and including all voices and co-creating new ways of working for future change.

This is continuing and always unfinished work with more to do in Canada and in Australia for genuinely teacher-led educational improvement. At first blush, the recent Gonski 2.0 (Gonski *et al.* 2018) report appears to embody features consistent with the four reflections I have outlined in this chapter. There is strong focus on the betterment of humanity, particularly defined as student growth and learning but also including professional learning. There is an emphasis on teachers' professional practice, use of evidence, de-privatisation of practices and importance of collaboration. Consistent with high performing education systems (Darling-Hammond *et al.* 2017), developing teachers and teaching is considered central. However, the recommendations embody an emphasis on *human capital*—individual talent development through recruitment, initial teacher education, induction, career pathways and certification—and *social capital*—collaborative professional development through professional learning communities, collaborative teaching and sharing of practices. What is less prevalent in Gonski 2.0 is the key feature of *professional capital* (Hargreaves and Fullan 2012), and an essential element for Flip the System, the *decisional capital* of valuing all teachers' expertise, experiences and professional judgement. The levers of change recommended in the Gonski 2.0 review are a formative assessment tool, measures of student growth and achievement, and "research-based teaching methods" (Gonski *et al.* 2018) to provide "tailored teaching" (p. 13) for each student. These are not inherently problematic—indeed, I support the use of—and need for—formative assessment, research, data and evidence in education. However, the danger is if reforms become centrally determined data-*driven* decisions and evidence-*based* practices combined with mandated collaboration bereft of vital professional judgement and genuine collaborative professionalism to value all voices, to engage in inquiry to inform action and to share co-developed professional knowledge and practices organically and authentically. Flip the System is about ecosystems of professionally led change not hierarchies of externally determined reforms.

Placing humanity at the centre and flipping the system to a new ecosystem of mutual respect and influence for collaborative professionalism amongst all involved in education is the goal. It begins with one person, then a group, then a network, then a system and it requires intentional, strategic, political, professional and personal work over the long haul. It's hard work; it's demanding work; it's energising and exhausting work; it's absolutely necessary work. Let's continue flipping!

References

Briscoe, P., Pollock, K., Campbell, C. and Carr-Harris, S., 2016. Finding the sweet spot: Network structures and processes for increased knowledge mobilisation. *Brock Journal of Education*, 25 (1), 19–34.

British Columbia Teachers' Federation (BCTF), 2010. *Worklife of BC teachers survey report*. Vancouver: BCTF.

Campbell, C., 2015. Leading system-wide educational improvement in Ontario. In: A. Harris and M. Jones, eds. *Leading futures: Global perspectives on educational leadership*. London: Sage, 72–104.

Campbell, C. (2016). Supporting teachers as a profession of knowledge developers and mobilisers. *Education Today*. 66 (2), 5–20.

Campbell, C., Lieberman, A. and Yashkina, A. with Hauseman, C. and Rodway, J. (2015). *The teacher learning and leadership program: Research report 2014–15*. Ontario Teachers' Federation: Toronto, Canada.

Campbell, C., Osmond-Johnson, P., Faubert, B., Zeichner, K. and Hobbs-Johnson, A. with Brown, S., DaCosta, P., Hales, A., Kuehn, L., Sohn, J. & Steffensen, K. (2016).

The state of educators' professional learning in Canada: Executive summary. Oxford, OH: Learning Forward.

Campbell, C., Lieberman, A., Yashkina, A. and Rodway, J. with Alexander, S. (2017). *The teacher learning and leadership program: Research report 2016–17*, Ontario Teachers' Federation: Toronto, Canada.

Campbell, C., Osmond-Johnson, P., Faubert, B., Zeichner, K. and Hobbs-Johnson, A. with Brown, S., DaCosta, P., Hales, A., Kuehn, L., Sohn, J. and Steffensen, K. (2017). *The state of educators' professional learning in Canada: Final research report*. Oxford, OH: Learning Forward.

Campbell, C., Pollock, K., Briscoe, P., Carr-Harris, S. and Tuters, S. (2017). Developing a knowledge network for applied education research to mobilise evidence in and for educational practice. *Educational Research*, 59 (2), 209–227.

Canadian Teachers' Federation (CTF), 2014. *Highlights of CTF survey on the quest for teacher work–life balance*. Ottawa, ON: CTF.

Canadian Teachers' Federation (CTF), 2015. *Teachers' perspectives on Aboriginal education*. Ottawa, ON: CTF.

Centre for the Use of Research Evidence in Education (CUREE), 2012. *Understanding what enables high quality professional learning: A report on the research evidence*. Coventry, UK: CUREE.

Dagen, A.S., and Bean, R.M., 2014. High-quality research-based professional development: An essential for enhancing high-quality teaching. *In*: L.E. Martin, S. Kragler, D.J. Quatroche and K.L. Bauserman, eds. *Handbook of professional development in education: Successful models and practices, PreK-12*. New York, NY: Guilford Press, 42–64.

Darling-Hammond, L., Burns, D., Campbell, C., Goodwin, A.L., Hammerness, K., Low, E.L., McIntyre, A., Sato, M. and Zeichner, K., 2017. *Empowered educators: How high-performing systems shape teaching quality around the world*. San Francisco, CA: Jossey Bass.

Desimone, L.M., 2009. Improving impact studies of teachers' professional development: Toward better conceptualisations and measures. *Educational Researcher*, 38(3),181–199.

Desimone, L.M. and Stuckey, D., 2014. Sustaining teacher professional development. *In*: L.E. Martin, S. Kragler, D.J. Quatroche and K.L. Bauserman, eds. *Handbook of professional development in education: Successful models and practices, PreK-12*. New York, NY: Guilford Press, 483–506.

Evans, L., 2014. Leadership for professional development and learning: Enhancing our understanding of how teachers develop. *Cambridge Journal of Education*, 44(2),179–198.

Evers, J. and Kneyber, R. eds., 2016. *Flip the system: Changing education from the ground up*. Abingdon: Routledge.

Garet, M.S., Porter, A., Desimone, L. M., Birman, B. and Yoon, K.S., 2001. What makes professional development effective? Results from a national sample of teachers. *American Educational Research Journal* 38 (4), 915–945.

Gonski, D., Arcus, T., Boston, K., Gould, V., Johnson, W., O'Brien, L., Perry, L.A. and Roberts, M., 2018. *Through growth to achievement: Report of the review to achieve educational excellence in Australian schools*. Canberra, AUS: Commonwealth of Australia.

Hargreaves, A. and Fullan, M., 2012. *Professional capital: Transforming teaching in every school*. New York: Teachers College Press.

Lieberman, A, Campbell, C. and Yashkina, A., 2016. Teacher learning and leadership program: professional development for and by teachers. *In*: J. Evers and R. Kneyber, eds. *Flip the system: Changing education from the ground up*. London, UK: Routledge.

Lieberman, A., Campbell, C. and Yashkina, A., 2017. *Teacher learning and leadership: Of, by and for teachers*. London, UK: Routledge/Taylor & Francis.

Ontario Ministry of Education, 2016. *Policy and program memorandum no. 159: Collaborative professionalism*. Toronto, Ontario.

Organisation for Economic Cooperation and Development (OECD), 2014. *New insights from TALIS 2013—Teaching and learning in primary and upper secondary education*. Paris: OECD.

Organisation for Economic Cooperation and Development (OECD), 2016. *PISA results (volume 1): Excellence and equity in education*. Paris: OECD.

9 Changing education in action
Lighting the collective efficacy flame

Gavin Hays and Adam Hendry

There is no easy way to 'flip the system'. This is especially true in education. However, it is not impossible, and this vignette offers readers a brief insight into how one Australian school has built a culture of empowerment, autonomy, and leadership amongst both teachers and students and has, seemingly, fostered feelings of efficaciousness amongst the school community to effect desirable educational outcomes – all within the confines of an established order.

Over the last decade, Parramatta Marist High School, a Catholic, systemic, non-selective boys' secondary school in Western Sydney, Australia, has undergone substantial whole school pedagogical change. The changes in the school were a response to both the increasing emergence and importance of technology in the early years of this millennium and wider societal and industry calls to address the development of certain key competencies or so-called 'enterprise' or 'twenty-first century' skills in students. These debates initiated an intense re-evaluation of the role of the teacher in our classrooms and the need to move towards more student-centred approaches to learning. After exploring various models in the middle 2000s, project-based learning (PjBL) was subsequently adopted as the primary instructional model for Years 9 and 10 as well as and in certain key learning areas in Years 7 and 8 in 2008. Subsequently, a problem-based learning (PBL) approach, derived from the "One Day, One Problem" model pioneered at Republic Polytechnic, Singapore, was adopted in Year 11 to help students gain a deeper understanding of content knowledge and further promote the development of key competencies. In 2013, a flipped classroom approach evolved for Year 12 students and PBL was fully implemented across Years 7 and 8; and, in 2016, a hybridised model of 'flipped PBL' was introduced into Year 11 so that students were provided the opportunity to move from surface to deep and to transfer learning. Hence, after ten years, a whole school approach to change had not only been adopted but also expanded and refined (Hendry *et al.* 2017).

It is quite evident that this evolution of pedagogical practice has had a profound effect on both students and teachers in manifold ways. In particular, the development of a learning community that promotes collaboration between staff (e.g. team teaching and timetabled professional learning);

between students (e.g. peer-coaching); and between teachers and students (and the curriculum). Moreover, the demystification and decoding of educational practices for students (explicitly addressing the 'how's and 'why's), the development of student agency and increased engagement are also observable features of the change in practice. Furthermore, the physical classroom environment has been designed to support these shifts in pedagogy and providing authentic and agile team teaching opportunities. Another obvious and clearly demonstrable effect has been the extensive student academic growth from 2008 to 2017 when comparing performance on the National Assessment Program—Literacy and Numeracy (NAPLAN) and the New South Wales (NSW) Higher School Certificate (HSC) examinations. The school has maintained a stable relationship to the state mean over this period of time in the NAPLAN examinations (showing no significant change in student academic ability upon enrolment). However, even though improving the school's HSC results was not the intended outcome in changing pedagogies, the school has experienced accelerated growth in the state-wide standardised exit exams, the NSW HSC. Since, 2010, growth has occurred peaking at 43rd in the state in 2014 and, in 2016 with every subject being above state average and reaching 4th in the state in Mathematics (Extension 1, 2 and Mathematics combined). Furthermore, the distribution of students in academic bands on the HSC has also increased significantly with a significant skewing of results towards higher achievement bands for all students. The school has also witnessed an improving rank, in general, in the HSC over the last decade.

Clearly, *something* has happened within the school in the attempt to develop a culture of empowerment, autonomy, and leadership amongst both teachers and students. These changes are quite palpable to the teachers, the students and visitors to the school; and it's a 'feeling', for want of a better term, that certainly runs much deeper and which is only partly reflected by the HSC results.

How then is this feeling best explained?

This is where collective efficacy enters, stage left.

Collective efficacy has been defined by Albert Bandura, the father of social cognitive theory, as a personal belief about the group's capabilities to organise and execute the courses of action required to produce given attainments (Bandura 1997). A sense of collective efficacy must first, however, emanate from an individual's own feelings of efficaciousness or 'self' efficacy. These kissing cousins are important motivational constructs as educational researchers, like Bandura, have shown them both to be good predictors of the level of individual and group performance. So, what exactly are the levers that can be pulled to generate a sense of collective efficacy? According to Bandura (1977, 1997), both individual and collective efficacy beliefs can be influenced by four sources of information: performance accomplishments, vicarious experience, verbal persuasion, and emotional arousal. Simply put, an individual or group who has repeated success and performs (in whatever field) tends to raise their self and collective efficacy respectively. For individual students at Parramatta

Marist, this may come in the form of project formative and summative tasks, problem resolution or assessments.

Feelings of self-efficaciousness can also be built by watching others perform (and successfully complete) a task that either we ourselves have never attempted or have attempted with varying or limited success. This may also hold true for class groups where they witness the success either via a PjBL group presentation, problem solution or assessment performance (as a whole). Such vicarious experiences can enhance the collective efficacy of a group and lead possibly to the transfer of these beliefs between groups of students. A group of students can also be persuaded by their teacher to believe in their capacities to accomplish a task, however, efficacy beliefs induced in this manner, whilst beneficial, are still not as powerful as those provoked by the group's own accomplishments (Bandura 1977). The last lever that contributes to collective efficacy is emotional arousal. As pointed out by Bandura (1997), people rely partly on their state of physiological arousal to assess their vulnerability to stress and therefore minimising this arousal leads to improved performance; essentially, groups that stay as cool under pressure are more likely to expect and experience success.

Naturally, teachers too are subject to the very same feelings as their charges.

Explorations of teachers' sense of efficaciousness have led to the coining of the term, 'Collective Teacher Efficacy' (CTE). CTE refers to "the judgments of teachers in a school that the faculty as a whole can organize and execute the courses of action required to have a positive effect on students" (Goddard et al. 2004, p. 4). Essentially, the stronger the staff's shared belief in their instructional efficacy, the better the school performed academically (Bandura 1993). If we again consider the four sources of information or levers that Bandura believes fosters efficacy beliefs in individuals and groups, it stands to reason that providing teachers an opportunity to collaborate, to team-teach and facilitate professional dialogue and to do so across disciplines, would surely lay the foundation for the development of CTE and, again, all achieved within a system of existing workplace agreements.

In theory, this all sounds great but building an efficacious learning community is not an easy task. Fundamental to a sense of collective efficacy is one's own belief in their ability to execute courses of actions with their ability and skills. This applies to both teachers as much as students. Hence, students who lack this self-efficacy are not easily convinced or beguiled into believing they can perform individually or as part of a group. Conversely, highly efficacious students may not perform as expected if they do not collaborate with peers. Moreover, collaboration in the form of peer-coaching is critical in building the confidence on learners and the sense of dependence and interdependence to achieve both individual and group goals like completing a project on time or performing in an exam.

What contribution collective efficacy has made to improving student outcomes in our learning community is not entirely clear although it is hoped that the current research initiatives within the school will go some way to unpacking its importance and shining a light on those factors that build it.

Establishing a learning culture where teachers and students feel empowered is hard; growing and sustaining it is harder; and, understanding (and proving) what contributes to its success, empirically speaking, is even harder. Nevertheless, it is most certainly possible to ignite the flame of collective efficacy within a school and within an existing system by affording both teachers (and students) *real* opportunities to collaborate, communicate and build confidence by trusting in their professionalism and increasing their autonomy to solve complex problems and determine courses of action that improve educational outcomes for students. The challenge we foresee is knowing what fuel to pour on the collective efficacy fire (and in what quantities) to keep it burning—intensely.

References

Bandura, A., 1977. Self-efficacy: Toward a unifying theory of behavioural change. *Psychological Review*, 84, 191–215.

Bandura, A., 1993. Perceived self-efficacy in cognitive development and functioning. *Educational Psychologist*, 28 (2), 117–148.

Bandura, A., 1997, *Self-efficacy: The exercise of control*. New York: W.H. Freeman.

Goddard, R., Hoy, A., and Hoy, W., 2004. Collective efficacy beliefs: Theoretical developments, empirical evidence, and future directions. *Educational Researcher*, 33 (3), 3–13.

Hendry, A., Hays, G., Challinor, K., and Lynch, D., 2017. Undertaking educational research following the introduction, implementation, evolution, and hybridization of constructivist instructional models in an Australian PBL high school. *Interdisciplinary Journal of Problem-Based Learning*, 11 (2). Available from: https://doi.org/10.7771/1541-5015.1688

10 From weakness to strength

Turning the challenge of 'out of field teaching' into a team that thrives

Yasodai Selvakumaran

'Out of field teaching' is a reality of the secondary education system that is not adequately addressed by the system. Many teachers are expected to teach outside their field of expertise, often without support or acknowledgement. As a Humanities teacher, I have personal experience in teaching outside of my chosen field. At a school trivia night a few years ago, our faculty team members light-heartedly renamed the HSIE (Human Society and Its Environment) team "Heaps Smart In Everything". Yet the fun name symbolised the challenge that secondary HSIE (or Humanities) faculties face in maintaining instructional expertise across various subjects. In 2016, the five most impacted subjects for out of field teaching in Australia were Geography, History, Social Studies, Media and Religious Studies (Wheddon 2016). Four of those subjects are taught in HSIE at Rooty Hill High School (RHHS). Although out of field teaching is often viewed as a deficit, this vignette shares personal and team reflections that highlight the positive impact when teachers view out of field teaching as an opportunity and a strategy to enhance the instructional capacity of the whole team. Working collaboratively, the HSIE team has evidence that it has strengthened teacher identities, better understood general instructional and subject-specific pedagogies, and adapted work practices to the lessons learnt. Our reflections show how valuing the experience of those working in schools is essential to flip less than ideal system realities such as out of field teaching into valuable opportunities to develop expertise.

The challenge

Caldis (2017, p. 1) highlights that out of field teaching can "disrupt the integrity of a subject" and can contribute to "heightened levels of student disengagement, lower than anticipated outcomes and an increasing lack of confidence amongst teachers about their skills to teach effectively". On average, our team of 12 teachers co-ordinate 24 courses across seven subjects (History, Geography, Commerce, Society and Culture, Business Studies, Economics and Legal Studies) from Years 7–12. This presents significant team workload and cognitive load for individual teachers in designing programs, assessment, and methods of timely feedback. Pressure can be further heightened if teaching outside one's original qualifications, especially the first time. A common out of field challenge in New South Wales (NSW) in HSIE continues to be in Years 7–10 when Geography teachers teach History and vice versa.

Transitioning teacher identities

Like many who pursue a career in secondary education, I entered teaching with a passion for particular subjects. Although in NSW graduating teachers are issued a provisional approval to teach based on university qualifications, the reality in seeking employment often means graduates accepting casual or temporary teaching appointments in out of field areas of the curriculum. Teachers may question their confidence in the ways they were prepared to act as a subject-based teacher and may limit their career progression. This, combined with the changes of beginning a teaching career, often contributes to low retention and burn out. Kenny and Hobbs (2015, p. 3) describe this as a "boundary crossing event" that will impact on a teacher's professional identity. Part of the frustration for individual teachers can be when the efforts of successful teaching out of field are not recognised or when the continuity of teaching needed for recognition is precarious.

I graduated with initial accreditation to teach English, History, Modern History and Ancient History and, one year into my teaching career, I completed my professional accreditation requirements with evidence that also included Geography, Commerce and Aboriginal Studies. In my second year, I taught Society and Culture in both Years 11 and Year 12 and, after two years I was granted approval to teach Society and Culture by the NSW Department of Education; the same status as being university qualified. This, for me, further developed my identity and confidence as a HSIE teacher. I now recognise that certification for successful out of field teaching by employers and accrediting authorities needs to be more consistent in developing individual and team identities in HSIE.

General and subject-specific pedagogies in secondary education

Secondary teachers graduate with deep knowledge and teaching methods related to the subjects they teach, and many hold a deep passion for learning and teaching in those subjects.

By teaching out of field, the HSIE team has developed its capacity in understanding the generic instructional pedagogies valued in humanities teaching to now further defining those specific to particular subjects. The work of our HSIE faculty in the implementation of the ACARA general capabilities (ACARA 2018) in each subject was featured by the Australian Learning Lecture (ALL) series in 2017 with the RHHS Creative Inquiry Cycle (Bridger 2017).

We are now continuing to explore the notion of subject-based *signature pedagogies* (Shulman 2005) to define ways of "knowing", "doing" and "being" for each subject. As a team, we are working collaboratively to define what makes learning in each subject unique and to identify the best ways to teach and learn in each subject. Out of field teaching has strengthened our faculty professional learning as we seek to define these signature pedagogies in each subject as team members now have multiple subject perspectives. In discussing History and Geography for example, we have noted and designed learning tasks that recognise that, while opportunities for analytical, practical fieldwork are critical in Geography, historical site studies demand a focus on contestability and source analysis.

An important lesson learnt

Out of field teaching within the HSIE faculty has thrived in the context of strong structures for induction, support, and ongoing collaborative professional learning in the school and faculty. Our initial faculty goal was to support new teachers and those teaching a subject for the first time, to have sample lesson plans and resources embedded as guides with options and flexibility to adapt team learning intentions and success criteria. One lesson the team has learnt through action learning was that over-scaffolding corporate programs, although providing examples of best practice, risked decreasing the capacity of some teachers to design and deliver lessons in some cases if they became too reliant on the work of other teachers.

This resonated with the 6th Principle of the Harvard Instructional Core:

> We learn to do the work by doing the work, not by telling other people to do the work, not by having done the work at some point in the past, and not by hiring experts who can act as proxies for our knowledge about how to do the work.
>
> (City et al. 2009)

This was a stark reminder to the team that although working from strengths is valuable, we also needed to ensure gaps between our most expert teachers and novices did not widen in ways that damaged the development of the novices. Induction initiatives and ongoing mentoring now focus on subject specialists "pairing" with those new to teaching a subject, no matter how many years they have been teaching. An individual professional learning approach to developing lesson and learning design capacity is delivered in faculty with the faculty Professional Practice Mentor (a school-based position to support accreditation and professional learning) working with teachers to target their professional learning on areas of classroom practice and subject-based instruction.

Out of field teaching, even in the same Key Learning Area, is not ideal for beginning teachers but success in out of field teaching should be acknowledged a highly skilled trait seen in the most expert teachers. The RHHS HSIE experience is an example of how a focus on developing expertise as a collaborative team can help faculties respond to both the system and individual challenges teachers may face when teaching out of field. The strong focus on professional learning has helped the HSIE team at RHHS use out of field teaching for "identity expansion and a reconceptualisation of practice" (Hobbs 2013, p. 274 cited in Kenny and Hobbs 2015, p. 5).

When I reflect on that school trivia night, even though we were not the winning table, we are confident that we can adapt to the changing needs of our students. Through ongoing targeted professional learning and faculty collaboration, we can build the capacity and sense of confidence in all teachers to teach the range of subjects our students want to study, not just those with original qualifications. Teachers are flipping the system like this all the time in collaborating and facilitating high quality learning. The system must acknowledge and support teachers as they tackle the complexities of their work.

References

ACARA, 2018. *ACARA general capabilities* [online]. Available from: www.australiancurriculum.edu.au/f-10-curriculum/general-capabilities. [Accessed 16 January 2018].

Bridger, E., 2017. Building critical skills at Rooty Hill High School [online]. *Australian Learning Lecture*. Available from: www.all-learning.org.au/resources/building-critical-skills-rooty-hill-high-school [Accessed 4 October 2017].

Caldis, S., 2017. Teachers having to know what they do not know [online]. *Geography Teachers Association NSW Bulletin*. Available from:www.gtansw.org.au/files/geog_bulletin/2017/1_2017/05_%20GTA%20Bulletin%20_Issue%201_17_Teaching%20out%20of%20field.pdf [Accessed 20 December 2017].

City, E. A., Elmore, R. F., Fiarman, S. E., and Teitel, L., 2009. *Instructional rounds in education: A network approach to improving teaching and learning.* Harvard Education Press, 21–38.

Kenny, J. and Hobbs, L., 2015. Researching with in-service teachers teaching "out of field" [online]. *Contemporary Approaches to Research in Mathematics*, Science, Health *and Environmental* Education *2015*. Available from: blogs.deakin.edu.au/steme/wp-content/uploads/sites/39/2018/01/Kenny-CAR_2015-Tas-TOOF.pdf

Shulman, L. S., 2005. Signature pedagogies in the professions. *Daedalus*, 134 (3), 52–59.

Wheddon, P., 2016. Out of field teaching in Australian Secondary Schools [online]. *Policy Insights*. Volume (6) June 2016. Available from: https://research.acer.edu.au/policyinsights/6/ [Accessed 8 June 2017].

11 Flipping their lids

Teachers' wellbeing in crisis

Andy Hargreaves, Shaneé Washington and Michael T. O'Connor[1]

Changing teachers, troubling times

Low pay. Declining status. School-by-school competition. Harmful and unwanted tests. Apart from a few exceptions—tiny pockets of professional pride in Northern Europe, Canada and Singapore—educational systems are going crazy and teachers are flipping their lids. In the United States, barely half of the teaching force is now prepared in universities. Applications for teacher education are in free fall. A movement known as #RedforEd has seen teachers turn out in their hundreds of thousands to demand salaries that will enable them just to pay their mortgage and feed their families. England faces a constant recruitment crisis. The decade-old global economic collapse, for which no public servants were responsible, condemned teachers in many countries like Portugal and Ireland to pay freezes and even pay cuts from which they are only now recovering. Norwegians have a parliamentary committee that proposes to restore long lost trust and autonomy to teachers. In Canada, the Nova Scotia government has forcibly separated school principals from the teachers' union to become the line managers of the government's will—dividing the education profession against itself (Glaze 2018). Rates of teacher stress are on the rise in Hong Kong and Japan, too (Asia Society 2018, Nakada et al. 2016).

Australians are not exempt from the teacher wellbeing crisis. The Deans of Southern Cross University (Bahr and Ferreira 2018) point to drops in teacher education applications in different universities ranging from 19–40% in just two years. Some of the key factors responsible for this declining attractiveness of teaching as a profession, they argue, are teachers experiencing decreasing autonomy in their own classrooms in the face of a bewildering list of competencies, an obsession with high stakes standardised testing, and an ever-escalating workload.

Policymakers are not blind to these problems; but most of the solutions they have adopted have been inappropriate and insufficient. Various governments promise to cut back on unnecessary regulations and paperwork, but this only removes some of the bad things. It doesn't actively improve the positive aspects of teaching. There is also a resurgent belief in the power and possibilities of more collaboration among teachers to provide mutual support and shared commitment. But what kind of collaboration do policymakers refer to, and will it always work? This chapter argues for the need to flip the ways in which teacher wellbeing is considered in the education system.

Six threats to teacher wellbeing

In Ontario, Canada, we have been studying how the province has been implementing reforms in four areas, including wellbeing (Hargreaves and Shirley 2018, Ontario Ministry of Education 2014). Some districts were as concerned about teacher stress and wellbeing as they were about student wellbeing. Our research points to six threats to teacher wellbeing, outlined below and supported by data from our participants.

1. Caring carries a cost

Like all caring professions that work with vulnerable people, the nature of teachers' work makes educators perpetually susceptible to illbeing. The greater the needs of the students, and the more challenging the schools, the more that teachers are prone to experience stress. As I found in my earlier work on teaching and guilt, one of the causes of guilt among teachers is the extent of their caring (Hargreaves 1994). Especially in a job with no limits where the work is never done, a common feeling among teachers is that they cannot care for everyone and can never care enough. As one Ontario principal remarked, "we've learned that the more we've gotten to know our students as people, the more our stress increases, because every story is heart-breaking".

2. Students are vulnerable

Teachers invariably encounter students who suffer or have exceptional needs. The international evidence, and the testimony of Ontario educators themselves, is that these needs are increasing. In Ontario, one in seven students has reported "a serious level of psychological distress" and over one-quarter indicated that during the past year there was a "time they wanted to talk to someone about a mental health problem, but did not know where to turn" (Boak *et al.* 2016, p. iv). A principal in Ontario explained, "We refer to our kids as 'trauma kids'" due to "poverty, neglect, and violence" so "we look at our role as addressing the whole student. Sometimes we clothe them, feed and shower them, and love them, really".

The greater the levels of concentrated poverty and social disadvantage, the more educators need help in finding ways to attain a work–life balance. An assistant principal observed how teaching is

> a messy profession. Our school has two teachers that are on stress leave, and there are other teachers that are on the verge of leaving. This is no longer a school where someone might start and end their career, because we don't know if they're going to last five years.

A director of one of the boards commented that "I have staff that are burning out, and I have admin that are burning out, and I have senior admin that are burning out".

3. Expectations have risen

There is increased awareness of and rightful attention to problems that have always been there. These include children in Indigenous communities who experience drug and alcohol dependency resulting from decades of oppression and forcible separation of children from their families; lesbian, gay, bisexual and transgender students who want to reverse cultures of bullying by ensuring they are included in the communities and curriculum of their schools; and a range of students with special needs who were once wrongly identified as badly behaved or unable to learn and whose parents now demand greater individualised attention for them. Teachers are being urged to address the whole child, not just the bit of the child that's connected to the subject they teach. They are also being asked to develop creativity and other global competencies without letting traditional performance standards drop. Teach more, care more, do more. Be on for all of everybody all of the time. Be resilient. Bounce back. No excuses. No let up. That's the nature of teachers' work today.

4. Too many initiatives; not enough initiative

There are too many initiatives coming at teachers from other people and there is not enough opportunity for teachers to exercise their own initiative. The 2018 *International Summit on the Teaching Profession* pointed to high levels of stress, anxiety and depression in 41% of Australian teachers, 46% of US teachers and 81% of teachers in the United Kingdom (Schleicher 2018). In England, the report continues, 84% of teachers have identified workload as a major issue (NASUWT 2017). It is not only teachers, but also principals and vice-principals whose wellbeing is impacted by their work today. A White Paper by the Ontario Principals' Council, for example, states that the province's principals "reported working 58.7 hours a week, with 72% of them feeling pressured to work longer hours" (Pollock 2017, p. 2). As the Introduction to this book makes clear, similar trends are also apparent in Australia (Riley 2017).

5. Implementing assessments teachers don't believe in

Threats to teacher wellbeing also arise when teachers have to implement high stakes assessments they do not believe in. They are expected to be inclusive of student diversity, but the tests push them towards mono-cultural standardisation. In Ontario, there has been a high stakes test since the 1990s in Grades 3, 6 and 9. It was one of the sources of inspiration for NAPLAN in Australia.

Our research in ten school boards unearthed considerable opposition to the tests. Although system administrators felt the test still "had a place in terms of accountability" and provided them with data that helped them to "see their students where they're struggling", the closer that educators' jobs got to the students, the more critical they became. Some test items were biased against children from the North, ones who live in poverty, or recent refugees, respectively. Teachers were less likely to risk innovation when they taught the grades that were tested. Teachers were also profoundly upset when students who were non-verbal, autistic, lived with their families in run-down motels, and so on, had to take the test. As one teacher put it, "It's hugely detrimental to my kids when we get into those scenarios. It's very stressful for them. It's very stressful for the teachers. And, quite frankly, it seems to be unfair". Teachers felt pressed into doing things they didn't believe in. "There's a lot of pressure", one principal remarked. "I can picture one of my Grade 3 teachers. She's carrying the weight of things she can't control."

All over the world, there are movements to pull away from high stakes testing. The US Federal Government withdrew from it in the 2015 Every Student Succeeds Act (2015). The Premier of Ontario accepted the recommendations of a review conducted by five other advisors and me to abolish standardised tests in at least Grades 3 and 9 (Campbell et al. 2018). Parents' movements in England are organising against standardised achievement tests (Belam 2018). Australia's NAPLAN will almost certainly follow suit.

6. Individualised solutions

Teachers in many schools are still trapped in a culture of individualism and isolation (DuFour 2011). They spend most of their time having to work alone with large groups of students. Cultures of individualism insulate teachers from the expertise and advice of their colleagues. They also withhold the solidarity and support that can help teachers cope with adversity by understanding that all of them deal with great challenges in their work. According to the second Gonski report (Gonski et al. 2018), Australian teachers spend less time on professional learning and collaboration than teachers across Organisation for Economic Co-operation and Development (OECD) countries. The report notes, however, that "the practice most strongly related to teachers' self-efficacy is taking part in collaborative professional learning" (Gonski et al. 2018, p. 57). Collaboration is itself a source of positive wellbeing that supports job satisfaction for teachers. But not only does teacher individualism sometimes linger on from the old days; competition between schools and sectors—like the public, Catholic and independent sectors in Australia—for families, students and teaching talent, exacerbates it still further.

Sometimes, the responses to the widespread occurrence of problems with teacher wellbeing have also been individualistic ones, such as encouraging teachers to take up courses in yoga and mindfulness. Some schools and school boards in our Canadian study adopted these kinds of strategies to improve educators' wellbeing. One board had partly funded several hundred teachers to take individual online courses in mindfulness. "We've been talking more and more about mental health with our staff and they're starting to take care of themselves now", one principal remarked. "They've got the yoga going. They've got after-school class where they're doing a lot of fitness." However, a teacher from the same school said, "There's this belief that, now that you've yoga-ed and meditated, you should be good to go". While meditation and physical exercise can be beneficial to all of us, the crisis of teacher wellbeing cannot be fixed by add-on programs for individuals alone. Wellbeing initiatives must also address the roots of the problem, such as reducing excessive workload demands, eliminating anxiety-inducing testing practices, and creating incentives for schools and their teachers to collaborate rather than compete.

Summary

There is no student wellbeing without teacher wellbeing. Teachers who are overwhelmed, exhausted, depressed, frustrated, burned out or unfit are poor role models for the young people they teach. Teachers' wellbeing is inherently at risk because teachers serve populations that are always vulnerable because of their dependence and immaturity. It is also increasingly vulnerable due to mounting social pressures and declining social support for families and children outside the school. Knowledge and awareness of children's needs has developed, expectations have risen, educational goals have broadened and deepened, and yet teachers are still inundated with external initiatives. They are plagued by lists of new competencies alongside inflexible demands for traditional high stakes testing that pull them in opposite directions. Competition between schools and sectors also inhibits the opportunities for collaboration and solidarity that could increase teachers' capacity to deal with the stresses they experience and the challenges they face.

Teachers are becoming increasingly frustrated and are flipping their lids. So it's time to flip the system so it can help them. The more emphasis we place on students' wellbeing, the more we need to support teachers' wellbeing. We need to not only protect teachers from excessive stress; we also need to create the conditions in which they can thrive. There should be not only more collaboration among teachers, but also better collaboration that yields benefits for students and teachers alike. We need better ways than NAPLAN for tracking students' progress that do not undermine innovation or lead to student ill being. There need to be fewer external initiatives, and more scope for teachers' own initiative. And we should seek greater equity between schools and sectors not by imposing more external funding mandates, however well-intentioned they may be, but by creating expectations and incentives for schools and sectors to work together for students' common good. Let's look at five specific ways in which these things can be done.

Five ways to think about enhancing teacher wellbeing

1. Collective autonomy

In many countries, big bureaucracies have taken away teachers' professional autonomy. Top-down bureaucracies dictate the curriculum with long lists of competencies. They replace teachers' professional judgments with high stakes standardised tests that narrow the curriculum and put teachers and their students under excessive pressure. They also subject teachers to endless cycles of analysing quantitative data about their students' performance so they can make speedy interventions to remedy any shortfalls.

At the same time, professional autonomy shouldn't mean individual autonomy from the learning, feedback, judgment and scrutiny of one's peers. Professional autonomy shouldn't allow poor practices to persist, or permit teaching to follow teachers' passions, even when this does not really fit with what students actually need. It shouldn't allow repetition of projects and content from one year to another, or omission of things that students really need to know.

The answer to this battle between top-down bureaucracy and individual autonomy from outside interference is collective autonomy (Hargreaves and Fullan 2012). In collective autonomy, educators have more independence from top-down bureaucratic authority but less independence from each other. Michael O'Connor and I have seen this principle at work in our study of five collaborative designs across the world (Hargreaves and O'Connor 2018).

2. Solidarity and specificity

On average, it is definitely better to collaborate than not collaborate. Collaboration improves learning and achievement (Hargreaves and Fullan 2012, Leana 2011), enhances the process of change, and increases the motivation of teachers by involving them in decision-making (OECD 2014). But not all collaboration is worthwhile. Deeper collaboration, or *collaborative professionalism* as we call it, benefits from two complementary features.

First, collaborative professionalism strengthens solidarity among educators. Solidarity is about, trust, loyalty and mutual support. It is traditionally most commonly associated with union allegiance and there are times when collective opposition to wrongs committed against the teaching profession, the children it serves, and the overall public good is warranted. But solidarity is also about holding things together, feeling you are all in the same boat, and exercising collective responsibility together. In the case study we conducted in the Pacific Northwest, solidarity was about teachers coming together in a network of isolated and remote rural schools, to share knowledge and problems with people whose work situation was just like theirs. In the forests of Colombia, solidarity occurred when teachers in the vast education network known as *Escuela Nueva*, which has helped prepare young people for peace and democracy, rode on their motorcycles to the teachers' network meeting to learn from each other, even though union work-to-rule action officially forbade it due to a strike.

Solidarity builds relationships and strengthens teacher communities, but the conversations and interactions that make up these communities need something else as well. They need precise tools, structures and protocols that give interactions a focus, ensure that everyone is included, and promote the sharing and use of expertise. In a school board in North Ontario we studied for *Collaborative Professionalism*, teachers took over the leadership of professional learning communities. In Norway, using cooperative learning strategies among teachers as well as with students, ensured that, in partnership with the principal, teachers were focused not just on small changes in their own classrooms, but also on reframing the big picture of the whole school. In Hong Kong, Lesson Study protocols, where visitors are divided into groups to provide different kinds of feedback to the teachers, ensured that criticisms were separated out from the complaints of habitual critics. In the Pacific Northwest, the network of teachers in rural schools didn't just meet and share ideas in an open-ended way. They got to work on curriculum planning with 'job-alike' teachers whose roles were very similar to theirs.

3. Collaborating with competitors

How do you build collaboration across schools when they are also competing? In Sweden, increased market competition between schools was associated with falling standards and growing inequality (Shirley 2017). In England, economists have found that the market-driven academies that have increasingly replaced schools that are democratically controlled by local authorities or schools districts, do not perform any better, on average, than the systems they replaced (Ladd and Fiske 2016). For historical reasons, inter-school competition in Australia operates in a different way. Public schools, Catholic schools and independent schools compete for the same students and teachers within the same communities.

The first Gonski report (Gonski *et al.* 2011) came up with a formula to create some equalisation of funding among the different sectors. This was partly implemented by the former Labour Government. Its purpose was not to eliminate the competition, but to make it fairer and base it on students' needs. Mandates to equalise funding, though, create perceived winners and losers, and if the losers are the most privileged, they will inevitably marshal their considerable social as well as financial capital to defeat the move in the long run. Efforts to equalise funding are rarely by themselves sufficient. Motivational strategies are also needed in addition to mandated ones that provide incentives and encouragement to work together for a common good.

Australian educators work in a system of historic competition, exacerbated by the publication of individual school test results on NAPLAN via the myschool website or on public ATAR (tertiary entrance rank score) league tables. It's time to flip the system to create incentives for the different sectors to cooperate together for the common good of a shared community of students and citizens, so everyone who participates feels invested and can share credit for a bigger win. Among the strategies that can be encouraged and supported are shared uses of high quality facilities, shared professional development, common and fair policies on student exclusions, selection criteria that span the full range of student ability and include an equal quota of students with special educational needs, and shared accountability for achievement results across entire towns, cities or regions.

4. External support and partnership

It's hard for teachers who take on more and more responsibility for students' wellbeing, when broader support in the society in terms of social services and mental health provision is inadequate. One school district we studied in northern Ontario contained high numbers of Indigenous Canadian (First Nations) students. As in Australia, Canada's Indigenous communities have suffered from a legacy of residential schooling that separated young people from their families, communities, language and culture, resulting in multiple forms of psychological trauma that have stretched across the generations. This district, for example, had "one of the highest suicide rate areas in all of Canada", that resulted from "a lot of despair, hopelessness, depression". Many students had witnessed suicide in their families or had seen family members self-harming. Some students had resorted to suicide themselves, due to high rates of suicide in their immediate environment, being in families with substance abuse issues, having an absence of positive role models, suffering instability from being raised in foster care, and being in a system where there was relative unavailability or complete absence of mental health services. Schools and their teachers should not be left to cope alone with the immense stresses suffered by families and their children. One key aspect of rethinking teacher wellbeing and collaboration, therefore, is investing more resources in support for families in the wider community and then building partnerships between these community agencies and the schools to provide 'wraparound' support for all young people, especially the most vulnerable. One example is the *City Connects* network of over 30 schools in Massachusetts, a program that yields demonstrable results for improved and lasting student achievement compared to a matched sample of schools (Walsh *et al.* 2014).

Then there is the remarkable story of Iceland, an entire country where, 15 years ago, there had been serious problems with drug and alcohol abuse, as well as school dropout among young people. The Icelandic government concluded that one contributory factor was that young people did not have enough to do or anything to belong to. So the government built leisure centres all over the country, constructed more than 70 indoor soccer pitches for year-round use, and hired 600 highly trained sports coaches to work with young people (Ronay 2016, Wahl 2018). Substance abuse problems dropped dramatically (Milkman 2017).

Too many systems are expecting schools to do all the work of compensating for shortfalls of public investment in the society. We need to flip the system so that schools and other agencies receive sufficient funding to support their young people together.

5. Less testing; better assessment

Subsequent to conducting and publishing our research with ten school boards in Ontario—research that included data pointing to systemic flaws in the province's high stakes testing system—a review of the Ontario testing system by the Ontario Premier's advisors, including me, presented survey evidence of the public and of stakeholders indicating that the test was perceived to be performing "poorly" or "very poorly" in terms of "ensuring student equity; recognising the culture and experiences of each student; (and) minimising the undesirable indirect effects of assessment on students' learning and wellbeing" (Campbell *et al.* 2018). The review recommended abolition of the tests in Grades 3 and 9 (two out of the three grades tested). It also proposed the further development of new continuous assessments that were already emerging in the province through the use of digital tablets to photograph, record and share student learning in real time, for example. Flipping a system of bad testing does not mean eliminating all testing. Instead, it poses one of the biggest challenges of the next five years in terms of developing better assessments that record, track and give feedback on students' learning in real time.

Conclusion

This chapter is by no means the first to comment on the problematic state of teaching in Australia. Field Rickards (2016), former Dean of Melbourne University School of Education, pointed to difficulties of low pay, oversupply, weak matches of teachers' expertise to the subjects they teach, poor career paths and a generally undervalued profession. Lawrence Ingvarson (2014), from the Australian Council for Educational Research, points to problems of entry qualifications and registration. But in the end, wellbeing and illbeing are not just results of how people pay you, what they think about you, and whether your career can progress. They are also in the nature of the job itself. Teachers are flipping their lids for all kinds of reasons, but a big part of it has to do with what the job feels like these days. Teachers feel they are losing control over their professional decisions, their sectors are working against each other rather than with each other, they are being asked to carry the mounting social problems of the world on their own shoulders, and, in the midst of all these things, they feel constrained and compromised by competencies and assessments that they do not always believe in.

So, if we don't want our teachers to boil over and flip their lids, we should pay them more and value them more. But mainly we should look at the job itself in terms of how we define it, how much teachers themselves control and believe in it, how well supported they are by other sectors in doing it, and what opportunities they have to work together to improve it. It's time to heed the words that Peter Garrett, Australia's former Education Minister once sang as the lead singer of Midnight Oil. While the song 'Beds are Burning' was written on behalf of Australia's Indigenous communities, it can apply equally well to the nation's teaching profession. The teaching profession belongs to teachers. It's time to give it back.

Note

1 Although this chapter is written in the first person by the lead author, it is co-authored by Shaneé Washington who led the authorship of the case study report of a school board in Northern Ontario, and Michael T. O'Connor who jointly conducted a study of designs for professional collaboration in five different countries. Both studies informed the writing of this chapter.

References

Asia Society. 2018. New challenges and opportunities facing the teaching profession in public education. Report from the International Summit on the Teaching Profession, 22-23 March 2018. Available from: https://asiasociety.org/sites/default/files/inline-files/2018-international-summit-on-the-teaching-profession-edu-istp.pdf [Accessed 7 June 2018].

Bahr, N. and Ferreira, J., 2018. Seven reasons people no longer want to be teachers. *The Conversation*, 16 April. Available from: https://theconversation.com/seven-reasons-people-no-longer-want-to-be-teachers-94580 [Accessed 4 June 2018].

Belam, M. 2018. 'These tests only measure a little bit of you'—the teachers' letters that go viral. *The Guardian*, 15 May. Available from www.theguardian.com/education/2018/may/15/these-tests-only-measure-a-little-bit-of-you-the-teachers-letters-that-go-viral [Accessed 7 June 2018].

Boak, A., Hamilton, H.A., Adlaf, E.M., Henderson, J.L. and Mann, R.E., 2016. *The mental health and well-being of Ontario students, 1991–2015: Detailed OSDUHS findings.* Toronto: Centre for Addiction and Mental Health.

Campbell, C., Clinton, J., Fullan, M., Hargreaves, A., James, C. and Longboat, K. D., 2018. *Ontario: A learning province*. Findings and recommendations from the independent review of assessment and reporting. Ontario Ministry of Education. Available from www.edu.gov.on.ca/CurriculumRefresh/learning-province-en.pdf [Accessed 7 June 2018].

DuFour, R. 2011. Work together, but only if you want to. *Kappan*, 92 (5), 57–61.

Every Student Succeeds Act, 2015. Pub. L. No. 114-95.

Glaze, A., 2018. Raise the bar: A coherent and responsive education administrative system for Nova Scotia. Halifax, Nova Scotia: Nova Scotia Department of Education and Early Childhood Development. Available from: www.ednet.ns.ca/sites/default/files/docs/raisethebar-en.pdf [Accessed 7 June 2018].

Gonski, D., Boston, K., Greiner, K., Lawrence, C., Scales, B. and Tannock, P., 2011. *Review of funding for schooling final report.* Canberra, Australia: Department of Education, Employment and Workplace Relations.

Gonski, D., Arcus, T., Boston, K., Gould, V., Johnson, W., O'Brien, L., Perry, L.A. and Roberts, M., 2018. *Through growth to achievement: Report of the review to achieve educational excellence in Australian schools.* Canberra, Australia: Department of Education and Training.

Hargreaves, A., 1994. *Changing teachers, changing times: Teachers' work and culture in the postmodern age.* London: Cassell.

Hargreaves, A. and Fullan, M., 2012. *Professional capital: Transforming teaching in every school.* New York: Teachers College Press.

Hargreaves, A. and Shirley, D. (2018) *Leading from the middle: Spreading learning, well-being, and identity across Ontario*, Council of Ontario Directors of Education Report. Available from ccsli.ca/downloads/2018-Leading_From_the_Middle_Final-EN.pdf [Accessed 7 June 2018).

Hargreaves, A. and O'Connor, M. T., 2018. *Collaborative professionalism: When teaching together means learning for all.* Thousand Oaks, CA: Corwin.

Ingvarson, L., 2014. Why don't we have the world's best or most respected, teachers? *The Conversation*, 20 July. Available from https://theconversation.com/why-we-dont-have-the-worlds-best-or-most-respected-teachers-29204 [Accessed 7 June 2018).

Ladd, H.F. and Fiske, E.B., 2016. *England confronts the limits of school autonomy.* (National Center for the Study of Privatisation in Education [NCSPE] Working Paper No. 232), 25 October. New York: Teachers College, Columbia University.

Leana, C.R., 2011, Fall. The missing link in school reform. *Stanford Social Innovation Review*, 30–35.

Milkman, H.B. 2017. Iceland succeeds at reversing teenage substance abuse: The U.S. should follow suit. *Huffington Post*, 6 December. Available from: www.huffingtonpost.com/harvey-b-milkman-phd/iceland-succeeds-at-rever_b_9892758.html [Accessed 4 June 2018].

Nakada, A., Iwasaki, S., Kanchika, M., Nakao, T., Deguchi, Y., Konishi, A., Ishimoto, H. and Inoue, K., 2016. Relationship between depressive symptoms and perceived individual level occupational stress among Japanese schoolteachers. *Industrial Health*, 54 (5), 396–402. http://doi.org/10.2486/indhealth.2015-0195

NASUWT (National Association of Schoolmasters Union of Women Teachers), 2017. *The Big Question 2017: An opinion survey of teachers and school leaders.* Birmingham: NASUWT. Available from www.nasuwt.org.uk/uploads/assets/uploaded/7649b810-30c7-4e93-986b363487926b1d.pdf [Accessed 7 June 2018].

OECD, 2014. *TALIS 2013 results: An international perspective on teaching and learning*, TALIS, OECD Publishing, Paris. http://dx.doi.org/10.1787/9789264196261-en.

Ontario Ministry of Education, 2014. *Achieving excellence: A renewed vision for education in Ontario.* Available from www.edu.gov.on.ca/eng/about/great.html [Accessed 7 June 2018].

Pollock, K., 2017. *Principal work-life balance and well-being matters.* International Symposium White Paper, Ontario Principals Council. Available from www.principals.ca/documents/PrincipalWellBeing-17-FINALb.pdf [Accessed 7 June 2018].

Rickards, F., 2016. What are the main challenges facing teacher education in Australia? *The Conversation*, 30 August. Available from: https://theconversation.com/what-are-the-main-challenges-facing-teacher-education-in-australia-63658 [Accessed 7 June 2018].

Riley, P., 2017. *The Australian Principal Occupational Health, Safety and Wellbeing Survey 2017 Data*. Fitzroy, Victoria: Australian Catholic University. Available from: www.principalhealth.org/au/2017_Report_AU_FINAL.pdf [Accessed 24 May 2018].

Ronay, B., 2016. Football, fire and ice: The inside story of Iceland's remarkable rise. *The Guardian*, 8 June. Available from www.theguardian.com/football/2016/jun/08/iceland-stunning-rise-euro-2016-gylfi-sigurdsson-lars-lagerback [Accessed 7 June 2018].

Schleicher, A., 2018. *Valuing our teachers and raising their status: How communities can help.* International Summit on the Teaching Profession, OECD Publishing, Paris, http://dx.doi.org/10.1787/9789264292697-en.

Shirley, D., 2017. *The new imperatives of educational change: Achievement with integrity* (Routledge leading change series). New York: Routledge.

Wahl, G., 2018. The little nation that can: Iceland's underdogs take on the World Cup stage. *Sports Illustrated*, 1 June. Available from www.si.com/soccer/2018/06/01/iceland-world-cup-soccer-nation-story-culture-heimir-hallgrimsson [Accessed 7 June 2018].

Walsh, M.E., Madaus, G.F., Raczek, A.E., Dearing, E., Foley, C., An, C., Lee-St. John, T.J. and Beaton, A., 2014. A new model for student support in high-poverty urban elementary schools: Effects on elementary and middle school academic outcomes. *American Educational Research Journal*, 51 (4), 704–737.

Part III
Social justice
Democratising the system

The influence of teaching and school leadership on student achievement is often at the forefront of discussions about improving education. Yet student achievement is most impacted by those factors over which teachers and schools have little control, such as socioeconomic context, indigeneity, gender, access, home life, parents' education and school funding. This section of the book wrestles with issues of equity and social justice in Australian education. It deals with serious issues often given lip service but not real action. These are issues often put in the 'too hard' basket or used as political pawns in election contests to win votes. The voices herein are examples of the kinds of voices often lost in the system or marginalised by the system. For instance, there is the 'working class girl' voice of Kelly Cheung, the Indigenous voices of Melitta Hogarth and Kevin Lowe, and the 'rough end of town' public school teacher voice of Tomaz Lasic. There are the echoes of student voices in these chapters, which advocate for students and families marginalised by or alienated from the current system.

Melitta Hogarth points out the inequities embedded in education policy rhetoric and its role in silencing and marginalising Indigenous peoples, a move that she terms 'discursive trickery'. She reveals the privileging of Western values and the perpetuation of racist ideologies in the policy treatment of Aboriginal and Torres Strait Islander peoples. She argues that Indigenous Australian educators need to 'speak up', but also that they need to be invited to sit at decision-making tables.

Kelly Cheung uses an autobiographical narrative frame to describe the education experience of working class girls in Australian education, including the reconstructed experiences of her grandmother, her mother and herself. She argues that the ideals of mass schooling have failed to overcome working class realities and social inequalities; that socially disadvantaged students are de-humanised and data-fied; and that working class, female ways of knowing and being are undermined in current schooling cultures.

Kevin Lowe makes the case for teachers and schools to open productive dialogues between themselves and Aboriginal families and communities. He argues that these interactions influence the needs of students and teachers, and that engagement provides teachers with the knowledge and skills required to contextualise their practice and affect real and sustained change in all students' learning.

Three chapters in this section share educational practice that attempts to redress inequities in the Australian education system. **Ben Lewis** explores his work at Wesley College Perth in engaging Aboriginal students, their families and communities, through the Moorditj Mob Indigenous Program. **Dan Haesler** and **Melissa Fotea** present the *Youth Off The Streets* program as an exemplar of alternative educational practice from which mainstream schools can learn. **Tomaz Lasic** presents a heartfelt vignette of the makerspace at his public high school as a place of 'soul', where students can connect, collaborate, succeed, and find value. These three chapters point to the agency of teachers and students in reclaiming the system for those neglected or ignored by it. They also point to the need for the education system to more seriously consider issues of equity, culture, identity and disadvantage.

Drawing together his international experience and now also his work with Australia's Gonski Institute for Education, **Pasi Sahlberg** challenges Australia to equitably fund its education system in order to meet the moral commitments and human development imperatives of an effective education system for all.

12 "In 2017 we seek to be heard"

De-tangling the contradictory discourses that silence Indigenous voices in education

Melitta Hogarth

Introduction

> For the last quarter century, [...], we've seen seminal reports which have repeatedly emphasised that our people need to have a genuine say in our own lives and decisions that affect our peoples and communities.
> (National Congress of Australia's First Peoples 2016, p. 5)

As the above quote from the *Redfern Statement—An urgent call for a more just approach to Aboriginal and Torres Strait Islander Affairs,* from here on referred to as the Redfern Statement, illustrates the struggle for Aboriginal and Torres Strait Islander peoples to have a definitive voice, and therefore self-determination, in the issues that directly affect and influence their lives is not something new. Indeed, policy and governmental rhetoric would suggest that this is happening or at least, seen as paramount. In the *Closing the Gap: Prime Minister's Report 2016*, Prime Minister Malcolm Turnbull asserted that, "in order for policies and programmes to deliver desired outcomes, they must not only be built on evidence, but be developed in partnership with the Aboriginal and Torres Strait Islander people and communities who will benefit from them" (Department of the Prime Minister and Cabinet 2016, p. 4). However, the notion of partnership is often misunderstood and therefore, marginalisation of Indigenous peoples continues; founded within the ongoing colonial values embedded within the societal and institutional constructs of colonial Australia.

A primary concern of this book is to flip the system, speak back to the dominant voices of government and give voice to the voiceless. Using the methodological approach, Indigenous Critical Discourse Analysis (Hogarth 2017b), I intend to make explicit how government and policy continue to marginalise and silence Aboriginal and Torres Strait Islander peoples. The continual dismissal of Indigenous voice and the assertion of deficit discourses homogenising Aboriginal and Torres Strait Islander students as 'failing' hidden within policy discourses perpetuate the notion of Indigenous peoples being 'inferior'. My intention is to illustrate the contradictory discourses within political rhetoric and policy with regards to the inclusion of Aboriginal and Torres Strait Islander voice in policy, decision making and planning as a whole with some focus on education. I consider how the various mechanisms 'put in place' by policy counter the goodwill intentions shared in policy discourses and the influence of social conditions on the recontextualisation of policy in education.

The contradictory discourses

A quick glimpse at the social conditions of production and interpretation and the unconscious series of processes that occur within all social interactions as evidenced in social media discourses illustrates how the explicit racist ideologies of colonial Australia still exist. The synergies and interrelationship between society and education ensure that policies produced to address and guide governmental actions to address the educational attainment of students continue to emanate assimilatory properties and ultimately, aim to shape the ideal citizen in this globalised neoliberal world (Brown and Lauder 1991). As a result, government and the anonymous policymakers enjoy a position of power that can influence attitudes, beliefs and stereotypes held in mainstream Australia about Aboriginal and Torres Strait Islander peoples.

Further to this, as Morgan *et al.* (2006, p. 231) highlight:

> invariably the nature, and consequently the outcome, of [the] education [provided is] constructed through and measured by non-Indigenous standards, values and philosophies. [Therefore,] the purpose of this education has been to assimilate Indigenous peoples into non-Indigenous cultures and societies. In other words, the education Aboriginal and Torres Strait Islander peoples are given access to, acts to privilege Western values and standards and maintains the colonial view that Indigenous children are "open to change, education and salvation.
>
> (Armitage 2014, p. 4)

What are political discourses suggesting is happening at a national level?

Indeed, policy and governmental rhetoric would suggest that Aboriginal and Torres Strait Islander peoples are involved in the decision making and planning of policy. In the *Closing the Gap: Prime Minister's Report 2016*, Turnbull asserts that, "as a nation we *will* walk side by side with Aboriginal and Torres Strait Islander people on the journey of recognition and reconciliation, to build a promising future for all" (Department of the Prime Minister and Cabinet 2016, p. 4). The use of the term 'will' indicates that the reader is obligated to perform the action as requested. Furthermore, as Turnbull is 'speaking' from a position of authority as a member of the power elite, the discourse indicates the desire of the speaker to improve the imagined future of Aboriginal and Torres Strait Islander peoples.

However, the representation of Aboriginal and Torres Strait Islander peoples in the decision-making process at a national level is minimal. Countering the ideological position of Turnbull, both the *Redfern Statement* (National Congress of Australia's First Peoples 2016) and the *Uluru Statement from the Heart* (Referendum Council 2017) speak about the need for Aboriginal and Torres Strait Islander peoples in Indigenous education decision making and policy-making. The *Redfern Statement* specifically highlights the lack of Indigenous representation in education at the national level.

The recent rejection of the *Uluru Statement from the Heart* (Referendum Council 2017) challenges the commitment of government to engage Aboriginal and Torres Strait Islander peoples in "decision making, planning, delivery and evaluation" at national levels (Conifer *et al.* 2017, Education Council 2015, p. 3, Turnbull 2017). Despite the extensive consultation process and the collective voice of Indigenous peoples found in the production of the *Uluru Statement from the Heart*, their voices have been silenced by government. The privileging of political agenda and Western values were upheld.

What are policy discourses in education suggesting?

So, while policy discourses exude the illusion of neutrality, their rhetoric is punitive. The influence of institutional and societal constructs, values, bias and assumptions and the dominant ideologies maintained in colonial Australia about Aboriginal and Torres Strait Islander peoples is mirrored in the education field. Deficit discourses of perceived failure are perpetuated through the unsaid in Indigenous education policy. The silencing of the Indigenous voice is hidden through the use of discursive trickery giving the illusion of space for Aboriginal and Torres Strait Islander peoples to engage in decision making and so forth (Hogarth 2018).

The notion of partnerships to build engagement and participation in the "decision making, planning, delivery and evaluation" of Indigenous education, as illustrated in the current Australian Indigenous education policy, the National Aboriginal and Torres Strait Islander Education Strategy 2015, from here on referred to as the Strategy, is fraught with assumptions (Education Council 2015, p. 3). The Strategy ignores the fact that the Australian education workforce is dominated by non-Indigenous peoples. In 2016, Aboriginal and Torres Strait Islander teachers made up just over 1% of the total Australian teaching population (Australian Bureau of Statistics 2017). The assumed hegemonic position of the coloniser as the 'knower' about Aboriginal and Torres Strait Islander peoples, histories and cultures, is established through the sheer number of non-Indigenous peoples involved in educating Aboriginal and Torres Strait Islander students. Partnerships in education are therefore bound within the parameters set by the coloniser and as a result, Aboriginal and Torres Strait Islander peoples can be further marginalised, excluded or encouraged based on the generosity of the White administrator.

Alternatively, the *Coolangatta Statement on Indigenous Peoples' Rights in Education* (Morgan et al. 1999, 2006), an Indigenous produced policy document founded in the international human rights charters and conventions, asserts that the involvement of non-Indigenous peoples in Indigenous education should be negotiated. It advocates for the need for a strong local involvement in Indigenous education where there is a need for parents and community to "determine how and to what degree non-Indigenous peoples are involved in Indigenous education" (Morgan et al. 2006, p. 235). Championing the notion of self-determination, the collective Indigenous voice asserts the rights and agency of Indigenous peoples to transform Indigenous education.

Lack of representation

An overview of the Australian educational context and the representations of Aboriginal and Torres Strait Islander peoples directly involved in Indigenous education is necessary. While the More Aboriginal and Torres Strait Islander Teachers Initiative (MATSITI) project sought to increase the number of Aboriginal and Torres Strait Islander educators in schools to provide mentors and role models for Indigenous students at the 'coal face', it also demonstrated the lack of Indigenous representation in executive roles (Johnson et al. 2016). Johnson et al. found that only 7% of the 3,100 Aboriginal and/or Torres Strait Islander teachers held the position of Deputy Principal with only 3% being in the role of Principal.

The lack of Indigenous representation at the local level and overrepresentation of other Australians, where the implementation of the Strategy (Education Council 2015) is enacted, demonstrates the power relations and struggle evident in Indigenous education. Where the Coolangatta Statement on Indigenous Peoples' Rights in Education (Morgan et al. 1999, 2006) asserts that non-Indigenous peoples' involvement is to be negotiated and controlled by Indigenous peoples, the realities of the current Australian context are that Aboriginal and Torres Strait Islander peoples are underrepresented and, therefore, their role in the decision making and recontextualisation of policy within schools is limited (Johnson et al. 2016). As a result, the coloniser maintains power and influence over the potential educational outcomes of Aboriginal and Torres Strait Islander students simply because they are in positions of power and clearly outnumber Indigenous peoples and therefore, can readily silence Indigenous voices.

The role of non-Indigenous peoples

At a national level, the role of non-Indigenous peoples in Indigenous education in positions of authority is extensive. The opportunity to include Aboriginal and Torres Strait Islander peoples within policy making at the national level, through their involvement within the Council of Australian Governments or Education Council, is minimised as it involves the election of

Aboriginal and Torres Strait Islander peoples within government. However, the opportunity for Aboriginal and Torres Strait Islander voices to be included at a national level of sorts is presented through the Aboriginal and Torres Strait Islander Education Advisory Group (ATSIEAG) (Education Council 2015). However, ATSIEAG is a discursive trick (Hogarth 2018). The term, discursive trick, indicates the deliberate 'play on words' to suggest the representation of Aboriginal and Torres Strait Islander peoples in ATSIEAG. It is easy to assume that a group with the explicit reference to Aboriginal and Torres Strait Islander in its name would be made up of, or at least be predominantly populated by, Aboriginal and Torres Strait Islander peoples.

However, the number of Aboriginal and Torres Strait Islander peoples in ATSIEAG is minimal with only two Aboriginal and/or Torres Strait Islander peoples being identified (Council on Federal Financial Relations 2016). The possibility and probability of the two Indigenous voices being silenced due to the discoursal elements 'at play', the hegemonic position of the senior officials within this group and the properties of orders of discourse are high. Due to the 'stacking' of non-Indigenous peoples within ATSIEAG, I argue this group is yet another non-Indigenous organisation involved in Indigenous education (Hogarth 2018).

Interestingly, despite the underrepresentation of Aboriginal and Torres Strait Islander peoples in the educational workforce as previously discussed, the Strategy (Education Council 2015) is written positioning non-Indigenous peoples as Other. The Strategy ignores the current disparities in the educational workforce and the fact that 97% of the executives (principals and deputy principals) who are interpreting and enacting the policy within schools are non-Indigenous (Johnson *et al.* 2016). Reference to non-Indigenous Australians is minimal and is used predominantly to illustrate the need for data collation to compare and contrast the educational attainment of Aboriginal and Torres Strait Islander students to "other Australians" (Education Council 2015, p. 3). In turn, the polarisation of Aboriginal and Torres Strait Islander students to other Australians creates a binary construct of difference and perpetuates the deficit view.

A vignette

Prior to entering the academy, I was a classroom teacher for almost 20 years working in all three sectors of the Queensland education system. In this narrative, I found myself (yet again) being the only Aboriginal teacher. Here, I was located in a small country school with a high Aboriginal and Torres Strait Islander student population. I was often drawn on by other colleagues and the school leader to 'handle' the Indigenous students who had been labelled as disruptive and disrespectful students. On other occasions, Indigenous students who may have been the only student in their class for any given school day were sent to my class despite the age difference because the students felt their classroom teacher was disrespectful and 'picked on them' when the others were absent.

My role became one of being like a 'cushion' between the school and the community. Any issues that the families had with regards to the school, it was seen as my role to 'get things changed'. Any issues the school had, it was my role to 'pass on' the expectations of the principal. My agency and voice in that position was minimised by the push and pull tensions of expectations.

Rather than recognising the opportunity he had to liaise and build partnerships; encouraging parents and community to engage with the decision making and planning, the school leader silenced them. He did not engage, and he did not speak with the community unless it was to inform parents that their child was being excluded from class or the school as a whole. The lack of engagement further widened the 'gap' with parents and therefore, the inclusion of Aboriginal and Torres Strait Islander voice in the "decision making, planning, delivery and evaluation" of Indigenous education was impossible (Education Council 2015, p. 3). The hegemonic position and the assumption of superiority exuded by the school leader put a metaphorical wall more than 6 foot high at the school gate and the Aboriginal and Torres Strait Islander parents and community were silenced.

Discussion

I share this story to contextualise how I have seen the power of the coloniser enacted. I have observed the patriarchal superiority of a school leader who privileges his colonial values and knowledges, and disregarded Indigenous knowledges. I have seen and heard the explicit racist views of colleagues who flippantly ignored my Aboriginality because I was one of the 'better ones' and 'not like those others'. It is because of these reasons and many more that the title and ultimately, the objective of this book, encouraging for the system to be flipped; to give voice to those involved in education to have a say in education, that I now speak to the need for change. In Indigenous education, I argue that there is a need for transformation (Hogarth 2018). As the authors of the *Redfern Statement* (National Congress of Australia's First Peoples 2016), the *Uluru Statement from the Heart* (Referendum Council 2017) and the *Coolangatta Statement on Indigenous Peoples' Rights in Education* (Morgan et al. 1999, 2006) advocate, Indigenous voice needs to be heard.

The international human rights charter that the *Coolangatta Statement on Indigenous Peoples' Rights in Education* (Morgan et al. 1999, 2006) drew on was the then draft of *The United Nations Declaration on the Rights of Indigenous Peoples* [UNDRIP] (United Nations General Assembly 2008). It hones in on Articles 3 and 4 of the UNDRIP that addresses some of the stated limitations of previous policy. As the *Coolangatta Statement on Indigenous Peoples' Rights in Education* is explicitly concerned with addressing the rights of Indigenous peoples in education, they also devote time to Articles 14 and 15 that are explicitly related to education.

In the Australian context, the current social conditions and the divisive environment that Aboriginal and Torres Strait Islander peoples are subjected to on a daily basis acts to silence their voices. The capacity of Aboriginal and Torres Strait Islander peoples to contribute is questioned. Indigenous peoples' understanding of policy is disputed. The recent dismissal of the *Uluru Statement from the Heart* by Prime Minister Turnbull illustrates how the value of First Nations peoples' contributions is diminished (Turnbull 2017).

The lived experiences, the knowledges, the values and beliefs maintained and held by Aboriginal and Torres Strait Islander peoples about how *they* are positioned and silenced in Australia echo in the widening chasm between Indigenous and non-Indigenous Australia. In education, government speaks of the 'gap' identified in the data and statistics when comparing and contrasting Aboriginal and Torres Strait Islander students' educational attainment to their non-Indigenous counterparts (COAG 2008). Little wonder there is a 'gap'; when in society, there is an ever-widening canyon founded within racist ideologies and separatist notions of a binary construct establishing the superiority of the coloniser and the inferiority of Aboriginal and Torres Strait Islander peoples.

The silences and hidden discourses of Indigenous education policy maintain the preservation of colonial values, biases and taken for granted assumptions about Aboriginal and Torres Strait Islander peoples in education and Indigenous education as a whole (Hogarth 2017a). Government and policymakers privilege and sustain the hegemonic position of the coloniser ensuring that, while policy rhetoric suggests collaboration and consultation, the reality of policy being informed by Indigenous voice is minimal. The recontextualisation and implementation of Indigenous education policy further looks to position non-Indigenous educators and administrators in position of power.

Concluding thoughts

The *Uluru Statement from the Heart*'s authors assert that "in 1967 we were counted, in 2017 we seek to be heard" (Referendum Council 2017). The need for change is now. Aboriginal and Torres Strait Islander peoples need to be more vocal and 'stand on toes'. We need to unite in our concerns for our children's futures, demanding a position at the table.

However, it won't be easy. While the call for the inclusion of Aboriginal and Torres Strait Islander voice within "decision making, planning, delivery and evaluation" is written within Indigenous education policy, the reality is that the role of Aboriginal and Torres Strait Islander peoples in education is dictated and dependent on the disposition of the dominant White administrators (Education Council 2015, p. 3). As Johnson *et al.* (2016) found within their report, Aboriginal and Torres Strait Islander educators are underrepresented. The roles and responsibilities of the majority of Indigenous educators are as classroom teachers and not in positions of power to speak into the space of school strategy and operation.

We need to be more assertive. The international human rights charters and conventions articulate our rights in education. We need to base our actions in these texts. We need to privilege the agency afforded to us in these texts. Our children and our future are dependent on it.

References

Armitage, A., 2014. *Comparing the policy of assimilation: Australia, Canada and New Zealand*. Vancouver: UBC Press.

Australian Bureau of Statistics. 2017. 4221.0 Schools, Australia, 2016. Available from: www.abs.gov.au/ausstats/abs@.nsf/mf/4221.0.

Brown, P. and Lauder, H., 1991. Education, economy and social change. *International Studies in Sociology of Education* 1 (1–2). 3–23.

COAG. 2008. National Indigenous reform agreement (Closing the Gap).

Conifer, D., Brennan, B., Higgins, I., Crothers, J., and Wellington, S., 2017. Indigenous advisory body rejected by PM in 'kick in the guts' for advocates. Online: ABC News.

Council on Federal Financial Relations. 2016. National Partnerships—Education. Available from: www.federalfinancialrelations.gov.au/content/npa/education.aspx.

Department of the Prime Minister and Cabinet. 2016. Closing the gap: Prime minister's report 2016. Canberra, Australia: Commonwealth of Australia.

Education Council. 2015. National Aboriginal and Torres Strait Islander education strategy 2015.

Hogarth, M., 2017a. The power of words: Bias and assumptions in the Aboriginal and Torres Strait Islander education action plan. *The Australian Journal of Indigenous Education*, 1–10. doi: 10.1017/jie.2016.29.

Hogarth, M., 2017b. Speaking back to the deficit discourses: a theoretical and methodological approach. *The Australian Educational Researcher* 44 (1), 21–34. doi: 10.1007/s13384-017-0228-9.

Hogarth, M., 2018. Talkin' bout a revolution: Transformation and reform in Indigenous education. *Australian Educational Researcher*, 1–12.

Johnson, P., Cherednichenko, B., and Rose, M., 2016. Evaluation of the more Aboriginal and Torres Strait Islander teachers initiative project: Final report.

Morgan, B., West, E., Nakata, M., Hall, K., Swisher, K., Ahenakew, F., Huges, P., Te Whanau-a-Ruataupare, T., and Blair, N., 1999. The Coolangatta Statement on Indigenous rights in education. *Journal of American Indian Education* 39 (1), 52–64.

Morgan, B., West, E. G., Nakata, M., Hall, K., Swisher, K., and Ahenakew, F., 2006. The Coolangatta Statement on Indigenous peoples' rights in education. *In*: P. Read, G. Meyers and B. Reece, eds., *What good condition? Reflections on an Australian Aboriginal Treaty 1986–2006*. Canberra: ANU E Press, 229–236.

National Congress of Australia's First Peoples. 2016. Redfern Statement – An urgent call for a more just approach to Aboriginal and Torres Strait Islander Affairs.

Referendum Council. 2017. Uluru statement from the heart.

Turnbull, M., 2017. Response to Referendum Council's Report on Constitutional Recognition.

United Nations General Assembly, 2008. The United Nations Declaration on the rights of Indigenous peoples.

13 Locked out, left out

Three generations schooled and classed

Kelly Cheung

Introduction

Working class girls in and out of school present problematic conceptions for educators. For the curriculum designers and education reformers of the early twentieth century, working class women and girls in the Australian state of New South Wales required the intervention of schooling in order to cultivate morality, frugality, and a temperament and skill set for a life disposed towards compliant domesticity (Kyle 1986). Despite the industrial and social transformations of the twentieth century, considerations of girls' education, particularly for working class girls, continued to be limited by conservative and parochial beliefs, values and attitudes (Campbell and Proctor 2014, Kenway and Willis 1993, Kyle 1986, Wyn 1990). Giving the old conservatism the flip is way overdue if we are going to truly include the children of the working class in our school communities today.

History from below

From a multi-generation working class woman, and a first-in-family university graduate, this chapter is deliberately claiming space (Ahmed 2017) for a working class writer to publicly write on education policies and practices under an auto(biographical) lens. This is consciously feminist work (Ahmed 2017, Johnson 2014) crossing two interdisciplinary fields (education and history) that does so with a meaningful stake in disrupting an—at times—overwhelming masculine club of correspondents.

In this piece, I will explore and question the ways in which the impact and influence of state educational interventions have been constrained by misunderstandings of class, culture and values, and consider ways in which to move forward through deeper understandings of gendered experiences of schooling. The use of narrative reflection of family stories shared and retold to one another is charted against extracted moments in the history of girls' education in New South Wales, Australia. As Grumet's (1990) exploration of the autobiographical form reveals, "autobiographical method invites us to struggle ... to develop ourselves in ways that transcend the identities that others have constructed for us" (p. 324). It is hoped that this weaving of (auto)biography and 'affective history' (Walkerdine 2015, 2016); history that is lived through the bodies of successive generations, enables readers to reflect upon institutional approaches for working class girls. Then, to evaluate whether our schools, then and now, are able to respect the ways in which working class girls negotiate schooling barriers and boundary crossings (Akkerman and Bakker 2011).

What is this 'social class'?

When exploring the school lives of working-class girls we must first consider what we mean by 'class'. In a capitalist society class identity comes from what one does and what one owns (Marx and Engel 1894), however older understandings of class identity may struggle to easily fit with newer perceptions of work and labour processes (Reay 1998). Problematically, women have been on the peripheral of theories of class identity; even now official reports struggle to accommodate a breadth of understanding of women's work—what she does and for whom she does it (Baird 2011). Yet, as Reay (1998) asserts: "class … shapes and goes on shaping, the individuals we are and the individuals we become" (p. 259). Much of what is understood as a working class identity comes through a deficit lens applied by those of different classes (Mills and Keddie 2012).

The stories we write within the body

When I sat with my nanna listening to her stories I'd think about recording her words for me and for others to listen to later. But I also thought on how we can hoard material things and in holding on to the physical forget to remember what we most want to keep. As I'd sit with Nanna in her sunroom, I chose not to record her. I didn't want her to live in a digital archive. I wanted her first to live on with me even if the memories became smaller vignettes rather than the longer conversation of a recorded transcript. There is power in story—the oral tale passed from one to another. As Grumet (1987) observes, "Our stories are the masks through which we can be seen, and with every telling we stop the flood and swirl of thought so someone can get a glimpse of us, and maybe catch us if they can" (p. 322). Some memories have now become too indistinct that I don't trust them enough to hold as stable. Nanna is slipping away from me, even as I struggle to catch and hold onto her tales. The vignettes I've chosen to share in this chapter come out of strong memories of stories repeated enough times by my nanna, my mother, and myself that the essence of them holds true.

Incorrigible dreamers

The ability of New South Wales schools to respond to the educational needs of working class girls in the 1920s and 1930s was limited by parochial considerations of what working class girls needed from an experience of schooling. Driving curriculum design were fears that in the absence of state intervention, the children of the working class would be fomenters of social discord, be easily led to crime and become a future burden on the state (McGowan 2006). Working class girls were of particular concern to authorities who believed that their knowledge—or lack thereof—of mothercraft, homemaking and domestic life, would perpetuate cycles of disadvantage and social unrest.

For working class girls in the 1920s and 1930s, schooling provided foundational skills in literacy and numeracy, but the conception of schooling for working class girls struggled to encompass deeper educational experiences beyond the development of compliant and obedient women whose service to their husbands and children was a sign of orderly family life. Working class boys may have been educated for a future that encompassed an identity beyond their gender, but girls first and foremost were educated for a womanhood whose defining features were qualifications in marriage and motherhood. It was a training in domestic service that so often featured within discussions of girls' education but for working class girls, more likely to contribute to the care of their siblings, their practical experiences of care were deemed inferior, and limited by the ignorance of their class. "It is not the fault of the mothers; they have never been taught any different. They never learned to give their children a sense of responsibility, to give them a sense of beauty in all things" said Mrs Francis Anderson, in an address in 'The Education of Girls' in 1921 (*The Armidale Chronicle* 1921, p. 8). It was the school that would bring the 'right' lessons to the working class girl and ensure the next generation would be unlike the unfit first (McGowan 2006).

It is 1931. My grandmother is 14. Dorothy is the eldest girl of five surviving children. She has a deft mind for mathematics, and will one day enjoy time to paint, to crochet, to read. She will teach herself how to play a (keyboard) piano. One day. But for now, there are four younger siblings to be fed and cared for, and a truancy officer to avoid.

> The truant officer kept coming because she was never at school. She had to look after all the brothers and sisters. So she left as soon as she could because they could send her off to work.
> (Reconstructed conversation, family anecdote, Linda (my mother) reflecting on Dorothy's experiences)

There appears to be friction between government authorities, who sent out truancy officers to report back on family behaviour, and families who needed their children to labour before they could learn. An understanding of economic and family circumstances contextualises the choices of working class girls and their families in how they approached schooling in the 1920s and 1930s. Dorothy's non-compliance with school attendance policies did not fit with the middle class morality of how a 'good girl' should be. She would have been perceived as one of the "incorrigibles" of the working class; her parents as exploiters of her labour; the family as ignorant of what their betters knew would be best for them. Yet, Dorothy's experiences throughout her lifetime reflect the very characteristics that shaped her schooling years: resilience, adaptability, independence, and a pragmatism in accepting circumstances for what they were while holding onto a dream for something better.

A conflict of class

It is 1961. My mother is 14. Linda is entrepreneurial and savvy with money, knowing ways in which to string pennies out and ways in which to call in more. She is torn between satisfaction in her spelling skills—Linda was recently awarded best speller in her old class—and a growing nervousness that lessons seem to move past her too fast, before she has a chance to focus on them.

By the time my mother began her journey in and out of New South Wales schools more female students were staying on beyond the leaving age of 14, working class girls amongst them. For the 1950s and 1960s Boomer children, the Australia of the post-war period provided opportunities within and beyond school that their parents couldn't entertain. For her final child, the baby of the family, my grandmother sought an experience of education that would support her daughter's eventual financial independence. Dorothy switched Linda out of the local public school to the more well-regarded Catholic school in an adjacent suburb, and sent her on again to an independent business college for secretarial training. The behaviour points to Dorothy's aspirational hopes for her daughter's future, at the very least to break Linda out of the domestic science pathway, the most common destination for high school girls.

Whether reflecting on her time in public education or in her Catholic school Linda's stories repeatedly centre around her struggles to pay attention to the learning in the classroom and repeated problems with school authority figures. As a left-handed person, she remembers the teaching nuns slapping her hand with a ruler in order to make her write right-handed. Then, academic streaming separated her from her friends. Over time, repeated negative experiences clouded her experience of school, although she rarely blamed her teachers or the schools. Rather, she perceived her educational struggles as personal failings.

> I had to do an IQ test—we all did, but mine wasn't good. I didn't want to go into classes without my friends. Mum put me into a new school in the hope I would be happier, and I repeated fourth class there. It was a good school. It had the best nuns, it was the best school. My education has nothing to do with working class or anything like that. My problem is me. I've never been able to concentrate. I still can't concentrate.
> (Reconstructed conversation, family anecdote, Linda)

If Linda attended a New South Wales school today it is likely some aspects of her learning difficulties may catalyse the intervention of a learning support team. In 1961, secondary schooling was a social sorting in which working class students had to perform to exemplary levels in order to overcome the barriers of class. At that time, only one in four teenagers had access to secondary education at all, and the numbers skewed more towards boys (Campbell and Proctor 2014). There was no accommodation for variations to a middle class (male, Anglo-Celtic) norm of expected pupil behaviour (Collins and Yates 2011). Psychological testing still held sway as a way of identifying children for schooling destinations (Campbell and Proctor 2014, Collins and Yates 2011) and, as seen in Linda's recount, held enormous psychological power in the way such tests shaped a child's lifelong sense of their schooling efficacy. For all of the 'special' Boomer children within May and Proctor's (2013) research on Sydney selective schools, many of those young people working their way through alternate pathways during the post-war years must have been left with a sense that they were anything but.

Big wins

> They just kept reading your name out … for English, for History, for Geography, for Religion. Dadda kept turning to me, saying, "she's got another, and another one". We were so proud that night. None of us ever thought any of us were any good at anything.
>
> (Linda, reflecting on the author's first academic prize night, circa 1993, end of Year 8)

I remember that night because my grandfather wore a suit. Nanna was in heels, and mum, of course, had 'put her face on'. There was a photo taken in the lounge room at home later that night, and I'm beaming, fanning these four white certificates bearing my name across my chest. The photo held place for at least another decade, even though never again in my school years did I perform at such a level of visible success, holding an announcer's tongue not for one or two or three but four records of achievement.

That night represents a culmination as well of many policy precedents for girls' education that had been laid in the intervening years between my mother's leaving of school and my own commencement. The IQ tests of the 1950s and 1960s had been replaced by entry tests for selective schools as a way of sorting students, and comprehensive options for girls had become far more ambitious than the earlier domestic science pathway (Campbell and Proctor 2014, Kenway and Willis 1993, May and Proctor 2014). The school girl of the 1980s and 1990s came of age at the same time neoliberalism and individualism changed the narrative and culture of what school could be (Gannon 2016). Just as significant, she matriculated during an era where girls' education received a policy push that recognised and aimed to overcome the gender barriers preventing women and girls from taking their rightful places in Australian society (Gannon 2016, Kenway and Willis 1993). The 1975 report Girls, School and Society laid the groundwork for women's liberation to reach the school curriculum and girls as a distinctive group with their own education rights and needs were prioritised for the first time within education policy. Successive initiatives, including the 1987 National Policy for the Education of Girls significantly reshaped educational approaches for girls and women.

Changing times

The 1990s proved to be a pivotal change in the schooling experiences of NSW students. The collapse of manufacturing and increasing automation across industries generated a prolonged period of youth unemployment across Australia (Carvalho 2015, Denny and Churchill 2016). It was no longer viable for young people to leave school early. They needed to stay on and accrue the highest qualification they could to improve their post-school labour prospects. As Vickers (2011) observed: "between 1982 and 1992, Australia's high school retention rates more than doubled, increasing from 36 percent to 75 per cent" (p. 135). For working class girls, a career of beauty therapy, hairdressing, and early childhood care was available through the new emphasis on (gendered) vocational streams (Vickers 2011) but the first step was a job—any job—as a resume with some experience was perceived by my mother (and many like her) to be far more advantageous than one without.

When I turned 14 my mother ramped up the pressure on me to take on a part-time job outside of school. Somewhat ironically, my paid work involved quite active computer literacy and mathematical numeracy. During this era, when there was significant concern that schools needed to do more to engage female students in computing, science and maths, I was getting paid to do just that outside of school hours. It is useful here to consider the ways in which social class values position student interactions with disciplinary subjects in particular ways. An educational goal was to change the ways in which female students used the new computing technologies and behaved around the hardware. For example, a 1995 article (Price 1995) in *The Canberra Times* is indicative of the gendered lenses that were becoming increasingly influential upon the manner in which computing and computer knowledge in the classroom was perceived. The headline of the article, 'Cyberpunks frighten girls away' is reflective of the patriarchal and conservative values at play. The pronoun 'cyberpunks' in this usage is a masculine identity that generates a fearful response in 'girls'. To be technologically savvy in this construction of who can (and cannot) be adept users of technology is to not be a 'girl'. Hardly a persuasive frame in which to embolden girls and women.

That women had long played instrumental roles in the development of computing technology and its uses was suppressed by a repositioning of technology in masculine terms (Keogh 2015). There is a class dimension within the consequences of disregarding women's work—under a masculinised vision of technology in which men and boys 'work' while women and girls merely 'help' (when, of course, they haven't been frightened away). The ways in which technology could be put to emancipatory purposes by working class youth in their paid employment did not fit within the middle class narrative of using computing technology in (gendered) ways within school culture. As such, possible outreaches to working class knowledges and interests failed to materialise within school cultures despite the promise of technology as a way to boost student engagement and extend the post-school aspirations of female students.

Conclusion

At times in my own experience, the feeling as a working class girl is not just that educational doors are closed but that there is some body, some force, straining to hold it closed, as I stretch my fingers in the slenderest of cracks to try and gain a finger hold. We owe it to current and future generations of working class girls to flip a system which marginalises their identity and disadvantages their knowledge in our current schooling cultures.

Real change will come when inequalities of birth circumstances are responded to in ways that brings significant and meaningful change in people's lives. That means State and Federal governments in Australia have a responsibility to fund students appropriately to bring all students up to an "average standard" (Cobbold 2014, p. 4). Such funding must take into account life circumstances whereby students bring multiple disadvantages with them when navigating an education culture made for a middle class norm. The backsliding over Gonski funding must be seen for what it is: deliberate social sabotage by those who shirk their civic responsibility for all Australian students.

It is not enough, however, to see appropriate needs-based funding applied to students fairly. The disadvantages of social class need urgent addressing with and through schools as hubs that can connect working class families with appropriately funded social services that middle class and elite families more easily access. Mental health support, general health support, literacy support, and numeracy support are vital if working class students, especially girls, are going to be able to thrive in and beyond their schooling lives.

School culture too needs changing in regard to the ways that working class girls are seen. There must be an understanding that while the educational patterns of working class girls may differ remarkably from their middle class peers, that does not mean that working class girls are less committed to their studies, to their future aspirations, or to a pattern of lifelong learning around competing responsibilities of home and family. Making working class stories visible, and ensuring schools are places that actively see working class families for the knowledges, cultures and histories that they bring, will be significant in overcoming the cultural discomfort that can arise when differences in beliefs, values and attitudes are brought to the fore. Connell *et al.* (1982) observed the lingering discomfort of working class families in and around school cultures. The school as a neoliberal site of markets and positional choice has only increased the disadvantages that occur when working class families are silenced by their affective histories.

Schools should be places where teachers and families can unite to push for equity and excellence on behalf of all students within the community. Speaking with working class families, listening to the experiences of working class students (former and current), and maintaining the historical record to capture what was, and what may yet come to be are vital polylogues if, as a society, we are going to value the breadth and diversity of all students within our educational communities.

Acknowledgements

This research was made possible thanks to a Research Training Program (RTP) Scholarship from Macquarie University.

References

The Armidale Chronicle, 1921. Higher education. 3 December, p. 8. Available from: http://nla.gov.au/nla.news-article189323245 [Accessed 16 January 2018 via Trove Australia].

Ahmed, S., 2017. *Living a feminist life*. Durham, NC: Duke University Press.

Akkerman, S.F. and Bakker, A., 2011. Boundary crossing and boundary objects. *Review of Educational Research*, 81 (2), 132–169, doi: 10.3102/0034654311404435.

Baird, M., 2011. The state, work and family in Australia. *The International Journal of Human Resource Management*, 22 (18), 3742–3754, doi: 10.1080/09585192.2011.622922.

Campbell, C. and Proctor, H., 2014. *A history of Australian schooling*. Crows Nest, NSW: Allen and Unwin.

Carvalho, P., 2015. Youth unemployment in Australia. *Research Report* 7. St Leonards, NSW: Centre for Independent Studies. Available from: www.cis.org.au/app/uploads/2015/11/rr7.pdf [Accessed 21 January 2018].

Cobbold, T., 2014. *The case for Gonski plus funding loadings for low SES students*. Save our Schools. Available from: www.saveourschools.com.au/file_download/167 [Accessed 6 March 2018].

Collins, C. and Yates, L., 2011. Confronting equity, retention and student diversity. *In*: L. Yates, C. Collins and K. O'Connor (eds.) *Australia's Curriculum Dilemmas: State Cultures and the Big Issues*. Melbourne: Melbourne University Press, 107–126.

Connell, R.W., Ashenden, D., Kessler, S. and Dowsett, G., 1982. *Making the difference: Schools, families and social division*. Crows Nest, NSW: Allen and Unwin.

Denny, L. and Churchill, B., 2016. Youth unemployment in Australia: A comparative analysis of labour force participation by age group. *Journal of Applied Youth Studies*, 1(2), 5–22. Available from: http://apo.org.au/node/62397 [Accessed 21 January 2018].

Gannon, S., 2016. Kairos and the time of gender equity policy in Australian schooling. *Gender and Education*, 28 (3), 330–342, doi: 10.1080/09540253.2016.1175783.

Grumet, M. R., 1987. The politics of personal knowledge. *Curriculum Inquiry*, 17 (3), 319–329, doi: 10.1080/03626784.1987.11075295.

Grumet, M. R., 1990, Retrospective: Autobiography and the analysis of educational experience. *Cambridge Journal of Education*, 20 (3), 321–325, doi: 10.1080/0305764900200311.

Johnson, C., 2014. Hard heads and soft hearts. *Australian Feminist Studies*, 29 (80), 121–136, doi: 10.1080/08164649.2014.928191.

Kenway, J. and Willis, S., 1993. *Telling tales: Girls and schools changing their ways.* Canberra: Department of Employment, Education and Training.

Keogh, B., 2015. Hackers, gamers and cyborgs. *Overland*, 218. Available from: https://overland.org.au/previous-issues/issue-218/feature-brendan-keogh/ [Accessed: 15 March 2018].

Kyle, N., 1986. *Her natural destiny: The education of women in New South Wales.* Kensington, NSW: NSW University Press.

Marx, K. and Engel, F., 1894/(2011). *The communist manifesto.* London: Penguin Books.

May, J. and Proctor, H., 2013. Being special: Memories of the Australian public high school: 1920s–1950s. *History of Education Review*, 42 (1), 55–68, doi: 10.1080/00220620.2017.1343289

Mills, C. and Keddie, A., 2012. 'Fixing' student deficit in contexts of diversity: Another cautionary tale for pre-service teacher education. *International Journal of Pedagogies and Learning*, 7 (1), 9–19.

McGowan, W.S., 2006. Rewriting the responsible parent. *History of Education Review*, 35 (2), 45–49, doi: 10.1108/08198691200600010.

Price, J., 1995. Cyberpunks frighten girls away. *The Canberra Times*, 11 March 1995, 3. Available from: http://nla.gov.au/nla.news-article127517248 [Accessed 13 March 2018 via Trove Australia].

Reay, D., 1998. Rethinking social class: Qualitative perspectives on class and gender. *Sociology*, 32 (2), 259–275.

Vickers, M., 2011. The senior secondary curriculum in New South Wales: Academic traditions face issues of retention. *In*: L. Yates, C. Collins and K. O'Connor (eds.) *Australia's curriculum dilemmas: State cultures and the big issues.* Melbourne: Melbourne University Press, 127–147.

Walkerdine, V., 2015. Transmitting class across generations. *Theory and Psychology*, 25(2), 167–183, doi: 10.1177/0959354315577856.

Walkerdine, V., 2016. Affective history, working-class communities and self-determination. *The Sociological Review*, 64, 699–724, doi: 10.1111/1467-954X.12435.

Wyn, J., 1990. Working-class girls and educational outcomes: Is self-esteem an issue? *In*: J. Kenway and S. Willis (eds.) *Hearts and minds: Self-esteem and the schooling of girls.* London: The Falmer Press, 119–130.

14 Learning with connection

Shifting teachers' practice through authentic engagement with Aboriginal and Torres Strait Islander communities

Kevin Lowe

This chapter is written expressly for those teachers who are concerned about their ability to affect the development of a productive learning relationship with Aboriginal students. What I have sought to highlight is that teachers have a capacity, in fact a responsibility, to reach beyond the school fence and actively examine the opportunities to connect with the families of students, and commence an educational dialogue that opens new possibilities for educational change.

The often-heard discussion for the importance of schools' engagement with Aboriginal and Torres Strait Islander peoples' centres on the efforts of schools to shift current unacceptable levels of Indigenous student underachievement. However, while it is accepted that the purpose of community engagement is to support the long-term engagement of students in their schooling, an unequivocal message from this chapter is that for many teachers this aspiration has proven illusory unless they have sought the assistance Indigenous families to broker relationships within the community, to share knowledge, and to advise teachers in the ways of this community. Martin Nakata (2007, 2010) speaks of this space and the '*cultural interface*', the place where new knowledge can be constructed between Indigenous and western knowledge systems. This space is highly productive in assisting both families and teachers to engage in constructive dialogue and as a consequence, is as highly beneficial for schools and teachers as it is for families and students. It is contended that if schools want to engage with Aboriginal people, then it should to be understood that, as the sometimes-synonymous terms engagement, partnerships and collaborations suggest—are two-way, relational and interactive and require both parties to shift their thinking and to challenge schooling practices and that have defined Indigenous students' underachievement.

This chapter is not written to be a checklist of 'how to' meet and/or engage with Aboriginal people, but instead to raise with you, the practitioner, questions to consider when contemplating the many issues that sit at the heart of Aboriginal student underachievement and the relational dissonance that has characterised the dysfunctional and intergenerational relationship between schools and Aboriginal families. The purpose here is to challenge and question how this relationship has come to be, to suggest ways for schools and/or other 'regulatory' institutions to recalibrate those practices that underpin this relationship of resistance, and to guide thinking about how the 'business of Aboriginal education' could be changed. While acknowledging that this task may seem insurmountable—'plainly' beyond your capacity as a teacher to make inroads—there are many examples of schools and/or teachers who have worked tirelessly to affect the happiness and educational opportunities, engagement and learning opportunities for Aboriginal and Torres Strait Islander students (Hands 2005). What I want to suggest, is that teachers have the ability to shift their own thinking and colleagues' thinking through their commitment to students' wellbeing, to challenge their own and institutional practices that have for too long conditioned everyone to tacitly accept the level of student underachievement. At the heart of these successful moments in education, are teachers who have sought to establish open, two-way dialogues that have proven to be productive in schooling teachers into establishing interrelationships within community and families, to hear first-hand their aspirations for their children and to understand what these communities see as the responsibility of schools to support their desire for genuine epistemic and cultural acknowledgement within their schools (Lampert *et al.* 2014).

There is a strong case to be made for all teachers to engage and partner parents in the education of their students, as it has been shown that these interactions have a significant impact on students' engagement with school, teachers' relationships with their students and the schools' positive interactions with parents (Jeynes 2011, Mapp 2004, Muller and Saulwick 2006). Yet, while this research clearly points to the positive outcomes that accrue to both teachers and students as a consequence of establishing these relationships, it conversely needs to be said that in a good number of cases, these efforts by schools have been seen to have little effect in meeting either the students and/or parents' real needs and consequently, is largely counterproductive. It has been shown that the actions of schools looking to establish these links with both families from low SES communities, or with other minority or marginalised communities, has had little impact as it seen as tokenistic, largely unsupported, having little impact on improving students' outcomes, or changing the structures of schooling that have underpinned student marginalisation (Fine 1993, Lareau 1996, Mills and Gale 2004).

Yet, as Vass (2017), Perso *et al.* (2012) and Savage *et al.* (2011) have all identified, where teachers were supported in establishing productive relationships with Aboriginal people, they were better able to affect significant change to their pedagogic practices and in their learning relationships with students. This nexus between parental engagement, significant teacher change and schooling success for students, was a central feature of the *Te kotahitanga* program, a highly successful 20-year project in New Zealand developed to deliver long-term improvements in Māori student achievement (Bishop *et al.* 2009, 2017). Ongoing research on the impact of this whole-school professional development and school leadership project, identified a clear link between the schools' commitment to community engagement, changed teaching practice and improved student outcomes (Alton-Lee 2015). The power of this research has provided a clear focus for schools across NZ as they have looked to establish multiple opportunities to professionally interact with Māori communities.

This is a critical jumping off point in this chapter, for although it is written from within the context of lifting the educational outcomes for Aboriginal students, the comments in this chapter are equally valid for teachers wanting to reach out to other groups of students who find themselves culturally marginalised in schools (Evers and Kneyber 2016). This is not just an 'Indigenous issue'—but one that all schools servicing diverse communities, need to pay attention to if they are going to meet the just claims of all students to a productive, relevant and supportive education.

What I have looked to demonstrate in this brief introduction to community and school engagement, is to identify that it is incumbent on schools and their staff to spend time developing an understanding of Aboriginal and Torres Strait Islander peoples' cultures and history. Secondly, that the establishment of these professional relationships with their Indigenous communities is a key to opening direct lines of communication between yourselves as teachers and the Aboriginal and/or Torres Strait Islander children in your care. In saying this, it is critical to acknowledge that this takes time, and that there is, like in all communities a range of voices, experiences and responses to the often-brutal histories of dispossession and enforced statelessness of Indigenous peoples from 'Country'. The notion of 'Country'—the space that is existential to Indigenous Australian's ontological existence, is critical to their individual and collective sense of belonging (Harrison and McConchie 2013, Tjapaltjarri, McGregor and Zimmer 2009, pp. 15–21). Yet, despite the realities of the 'colonial' legacy of dispossession and 'loss' of Indigenous peoples' legal sovereignty over their Country, I will go onto discuss how inclusive educators have set about constructing effective and authentic connections with Aboriginal people, which over time have enabled them to positively affect students' resistance to schooling through their engagement with their families through listening and learning, and finding ways to address the educational needs of students through establishing an inclusive and culturally affirming curriculum and pedagogical practices.

Why community engagement?

School and community engagement can be best defined as the interconnections between educational sites and individuals, businesses, formal and informal institutions and members of community itself (Department of Education Training and Workplace Relations 2010). In the formal sense, effective engagement is seen to be relationally focused, be purposeful and with an emphasis on reciprocal interactions that supports learners. This notion of authentic action is critical to this discussion, as it goes directly to the question the underlying intention of the school. You may hear Aboriginal people question a proposal to 'engage them' in a school program, and where the question the school's intent and commitment is challenged when asked—'are you gammon us' or are you leading us on to? This may sound harsh, but remember—promises are often made—maybe even with good intention, but your intent will become all too clear if you are incapable of understanding that the very structures of schooling have long supported the exercise of power over Aboriginal communities and where the classroom remains the primary site of conflict where teachers are seen to perpetuate epistemic and historical untruths about Aboriginal peoples' histories, cultures, and experiences of displacement. These and other issues are ones that schools need to consider as they move to 'engage' parents (Lowe 2011). What research has shown is that the relationships between Indigenous communities and schools are best developed within an environment of honesty, integrity, trust and two-way respect and that it is constantly re-constructed, nurtured, advanced and advocated for by each key stakeholder group (Goos 2004, Muller and Saulwick 2006).

There are many reasons for the underachievement of Aboriginal learners, and though many educators and parents rush to claim to know the reasons for this, they are by and large the aggregated localised consequences of the complexities of colonisation, and the enacted histories of intergenerational educational disadvantage.

However, notwithstanding this, what has been established across many schools sites, is that there have always been those few teachers who, having made their own opportunities to collaborate with Aboriginal Elders and/or community members, are enabled to speak of being professionally liberated, through developing the skills to reflectively interrogate their 'knowledge' of where they find themselves, of being able to see how negative and normalised constructs of 'the Aboriginal students and parents impacts on school success, of gaining contextual insights into the acts of dispossession and how all of these issues continues to affect teachers' professional attitudes towards Aboriginal students. What we know, is if these remain uncontested and unchanged, they continue to affect the everyday pedagogic attitudes and practices that have misguided teacher understanding of Aboriginal and Torres Strait Islander students, their uniqueness, their sense of identity and fail to see the policy mechanisms that paralyse school system's ability to affect those changes needed to improve students' schooling trajectories (Lowe 2017). Research from both New Zealand (Bishop *et al.* 2009, Glynn *et al.* 2010) and North America (Battiste 2012) demonstrates that change occurs for teachers when they truly understand how both systemic and personal practices and policies underpin a purpose of schooling that have had the effect of collectively supporting the policies of assimilation.

What are the benefits of community engagement?

There are several key assumptions that sit behind the calls for schools to actively seek to partner students' families and communities. Typically, the research has pointed to the positive effects that have been seen to accrue to students and teachers alike when parents and the wider community are enabled by inclusive policy strategies to forge productive collaborative relationships with local schools (Muller 2012). Some of these benefits have been shown to include the following.

- Challenging underpinning cultural discontinuities between largely unchallengeable 'western' knowledge embedded in curriculum and teachers' professional and pedagogic discourses, as opposed to what is characterised as 'unscientific' and unsophisticated Indigenous knowledge systems (Harrison and Greenfield 2011, Lowe 2009, Snively and Williams 2016).
- Identifying, challenging and reconceptualising those educational discourses where deficit theorising directly impacts on the teachers' everyday interactions with students such that it affects their teachers' decisions about students' educative capacity, aspirations and interests, the implementation of school policies, quality curriculum development, and pedagogic practices and assessment (Fforde et al. 2013).
- Developing cultural, language and other local programs with direct and on-going collaboration with the community (Lowe 2017).
- Working collaboratively in identifying where and how schools are enabled to share Aboriginal peoples' knowledge and skills to initiate curriculum, teaching and or new programs that directly support learners (Board of Studies NSW 2008, Lewthwaite et al. 2015).
- Understanding how power, as exhibited within schools is enacted, used and possibly shared, the responsibilisation of parents to co-lead and programs, and knowledge sharing within and across a variety of educational settings (Denzin et al. 2008).
- Developing an understanding of the sensitivities of teaching about a local community's cultural business (inclusive of sacred Dreaming places and narratives) and appreciating the need to work with and to seek advice from the local community. Many school systems and curriculum authorities will provide you general and syllabus specific advice on these matters (see Queensland Studies Authority 2010).
- Defining Community engagement and understanding protocols for engagement (Board of Studies NSW 2008, NSW AECG 2011).

Consultation is an ongoing process that benefits all participants to ensure that Aboriginal voices are effectively incorporated into the curriculum. It involves establishing a respectful relationship with communities, and demonstrating a willingness to share, learn and negotiate. At their heart, protocols are a way of acting that is respectful, and emanates from an understanding that there is an appropriate way to engage with people (Board of Studies NSW 2008). It is about showing respect for the diversity of Aboriginal and Torres Strait Islander peoples, their lived experiences, histories, cultural knowledge and languages. The best advice will come through engaging with local people and where possible, having them support your introduction to that community. At all times teachers need to be mindful that there many issues which need to be approached, understood and then managed with sensitivity if you are to bring people along in your journey.

Once starting on this path, teachers should seek advice to ensure that these general protocols are appropriately applied to the local contexts in which they find themselves. Useful examples of practical and 'school tested' protocols include NSW Board of Studies (2008), *Working with Aboriginal Communities* and resources from the Queensland Curriculum and Assessment Authority (QCAA n/a).

Meaningful discussion: key questions to consider

The following questions and strategies will aid in developing a collaborative and productive relationship with Indigenous staff who may either be in a local school, regional or diocesan office, or in another agency in each community. If that is not available, an alternative strategy is to seek advice from Aboriginal parents, talking directly with a peak Indigenous body, such as Aboriginal Education Consultative Groups (AECG) or another community agency such as the Aboriginal medical, health and/or legal service. Each of these bodies are an invaluable resource in helping you make contact with the right people, to ask the right questions, to provide the context of this community and to help you understand the appropriate protocols for each occasion.

Remember—as a teacher, you are looking to connect, to get advice and to begin a dialogue with Aboriginal and Torres Strait Islander parents, workers or agencies, for the purpose of helping you to learn about this local community and to understand their fears and aspirations for their children. Talking, listening and enacting this knowledge in the classroom is seen to improve the levels of trust and respect, which in turn will facilitate greater access to more insights about cultural knowledge, events and students (Owens *et al.* 2012).

Asking questions may appear simple, but always remember they are laced with preconceived assumptions about motivations, power relationships between parents and schools, or assuming that everyone is motivated by the same immediate outcome. Only through broad-based discussions, will issues be raised and schools hear family's aspirations for their children. There are a number of critical issues that need to be managed when embarking on a program to engage with Aboriginal people. One of these is to remember that there is a 'history' that needs to be known and addressed—a record of past and current interactions that will, if not understood, impact on the efforts of those seeking to engage families and Elders. As a rule of thumb, the greater the level of authenticity in this engagement, the more that families are likely to share and the bigger the dividend in establishing a relational learning environment within which to students in their learning.

While there are common experiences that characterise the educational encounters that many Aboriginal and Torres Strait Islander people have had with schools, this does not mean that their responses are going to be the same. The development of a communities standpoint position (Rolin 2009, Tur *et al.* 2010) or acute understanding and reaction to their histories of dispossession are unique, idiosyncratic and sometimes representative of a particular family's voiced experiences. When teachers are cognisant of this complexity, they are enabled to embark on developing a relationship that genuine in purpose and possible in liberating their capacity to understand the 'other' in their classrooms (Fluckiger *et al.* 2012).

In summary

This short chapter has explored the importance of teachers establishing authentic links with communities. Every text you read will tell you that this is critical for teachers wanting to develop high-quality teaching and learning programs that include Aboriginal and Torres Strait Islander peoples. In summary, I have argued that education and community engagement is about trust, respect and two-way interactions that value the knowledge of both teachers and Aboriginal people alike. Second, that these interactions must be reciprocal as it is the relationship that provides the links across these different world views. Third, that an authentic engagement facilitates key players to develop insight into the lived experiences, histories, attitudes and beliefs about the schooling of Aboriginal students. Lastly, that in the establishing and maintaining these two-way learning relationships, educational settings begin to understand and become responsive to the aspirations of communities about what school success could be for Aboriginal students.

References

Alton-Lee, A., 2015. Ka Hikitia: A demonstration report: Effectiveness of Te Kotahitanga Phase 5, 2010–2012. In *Iterative Best Evidence Synthesis (BES) programme: Hei Kete Raukura evidence, data and knowledge*. Wellington, NZ: Ministry of Education.

Battiste, M., 2012. Enabling the autumn seed: Towards a decolonised approach to Aboriginal knowledge, language and education. In S. Bourke and P. Milewski, eds., *Schools in transition: Readings in Canadian history of education*. Toronto: University of Toronto, 275–286.

Bishop, R., Berryman, M., Cavanagh, T., and Teddy, L., 2009. Te kotahitanga: Addressing educational disparities facing Māori students in New Zealand. *Teaching and Teacher Education*, 25 (5), 734–742.

Bishop, R., Berryman, M., Wearmouth, J., and Peter, M., 2012. Developing an effective reform model for indigenous and other minoritised students. *School Effectiveness and School Improvement*, 23 (1), 49–70.

Board of Studies NSW., 2008. *Working with Aboriginal communities: A guide to community consultation and protocols*. Sydney: Board of Studies, NSW. Available from: https://goo.gl/hqYkW4.

Denzin, N., Lincoln, Y., and Smith, L.T., eds., 2008. *Handbook of critical and Indigenous methodologies*. Los Angeles, CA: Sage.

Department of Education Training and Workplace Relations, 2010. *Sustainable school and community partnerships. A research study. School and community working together What Works. The Work Program.* Available from: https://goo.gl/hhxjgb.

Evers, J., & Kneyber, R., eds., 2016. *Flip the system: Changing education from the ground up.* London: Routledge.

Fforde, C., Bamblett, L., Lovett, R., Gorringe, S., and Fogarty, B., 2013. Discourse, deficit and identity: Aboriginality, the race paradigm and the language of representation in contemporary Australia. *Media International Australia*, 149 (1), 162–173.

Fine, M., 1993. [Ap]parent involvement: Reflections on parents, power and urban public schools & responses. *Teachers college record*, 94 (4), 682–729.

Fluckiger, B., Diamond, P., and Jones, W., 2012. Yarning space: Leading literacy learning through family—school partnerships. *Australasian Journal of Early Childhood*, 37 (3), 53–59.

Glynn, T., Cowie, B., Otrel-Cass, K. and Macfarlane, A., 2010. Culturally repsonsive pedagogy: Connecting New Zealand teachers of science with their Māori students. *The Australian Journal of Indigenous Education*, 39, 118–127.

Goos, M., 2004. Home, school and community partnerships to support children's numeracy. *Australian Primary Mathematics Classroom*, 9 (4), 18–20.

Hands, C., 2005. It's who you know and what you know: The process of creating partnerships between schools and communities. *School Community Journal*, 15 (2), 63–84.

Harrison, M.D., and McConchie, P., 2013. *My people's dreaming: An Aboriginal elder speaks on life, land, spirit and forgiveness.* Sydney: HarperCollins Australia.

Harrison, N., and Greenfield, M., 2011. Relationship to place: Positioning Aboriginal knowledge and perspectives in classroom pedagogies. *Critical Studies in Education*, 52 (1), 65–76. doi:10.1080/17508487.2011.536513.

Jeynes, W., 2011. Helping families by fostering parental involvement. *Kappan*, 93 (3), 38–39.

Lampert, J., Burnett, B., Martin, R., & McCrea, L., 2014. Lessons from a face-to-face meeting on embedding Aboriginal and Torres Strait Islander perspectives: 'A contract of intimacy'. *Australasian Journal of Early Childhood*, 39 (1), 18.

Lareau, A., 1996. Accessing parent involvement in schooling: A critical analysis. In: A. Booth and J. Dunn, eds., *Family-school links: How do the affect educational outcomes?* Mahwah, New Jersey: Lawrence Erlbaum Associates, 57–67.

Lewthwaite, B.E., Osborne, B., Lloyd, N., Boon, H., and Llewellyn, L., 2015. Seeking a pedagogy of difference: What Aboriginal students and their parents in North Queensland say about teaching and their learning. *Australian Journal of Teacher Education*, 40 (5), 132–159.

Lowe, K., 2009. Opening the doors—collaborative community and school engagement to establish a sustainable Aboriginal language programs. *Journal of Australian Indigenous Issues*, 12 (Special Issue: 2008 World Indigenous Peoples' conference on education. Refereed Conference proceedings), 333–349.

Lowe, K., 2011. A critique of school and Aboriginal community partnerships. In: N. Purdie, G. Milgare, and H. Bell, eds., *Two Way Teaching and Learning—Toward culturally reflective and relevant education.* Melbourne: ACER, 20.

Lowe, K., 2017. Walanbaa warramildanha: The impact of authentic Aboriginal community and school engagement on teachers' professional knowledge. *The Australian Educational Researcher*, 44 (1), 35—54. doi:10.1007/s13384-017-0229-8.

Mapp, K., 2004, Dec 2. *Supporting student achievement: Family and community connections with schools*. Paper presented at the Family, School and Community Connections symposium: New Directions for Research, Practice and Evaluation, Cambridge, MA.

Mills, C., and Gale, T., 2004. Parent participation in disadvantaged schools: Moving beyond attributions of blame. *Australian Journal of Education*, 48 (3), 268–281.

Muller, D., 2012. Parents as partners in Indigenous children's learning. *In: Canberra: Family-School and Community Partnerships Bureau*, 75.

Muller, D., and Saulwick, I., 2006. *Family–school partnerships project: A qualitative and quantitative study*. Melbourne: Australian Council for State Schools Organisations and Australian Parents Council.

Nakata, M., 2007. *Disciplining the savages: Savaging the disciplines*. Canberra: Aboriginal Studies Press.

Nakata, M., 2010. The cultural interface of islander and scientific knowledge. *The Australian Journal of Indigenous Education*, 39 (Supplement), 53–57.

NSW AECG, 2011. *Connecting to country*. Stanmore, NSW: Aboriginal Education Consultative Group. Available from: www.aecg.nsw.edu.au/policies-programs/connecting-to-country/.

Owens, K., Doolan, P., Bennet, M., and Paraide, P., *et al.*, 2012. Continuities in education: Pedagogical perspectives and the role of Elders in education. *Journal of Australian Indigenous Issues*, 15 (1), 20–39.

Perso, T., Kenyon, P., and Darrough, N., 2012. *Transitioning Indigenous students to western schooling: A culturally responsive program*. Paper presented at the 17th Annual Values and Leadership Conference: Ethical Leadership: Building Capacity for those Moments of Challenging Choices, Brisbane. Available from: https://goo.gl/VDaRhA.

QCAA, n/a. *Protocols: Aboriginal and Torres Strait Islander ways of working*. Brisbane: Queensland Curriculun and Assessment Authority. Available from: https://goo.gl/vfeS9h.

Queensland Studies Authority, 2010. *Aboriginal and Torres Strait Islander studies: Handbook 2010*. Brisbane: Queensland Studies Authority.

Rolin, K., 2009. Standpoint theory as a methodology for the study of power relations. *Hypatia*, 24 (4), 218-226.

Savage, C., Hindle, R., Meyer, L. H., Hynds, A., Penetito, W., and Sleeter, C.E., 2011. Culturally responsive pedagogies in the classroom: Indigenous student experiences across the curriculum. *Asia-Pacific Journal of Teacher Education*, 39 (3), 183-198. doi:10.1080/1359866X.2011.588311.

Snively, G. and Williams, W.L., eds., 2016. *Knowing home: Braiding Indigenous science with Western science (Book 1)* (Vol. 1). Victoria, BC: University of Victoria, BC.

Te Kotahitanga: Raising Māori student achievement. (2017). Available from: http://tekotahitanga.tki.org.nz.

Tjapaltjarri, B. W., McGregor, K., and Zimmer, J. (2009). *Bill Whiskey Tjapaltjarri* Melbourne: Macmillan Art Publishing.

Tur, S., Blanche, F., and Wilson, C., 2010. Developing a collaborative approach to standpoint in Indigenous Australian research. *Australian Journal of Indigenous Education*, 39 (Supplement), 58–67.

Vass, G., 2017. Preparing for culturally responsive schooling: Initial teacher educators into the fray. *Journal of Teacher Education*, 68 (5), 451–462.

15 Empowering Aboriginal and Torres Strait Islander students in schools

Ben Lewis

Educational outcomes for Aboriginal and Torres Strait Islander students are plagued by poor attendance, poor health, intergenerational poverty and disadvantage. The system is failing to address many of these issues as it is currently unqualified to promote Aboriginal and Torres Strait Islander culture or seek out the voices of Indigenous communities in the education of their own children. There are a number of schools, community groups and organisations who challenge the current system to ensure culture is at the centre of any Indigenous student's education. These programs can be unorthodox and challenge the mainstream conception of what education is supposed to look like. These are programs that often fly in the face of what the highly Westernised education system deems appropriate. The strongest programs are based on blood, sweat and tears (a lot of tears); they're not glamourous, just passionate people working hard, consistently, over long periods of time. Programs like these don't tend to attract huge amounts of funding but the results they are achieving demonstrate the significant role schools have in making a difference in students' lives and the lives of their communities.

In the south western corner of Western Australia, I am known as a Wadjela or white person. I was born on the lands of the Gadigal people of the Eora nation in Sydney, New South Wales. I spent my early years in the Western Australian Goldfields on Wongatha country, travelling frequently to remote communities with my father. I was educated here in Perth on Nyoongar country and started teaching with the Martu people of the Great Sandy Desert. I acknowledge the importance of the land in which I live and share, and recognise that for most of its history, the languages and stories of my significant places, my homes, are Aboriginal ones. These people and places led me to my current role as the Indigenous Program Coordinator at Wesley College, an Independent, Uniting Church boarding school on the banks of the Derbarl Yerrigan (Swan River) in Perth, Western Australia.

Since 2005, Wesley College has worked with local Aboriginal communities to create a programme that attempts to facilitate authentic and informative cultural experiences for both Aboriginal and non-Aboriginal students. In the Nyoongar language, Moorditj means 'great', 'strong' or 'excellent', and the Wesley College Moorditj Mob aims partly to provide the highest quality

Western education for Indigenous boys, but one integrated with a deliberate and explicit focus on their own culture while developing pride in their Aboriginality. It is also intended to educate non-Indigenous students and to model taking action on the significant issue of the discrepancy between education outcomes for Indigenous and non-Indigenous students in Australia. Students are encouraged to take ownership of their own cultural identities and create 45-minute traditional dance and music workshops based on the National Aborigines and Islanders Day Observance Committee (NAIDOC) Week theme of the year. These workshops are then presented around the state. In 2017, 25,000 Western Australian students engaged with the Moorditj Mob, and the Mob performed over 100 times for various school, corporate and government events. These performances empower students within the program to take on the responsibility of educating the community while at the same time educating teachers on what it is to live and learn in the world today as an Aboriginal person.

The success of any Indigenous program comes from establishing strong relationships, relationships with and between students, families and community members. Wesley College believes that establishing relationships with Aboriginal and Torres Strait Islander communities requires unique thinking and trust in the people involved in the program and sharing the responsibility with those outside the College. There are no secrets to building these relationships, it requires hundreds of hours. Students and staff attend community events, public lectures, theatre and cinema, festivals and concerts, weekend sporting matches and art exhibitions. At times students come from backgrounds where the relationships they have with adults can be complex. It is common for students to develop trust in staff and this often results in staff members being required to take on more of a paternal role, a role shared with the students' parents.

I have told the story below many times, it is always on my mind each time the Moorditj Mob are invited to perform and share culture at primary schools across the state. I tell it because it reflects some of the challenges we have as staff, working in a highly regulated environment with a number of policies and procedures that are meant to enable Indigenous students to 'succeed' in education. These structures and regulations are necessary, but at times can be problematic and can become a barrier for Indigenous students to participate in cultural experiences. Aboriginal and Torres Strait Islander communities are over-represented in many statistics that confirm that for many within these communities there is the presence of severe trauma and a lack of strong, trusting relationships. These create obstacles for students when participating in the educational environment. The story below demonstrates the flexibility and open-mindedness required when trying to serve Indigenous students in our care, whose cultural needs are necessary in order to achieve success, however, might not neatly fit into what is considered 'mainstream' education.

> Michael reflects on a day back in 2008, he was in his final year of primary school on the outskirts of town when the Moorditj Mob performed during their NAIDOC Week celebrations. Michael remembers the

performance and the way he felt when he saw how much pride the Wesley boys had when they danced and shared their culture. He was motivated to ask one of the boys after the performance "how do you do that?" The boy replied that they perform at a number of schools and it was a part of school at Wesley to learn about Aboriginal culture and to share it with others. Michael remembers asking the boy how you get to go to Wesley College and the boy said he needed to fill in lots of papers and send them into the College. Michael went straight to the school's Aboriginal Liaison Officer and asked for help. Together with his family they got the paperwork done, attended an interview and were accepted into the College on a MADALAH Indigenous Youth Leadership Program Scholarship.

During Michael's five years at Wesley College he learnt how to dance, he learnt how to play the didgeridoo and he had opportunities to meet members of the local community who taught him about culture. He had many opportunities to share this knowledge with others, but he also achieved academically and was recognised with various leadership roles. Since graduating, Michael has travelled around the world, he has lived and worked in England and is now completing a teaching degree at Curtin University while working at Wesley College within the Indigenous Program.

When I think of that day, and the many other days like it, I think of what would have happened if Michael did not see the boys perform, if he did not have *culture* as the basis of his motivation to seek out an education for himself and without it, the negative effect it may have had on his life. Culture is that missing link, lack of culture in the education of Aboriginal and Torres Strait Islander students causes trauma, it further discriminates and isolates students from their peers and limits their ability to find meaning and purpose. In facilitating culture as the centre of Indigenous education we also recognise that in most cases non-indigenous teachers and the current education system are ill-equipped to provide this in isolation. Recognising that Aboriginal and Torres Strait Islander people alone have these skills is reflected in successful programs. Schools' and organisations' abilities to engage local communities, to recognise their own limitations, and their willingness to share responsibilities, are all factors in their success.

Wesley College is a well-resourced school that has been willing and able to utilise its resources to ensure that Aboriginal and Torres Strait Islander students can access simultaneously, both a cultural and mainstream-western education. Indigenous students often begin their journey at Wesley College not knowing their background, not having a strong cultural identity and not understanding their own ability to share culture with the wider community. In building relationships students are engaged and communities recreated, students develop a pride and confidence, and this can change their worlds. It also changes the worlds of non-Indigenous students and staff, showing us that Australian society can still be unjust; it can still discriminate and alienate children from our educational environments. While there is much to celebrate for the Moorditj Mob, there remain challenges when primarily non-Indigenous teachers in predominantly non-Indigenous schools have the privilege and responsibility of working with Indigenous students. If the system is to be flipped in favour of Australia's Indigenous population, power structures and inequities in Australia need to be challenged. The education system needs to value, listen to, and include Indigenous experiences, voices and ways of knowing, and to integrate opportunities for Indigenous students throughout the system, not in infrequent and isolated programs.

16 Reach them then teach them

Engagement in alternative education settings

Dan Haesler and Melissa Fotea

Assuming that the primary aim of education is not just to improve scores, but to improve life outcomes for individuals, and enhance society as a whole, it is important to explore how adolescents for whom the mainstream doesn't work are catered for by the education system. It may be beneficial for those in mainstream schools to consider what can be learnt from educators who work with 'disengaged' students on a regular basis. This chapter explores traditional notions of engagement in schools, and offers up an example of the ways in which one Australian alternative education setting thinks differently about engagement. In this chapter, the authors Dan Haesler—a former teacher—and Melissa Fotea—an educator with Youth Off The Streets—will discuss how the alternative education program offered by Youth Off The Streets aims to support students who have experienced difficulties conforming to 'mainstream'. The schools at Youth Off The Streets are 'alternative' in that, although they adhere to the curriculum, they include programs for anger management, counselling, and health and wellbeing to ensure all students are provided the opportunity of an education. This chapter aims to explore whether there is the need for mainstream education to flip its approach to engagement, or more specifically 'disengaged' students.

Talking about engagement

Anecdotally there is talk of the 'youth of today' becoming disengaged, glued to their screens and lacking the skills required in the modern workplace—even if they do perform well in school. To attempt to ascertain levels of engagement in classrooms around the world, since 2009, Gallup has conducted its Gallup Student Poll. In the US alone, Gallup has surveyed over 1.5 million students, and was administered in Australia for the first time in 2013. In Australia, the Gallup Student Poll takes place with around 10,000 students across the mainstream education sector in order to determine the extent to which students engage with their learning, feel hopeful for the future and their levels of wellbeing. The survey contains 20 items and takes around 10 minutes to complete. Gallup defines students as being engaged if they "are highly involved with and enthusiastic about school". They also draw a distinction between those students who are *not engaged*—present but not involved or enthusiastic—and those who are *actively disengaged*—students who undermine the educational process for themselves and others. Each year Gallup release their latest findings into student engagement in Australian schools and they make for compelling reading. Each year in Australia, they find that students become less engaged as they make their way through the school system and only 1 in 3 students believe they will find a good job when they leave school (Gallup 2016).

In their latest survey, Gallup found that according to their definition, 31 per cent of students have disengaged from their learning by the time they are in Year 5, and, by Year 12, Gallup contend that only around one in two are engaged. To be clear, these are the students who *turn up* to school—they had to be there to take the survey—so what of those students who for one reason or another do not attend a mainstream school?

'Engagement' is a term widely used in schools, particularly when referring to students, but what constitutes engagement in any given school can vary. In some schools, a fairly simple set of criteria based around behaviour may be enough. In schools who are veering towards a more disciplinarian approach ensuring that students follow the rules, sit quietly in class, raise their hand to speak and wear the uniform correctly, whilst completing the set task will constitute engagement. This brings with it a risk that compliance can be seen as synonymous with engagement, leaving some adults to describe a student as engaged if they do no more than conform to what is expected. Whilst the compliant student may still do well in school, by mistaking conformity and compliance for engagement we misunderstand the benefits of genuine engagement, whilst at the same time, ostracising those students who don't comply. We may view these students as being disengaged, and depending on our context, perhaps less desirable, particularly in today's education climate of performativity. So, if left unchecked, it is possible these students may be viewed as a burden in particular classrooms, or on the school more broadly.

In NSW, the Department of Education has utilised a survey called *Tell Them From Me*, with the majority of NSW public schools in which they seek to dig deeper into engagement. It seeks to understand a student's sense of engagement on three levels:

- a social level, i.e., do they enjoy being at school, do they have friends, do they feel like they belong etc.;
- an institutional level, i.e., do they follow the rules, are they proud of their school etc.; and
- a learning level, i.e., do they value school outcomes, do they put effort in to their learning etc.

The constant that emerges from these surveys, which New South Wales has been running since 2013, is the need for a sense of school belonging for students to engage (NSW CESE 2017).

Students can become disengaged for a multitude of reasons—poor academic performance, bullying, family breakdown, low self-esteem, health issues—just to name a few (Hancock and Zubrick 2015). It may start with talking in class, not getting homework done, having a few days off then quickly move to the extreme end with angry outbursts, violent or aggressive behaviour to students and staff, and/or refusing to go to school at all. Some students may find excuses to stay home—such as looking after a younger sibling; undiagnosed illness or symptoms such as pain, headaches or nausea; transportation issues; and a multitude of other possibilities and reasons for non-attendance. When educators recognise that an individual's sense of engagement—or ability to engage—is not confined to school, but is interdependent on that of their parents/caregivers (even extended family) and peers, they can begin to recognise the need of many parties to be involved in the learning process to ensure best outcomes for attendance and learning.

A quick test to ascertain engagement is to ask yourself, "How many of my students would turn up if they didn't have to?" Whilst the classroom is not empty, how many empty chairs might there be? It is the approach to these empty chairs that determines a school culture. In some schools, these empty chairs are seen as a sign they can *finally* get on with some teaching, whilst elsewhere, schools go out of their way to find out *why* these students don't want to be there and then work to change that. Of course, many of the students whose chairs remain empty are likely to have significant issues in their personal life and some of these students are dealing with issues such as domestic violence, drug addictions or other such challenges.

Who is there to inspire these 'disengaged' students if they fall through the cracks?

Youth Off The Streets was founded by Father Chris Riley AM and is a non-denominational community organisation working for disadvantaged young people who may be homeless, drug dependent and/or recovering from abuse. Since opening in 1991, Youth Off The Streets has grown from a single food van delivering meals to young homeless people on the streets of Kings Cross in Sydney, to a major youth-specific agency offering a full continuum of care through delivery of a wide range of services to support young people as they work to turn their lives around and overcome immense personal trauma such as neglect, physical, psychological and/or emotional abuse.

Their stated goal is: "To see that no young person is denied the right to education, safe accommodation, drug and alcohol rehabilitation, counselling and other support services aimed at breaking the cycle of disadvantage, abuse and neglect."

In order to provide an education, Youth Off The Streets currently operates six registered, accredited independent high schools over six campuses and a Registered Training Organisation (RTO), which offer young people the opportunity to go back to school and achieve the Record of School

Achievement, Higher School Certificate or vocational qualifications. Whilst most schools are constantly exploring ways in which to motivate their students using grades, punishments, report cards, badges or certificates as either carrots or sticks to improve their work, effort or behaviour, much of Youth Off The Streets work reflects a theory of motivation called *Self Determination Theory (SDT)*. The methods mentioned above are all *extrinsic* motivators and are seen by many as the most likely to succeed in getting the desirable outcomes and with students who are, for the most part, compliant or don't face the extenuating circumstances outside of school that Youth Off The Streets students encounter. However, people can be just as motivated from within by their interests or passions, curiosity or a deeply held set of values (Thomas and Mueller 2017) and it is this form of motivation that is most likely to connect with students at Youth Off The Streets. It is also this model of motivation that is more likely to encourage authentic engagement.

Beyond compliance

Self Determination Theory is concerned with the relationship between these intrinsic and extrinsic motivators. Too often we may hear, "Well that's it. I've done all I can do, if he doesn't want to learn, then there's nothing I can do about it". However, by exploring the world with SDT we can see the factors that need to be at play in order to enhance our students' intrinsic motivation and at the same time consider our own personal and organisation roles as to whether or not some of our most common practices may be undermining a student's innate desire to learn.

SDT was originally developed by Richard Ryan and Edward Deci from the University of Rochester and gained a lot of mainstream coverage when Dan Pink used it to frame much of his 2009 TED Talk, *The Puzzle of Motivation* and his 2011 book, *Drive*, in which Pink goes to great lengths to explore how leaders and educators can create environments and conditions to support an individual's sense self-determination. Such conditions can be created by being mindful of what are known as the three pillars of SDT, which are:

- Autonomy;
- Competence; and
- Relatedness.

SDT proposes that when leaders or educators cultivate a sense of these three pillars in their community, not only is intrinsic motivation enhanced, but also performance, effort, creativity and wellbeing. In contrast, when experiences and environments do not recognise these three pillars, motivation, performance effort, creativity and wellbeing suffer. In schools, the facilitation of more self-determined learning requires classroom conditions that allow satisfaction of these three pillars (Ryan and Deci 2000), so it is pertinent to explore how each of these is addressed.

Competence

One would assume that developing a sense of competence in students would be core business for schools, yet research suggests that one of our most common behaviours in schools can actually curtail learning.

That behaviour? Grading.

Most educators are aware that giving a grade, or a mark on its own is unlikely to aid learning (Black, Buoncristiani, and Wiliam 2014) as the student who receives 20/20 feels they don't *need* to learn anymore, and from the point of the syllabus perhaps they are right, but, of course, they *can* learn more, yet their behaviours rarely reflect this. The student who receives 15/20 is either happy because it keeps everyone off their back, or they are unhappy because a friend scored higher, whilst the student who gets 7/20 rarely cancels their weekend plans to address the short-comings in their work, instead determining that they do not like this subject, or worse—they are incapable of learning this subject. As pointed out, educators know this, that is why students rarely receive a mark in isolation, and instead teachers include lengthy comments as part of the feedback. The issue is, of course, kids don't read the feedback. Why would they? When students get both a mark and a comment, the first thing they do is look at their mark. The second thing they do is look at their neighbour's mark. They rarely look at the comments. Wiliam (2002) argues that teachers who spend time crafting helpful comments are therefore wasting their time if they also give a mark as the students who get high marks feel they do not *need* to read the comments, and those who get low marks do not *want* to. As their sense of competence is eroded, so is their ability and willingness to engage.

Prior to attending Youth Off The Streets schools, many of the students have spent their entire school life receiving poor grades. With this in mind, educators at Youth Off The Streets find different pathways for young people to succeed. For example, if a student struggles academically they find suitable employment or a traineeship focused on strengths and interests of the young person. Although these schools are part of the education system and must follow the curriculum and conduct assessments and exams, the teaching staff will focus on the strengths of the students to encourage engagement using peer support to assist where needed. Education staff and student support workers also conduct interviews at the beginning of each term to determine the wants and needs of the students and to collaboratively set goals for the term and the rest of the year. The staff at Youth Off The Streets go to work with a certain mindset that recognises everyone is entitled to a bad day, and when this happens with one of their students, they empathise and give them the space they need to either work it out themselves, or find a way to help them if they want help. It is this positioning as allies, as opposed to mentors or authority figures that accounts for the biggest differences in the way mainstream and Youth Off The Streets educators work.

A challenge for some schools could be to reduce the number of times they use grades in their feedback. Perhaps they may only offer three pieces of feedback as to how work could be improved. This could be done for the student who received 20/20 as well as the one who received 7/20. Most guidelines across Australia require teachers to report to parents with a grade twice a year, not twice a term or twice a week, so by removing the focus on marks and placing it squarely on improvement we may move closer to achieving that sense of competence for more of our students. Of course, teachers still record the marks in their documentation, but they control the flow of information so that learning continues as opposed to ceases when work is handed back.

Autonomy

For an individual to be intrinsically motivated they need a level of autonomy, and research has shown that teachers who support student autonomy see an increase in their students' levels of—not only motivation—but curiosity and desire for challenge (e.g., Deci, Nezlek, and Sheinman 1981, Ryan and Grolnick 1986). In contrast, students who are overly controlled by their teachers not only lose initiative but also learn less well, especially when learning is complex or requires conceptual, creative processing (Benware and Deci 1984, Grolnick and Ryan 1987).

Staff at Youth Off The Streets recognise that many of their students may have had poor relationships with teachers in the past, and in many cases much work needs to be done around nurturing autonomy, student voice, choice and agency.

To address this, Youth Off The Streets utilise Restorative Practices across their schools. Restorative Practice is widely used in schools to address issues of bullying or classroom management issues (Vaandering 2014), but at Youth Off The Streets it is used to address many behaviours. Given the nature of students' lives, it is quite common for them to experience the 'bad days' and act out as a result. Restorative Practice focuses on the behaviour and the impact of behaviour on others, rather than their moral character. This provides an opportunity for the young people to have a voice and to be heard. It also empowers the young people to take ownership of their behaviour, accept it and address it. Behaviour rarely changes just because one is told it must.

Belonging/Relatedness

As previously discussed, every year the NSW Department of Education invites government schools to take part in the *Tell Them From Me* survey, in which students and parents are asked to reflect on their experiences of education. The student survey specifically focuses on student engagement, exploring issues such as participation in extra-curricular activities, motivation and teacher—student relations. Of particular interest is the rate at which students report a positive sense of belonging at school. State-wide, by around Year 6, approximately 80 per cent of students report experiencing a positive sense of belonging. And then they go to high school. From Year 7 to Year 9 there is a steady decline to a point where only approximately 58 per cent of Year 9 students report a sense of belonging. It is important to note, of course, that this is not to say the students attend school; again as with the Gallup Student Poll, they had to be there to take the survey. So, what of those students who *aren't* there? What of those students for whom the mainstream doesn't work? For many it is a case of out of sight, out of mind.

At Youth Off The Streets, a great deal of effort goes into developing a sense of belonging and relatedness. As well as sporting competitions and cultural days celebrating the various nationalities within Youth Off The Streets and the community, students and staff also take part in Service Learning to improve and build relationships between themselves and within the community. Service Learning, the combination of learning objectives and community service, allows students to learn in different environments, with different people in different contexts to their own, whilst also engendering civic responsibility. Through Restorative Practice, issues are dealt with in an inclusive way to increase awareness of self and others thereby promoting respectful relationships. In the mainstream, it is sometimes the case that parents only hear from the school when a problem arises, and whilst some schools actively challenge this by making phone calls to the parent or caregiver, or using smartphone apps to sometimes share student successes, at Youth Off The Streets, educators maintain consistent, almost daily, contact with an appropriate adult (parent/caregiver) wherever this is possible. And whilst in the mainstream it may be uncommon for students to sit with staff for lunch, at Youth Off The Streets, group lunches are the norm. Students and staff prepare meals for each other and then sit, talk and eat together. It's through these efforts and activities that educators can really get to know each young person and help them find their place where they belong through education, work, outreach and housing.

Can mainstream schooling learn from alternative education settings?

In Alternative Educational Settings, and Youth Off The Streets exemplifies this perfectly, all educational work is built on two pillars. Time and Relationships. The nature of their schools means that most classes are small in number, and add to that, all Youth Off The Streets campuses have, in addition to the educators on site, a psychologist and a student support worker. This enables the students and educators to connect on a more personal level to define and then achieve individual and collaborative success. Time is used to meet the needs of the students, and without the need for bells, the school day is more flexible than you may find in a larger mainstream school. Staff collaborate when students need more time on assignments or tasks or when a student is having a particularly bad day and wants to complete individual work.

The logistics of running a large mainstream school means that such flexibility is rarely afforded to educators or students. Bell times, separate subjects, ability setting, assessments and competing priorities within the school community often means the need for compliance is even more exaggerated. As schools, particularly in our cities, continue to take on more and more students to accommodate the growing population, whilst at the same time feeling the pressure of the performative nature of the education debate, the need for compliance will continue to grow. And as this need grows, so will the number of students who fall through the cracks. Whether or not organisations like Youth Off The Streets will be on hand to pick them all up will be largely left to chance, so it is up to mainstream education, the politicians and society in general to be a little less hasty when writing off young people as being disengaged and somebody else's problem.

References

Benware, C.A. and Deci, E.L., 1984. Quality of learning with an active versus passive motivational set. *American Educational Research Journal*, 21 (4), 755–765.

Black, P.J., Buoncristiani, P. and Wiliam, D., 2014. *Inside the black box: Raising standards through classroom assessment*. Moorabbin: Hawker Brownlow Education.

Deci, E.L., Nezlek, J. and Sheinman, L., 1981. Characteristics of the rewarder and intrinsic motivation of the rewardee. *Journal of Personality and Social Psychology*, 40 (1), 1–10.

Hancock, K.J. and Zubrick, S., 2015. *Children and young people at risk of disengagement from school*. Commissioner for Children and Young People, Western Australia.

Gallup, 2016. Gallup Student Poll Report, Australia and New Zealand.

Grolnick, W.S. and Ryan, R.M., 1987. Autonomy in children's learning: An experimental and individual difference investigation. *Journal of Personality and Social Psychology*, 52 (5), 890–898.

NSW CESE, 2017. The role of student engagement in the transition from primary to secondary school. *The Learning Curve*. New South Wales Centre for Education Statistics and Evaluation. Available from: www.cese.nsw.gov.au/publications-filter/the-role-of-student-engagement-in-the-transition-from-primary-to-secondary-school [Accessed 13 May 2018].

Pink, D.H., 2011. *Drive: The surprising truth about what motivates us*. New York: Riverhead Books.

Ryan, R.M. and Deci, E.L., 2000. Self-determination theory and the facilitation of intrinsic motivation, social development, and well-being. *American Psychologist*, 55 (1), 68–78.

Ryan, R.M. and Grolnick, W.S., 1986. Origins and pawns in the classroom: Self-report and projective assessments of individual differences in children's perceptions. *Journal of Personality and Social Psychology*, 50 (3), 550–558.

Thomas, A.E. and Mueller, F.H., 2017. A magic dwells in each beginning? Contextual effects of autonomy support on students' intrinsic motivation in unfamiliar situations. *Social Psychology of Education*, 20 (4), 791–805.

Vaandering, D., 2014. Implementing restorative justice practice in schools: What pedagogy reveals. *Journal of Peace Education*, 11 (1), 64–80.

Wiliam, D. 2002, Assessing the best method of learning. *The Scotsman*. Available from: www.scotsman.com/news/professor-dylan-william-assessing-the-best-method-of-learning-1-941504 [Accessed 13 May 2018].

17 Makerspace as 'soul work' of public schooling

Tomaz Lasic

Imagine this. A large manual arts workshop at the back of a suburban public school in Perth, Western Australia, built around the time when Pink Floyd were at the top of the charts with 'Another Brick in the Wall', pun intended. From serving over a thousand students a year in its heyday, the school gets restructured, student numbers drop, programs are cut. It is a middle school only now. The workshops get used less and less, seeing only the occasional part-timer and a few interested kids here and there. Over the past ten years, barely anyone goes there, other than to dump unwanted stuff or 'borrow long term' any handy tools and materials still openly lying around. Birds nest. Spiders weave. Dust gathers. The place is dirty and dangerous for anyone, let alone kids, to use. But it has good bones and enormous potential.

We are in the poor, 'rough' end of town. Two-thirds of the school's students come from families in the lowest socioeconomic quartile in the country. Most of the rest pretty much from the next lowest. This is blue collar and welfare territory. One-third of the school population is Indigenous, one-third migrants, many of them refugees escaping wars you see on TV. Rampant generational poverty ensures many childhoods around here are those of constant 'no'. Plenty of students may not look and sound like 'good students' at first but if you build a relationship and trust, they would do things for you that colleagues in the more affluent schools couldn't dream of.

Since the restructure, the school has been a flagship school using the Big Picture learning design. Big Picture is all about students learning about and through their interests. And not just learning about it but doing it. The school motto is 'One student at a time'. The aim is the trifecta of engaged minds, hearts and hands, unique to each kid. We have kids whose interest fits this trifecta and would love to use their hands to make, fix, build, bash, paint, shape, pull apart, connect, learn stuff. But the hands are missing out as we have nowhere safe really for them to do so. Can we do something with these workshops for these kids and their families?

The deputy principal and I both think that not using the workshops is bordering on criminal, especially given our student cohort and the Big Picture framework. Trouble is—we have no qualified Design & Technology teacher on staff. I put my hand up and after a hectic semester of full-time teaching and full-time additional graduate study, I get the ticket to run the place. Nothing terribly remarkable, but what comes next is.

The place is still a dangerous, ugly dump. We lack the funds and hands to make it full of kids again. We are a government school, yes, and the tight budgets would make many laugh. Or cry. Soon, a casual conversation with a family member who works for Australia's largest fully Indigenously owned engineering and mining company ends up in a high-level meeting.

"I would like to see football and arts not to be the only viable career options for Indigenous kids around here. We need to give them a fighting chance for something else, especially when they are young."

"You've just described my story", says the company founder, and soon after approves $10,000 dollars of 'seed funding'. "This is for all, not just Noongar[1] kids." The man knows, we know, that ten thousand goes a long way here This will allow us to do the place up and perhaps order some technology of the future, not just that of the past. We also win a small Federal grant. We have the funds. Now to hands.

I recruit a couple of trusted students to help me out with clearing, cleaning, fixing and stocking. A keen graduate from last year joins us for a day a week as part of his workplace learning course. Soon, more students ask if they can come and help. I ask a few kids skipping class and hiding around the school to help us. When invited to help throw stuff in the bin, drill a hole, shift a table, help make a cabinet, sweep, wield a paint roller instead of 'getting into trouble', they respond with "sure", most of them. A handful of helpers grows into a platoon-sized bunch, eager and able to help to the limit of their abilities. Anyone coming to fool around is sent back to class, often by the helpers themselves. This is fun but serious and meaningful at the same time. The more experienced helpers are put in charge of small teams, informally. The radio plays, surrounded by work, lots of humour and laughter. Technical and social skills are growing. Relationships are building. The principal comes often to see what we are up to.

After months of steady progress, we open our own Makerspace, our "space with tools and materials where people gather to design, invent, make and learn by doing". Safe, clean, stocked, inviting. At the opening, students, staff, families, guests and dignitaries effuse about the space and opportunities ahead. In a brief speech, I remark how this place 'has a soul' of effort and care. These are not empty words. The space doesn't look as if a contractor got hold of it over the holidays and made it into something spectacular. The space looks like it is done by students for students, made and owned by them. Because it is.

Something else happens in this space where students work on things they want. In here, they are free to 'have a go' without the pressures of schooliness and measured performance. They are the ones who judge, compare, evaluate. Curricular but also other, different knowledge is validated here. Where else in the school would knowing how to fix fibreglass they have learned with their uncle, or learning how to weave from their grandma, be welcome, useful?

There are no grades to stream them in low (or high) ability classes. They are not required to sit still. There is minimal teacher-planned activity to follow. Many students see themselves in a different light in this space. Some of them resist, challenge and change their ontologies. They embrace, rather than resist or suppress, who and what they are. A few troublemakers and rebels elsewhere become responsible leaders and knowers in here. A self-proclaimed 'dumb' student shows things to the 'smart' students he is working together with in his team. Some 'academic students' struggle with, some enjoy purposes beyond grades, and more. Much more. We have flipped student identities. We have flipped the teacher–student control. We have flipped notions of accomplishment. We have flipped schooling itself and operate as a thrumming microcosm of what education could be like for students who are disadvantaged, marginalised, or who do not fit within the strictures of traditional classrooms and traditional measures of success.

What about learning? Or teaching rather? School is after all a place of, for it.
"Mister, how do you work out how much yellow paint we need for this?"
"Remember calculating the area in Maths?"
"Um, sort of . . . No."
"Well, length times width. Have a go."
Fifteen minutes later, the same child who flunked the standardised numeracy tests and 'hates maths' (re)learned the difference between millimetres and centimetres, measured the sides accurately, multiplied the length and width to calculate the area and quantity of paint required for two coats of paint over it. I was there to help if perhaps terminally stuck, but she worked it out with minimal help from me. She had a positive experience of being numerate. She was pleased, proud even. Writing her compulsory log entry, her classmate asks how to spell "persisted". Vocabulary. Literacy. Strings of small, positive, meaningful, validating and unmeasurable acts.

Some may see our Makerspace as a fanciful 'student-centred' space where teachers don't run the show. But I ask: Is a student being proud of their own, meaningful effort, seeing value in literacy, numeracy, asking questions, concepts to learn or make sense of in that next Science or Humanities class, a waste of time?

I pride myself on being student-centred in the things I do as a teacher. As I write this phrase, I acknowledge that its meaning has become very fluid thanks to increasing (over)use. To explain, I have always sought to understand the context of the school, space, group and individual students I am working with, as much as it is practically possible. Understanding these helps develop and encourage learning activities that are not only effective in terms of student learning, but are respectful of student's circumstances, needs and hopes. For years, I have been trying to give students a genuine choice and voice in what they learn, how they learn and what they learn for. I acknowledge that this is not perfect, ideal or possible in every situation. But a sense of personal agency, purpose and value of education to self and others cannot be built without allowing one's own voice to be heard and tested.

This is what I mean by student-centred. This is the soul of our Makerspace. Together, teacher and students have rewired the system in order to reclaim education on our own terms.

Note

1 The Noongar people are members of the local Indigenous language group and traditional owners of the large part of the south-western area of Western Australia, including the Perth metro area.

18 Equitable education in Australia
Empowering schools to lead the way

Pasi Sahlberg

Horizons of school education

During the last two decades I have travelled around the world for work. It has been a privilege to meet top-level education leaders, teachers, school principals and children in a wide range of countries. My prime principle as a school improvement activist or education policy advisor to ministers and governments is to listen to students and take a good look around the place where they are learning every day. Oftentimes, I also go to school in a foreign country to teach children mathematics so that I can understand their perceptions and beliefs about teaching and learning in school. This *modus operandi* has proved to be powerful. It has taught me first-hand how children's experiences of school education are often distant from what adults and policymakers think. Curiosity to figure out how to address this complex conflict of perceptions led me to write this chapter.

Another observation en route around the world is that schools look very similar from one country to another. Of course, there are schools that derail from this mainstream image. I have seen them in every country I have visited. But when I look at what subjects dominate school curricula, how they are taught, school architecture or classrooms design, and students' opinions about their school, differences are not significant from one place to next.

The school systems do, however, tend to vary significantly in one area: how they deal with inequalities and diversities that accompany children to school daily. Nordic countries, for example, place great emphasis on inclusiveness and fairness in schools. Inclusion in schooling means that all children have access to learning and support that ensures they will attain essential knowledge and skills required in their education. When a large number of children are out of school or segregated in special institutions or classes, inclusiveness becomes at risk. Fairness, as the OECD (2016) defines it, in education refers to the strength of the relationship between children's family background and achievement in school. Fairer education systems assure that all students, regardless of their home background, individual characteristics, race or ethnicity, place of residence, or other life circumstances have similar opportunities to succeed in school than others. Other education systems that focus on inclusion and fairness are Estonia and many of the provinces in Canada. Both Canada and Finland, both known for their education systems built on ideals of equality and social justice, turned out to be the leaders in overall educational success.

Australia was among the top-performing school systems in early PISA surveys in the 2000s. Since then, however, students' learning outcomes in Australia have dropped in PISA and other internationally comparative student assessments. National assessment program—literacy and numeracy (NAPLAN) has confirmed the stagnation of students' academic learning in Australia. A lot of research and analysis exists about what is keeping education systems in Australia that way (ACARA 2017, OECD 2016). Debates range from lack of real competition and market-drivers within the education system to unequal resourcing and student segregation due to a push for parental choice for children's schooling. In light of international data, it appears that the actual problem in Australian school education is eroding equity and increasing segregation in education that manifests itself especially in remote and rural parts of the country. What would be required to improve educational performance in Australia is to flip the education policies to focus more on equity, in other words, on inclusion and fairness, and less on narrowly measured academic test scores and excellence as the key indicators of educational success.

The Finnish way of equity

Finland chose *enhancing equity* as the key idea in reforming its education system when the Basic School Reform was launched in early 1970s. Today, national education policy and the legislation behind it are still based on values and principles of equality of educational opportunity and equity of education outcomes. In this sense, the focus of the educational policy has not changed over the last four decades. However, there have been two distinct phases regarding how schools have addressed educational equality.

The first phase, the 1970s and 1980s, was characterized by strict central steering and external control of schools. Prescribed state curriculum, detailed common syllabi, inspection of schools, and strict state regulations gave the Finnish government a strong grip over schools and teachers. These central directives also insisted that all schools must have health services, warm school meals, and appropriate support for children with special needs available nationwide. In other words, equality of opportunity was ensured, and equity of outcomes promoted through control by the central government.

The second phase since the early 1990s to the present has represented a time of increased local control for schools and professional autonomy of teachers. In 1994, schools became responsible for managing their core work, assessing their students, involvement in professional learning and school improvement, and also "self-inspection" of their own work. State school inspections were eliminated, fiscal control moved to the districts, and a sample-based educational evaluation system was designed to help to monitor the overall performance of the Finnish educational system (Sahlberg 2015). A critical aspect in this radical transformation of education governance was a school-based curriculum, requiring that all schools create their own curriculum that included detailed descriptions of school values, a mission statement, pedagogical principles, and the overarching goals of the school. School-based curriculum planning is steered by the National Curriculum Framework (NBE 2014), which is a loose guide and collection of legally binding conditions that schools and municipalities must follow in their curriculum planning.

During my time as a government school improvement officer at the time of abovementioned changes, I read hundreds of school-made curricula to understand how teachers thought about what is important in education. All of them, with very few exceptions, had formulated their values and goals with equity, inclusion and fairness as central principles of the declared work of the school.

According to the latest OECD PISA study, Finnish 15-year-old students did very well in reading, mathematics and science and had one of the weakest impacts of socioeconomic background as shown in Figure 18.1. At the same time, variation of students' science achievement between schools is one of the smallest in the world. Many observers of international education have asked what makes the Finnish school system equitable. According to my own analysis, Finnish schools have had two influential strategies to enhance equity in education: (a) school-based curricula that give teachers and principals the

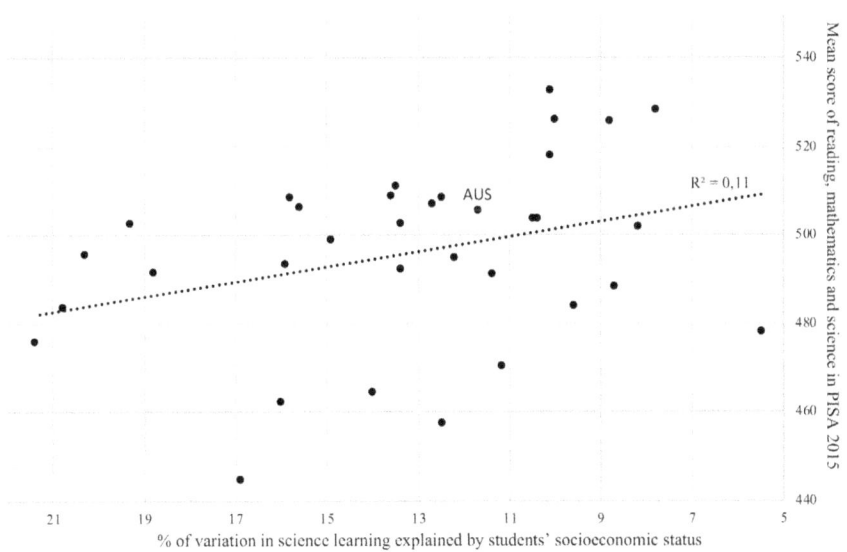

Figure 18.1 Student academic achievement and the strength of socioeconomic gradient in OECD countries in 2015

Source: OECD 2016

power and responsibility to define values, purpose, and overall educational goals for their school, and (b) access to purposeful professional learning to help teachers and schools to improve their work towards these goals.

As a consequence, teachers and school leaders are able to influence the formulation of the values, purpose, and goals of their schools, based on their own professional wisdom and judgment after having a dialogue with parents and the community about their expectations regarding what schools should do. The terminology and style of school curricula in Finland are very down-to-earth; reflecting the moral aspects of education rather than the political rhetoric typical of centrally prepared policy documents and directives. Finnish experience shows that if we allow schools to formulate the details of what is important in school from children's perspective, they typically say things like "everybody has the opportunity to succeed", "no child is left behind", and "all children can learn anything if they are properly helped to do so" in ways that are possible to accomplish in practice. Common to the mission statements of Finnish schools is a strong emphasis on equity in schooling. That is, ensuring that pupils' home background, life situation, or mother tongue don't determine their learning in school. School-based curricula are, therefore, an important strategy to convert system level strategies and equity policies into concrete actions and structures within schools and how to monitor them (UNESCO 2018).

All teachers and principals are professionals in Finland who must hold advanced academic credentials (Hammerness, Ahtiainen, and Sahlberg 2017). However, just like medical doctors or lawyers, educators also must update their professional knowledge and skills continuously. The Finnish government has maintained teachers' and principals' professional learning and development as one of the main policy priorities since the start of the era of stronger school autonomy in the early 1990s. In recent years, for example, the state budget has allocated over AUD40 million to teachers' professional learning and leadership development. Local municipalities (310 in total) that govern and provide most of the funding for schools also significantly invest in continuous improvement of their schools. Professional learning and school improvement are based on the demand and needs of schools and, therefore, primarily focus on implementation of the school's own curriculum. Finnish teachers and principals spend, on average, about seven days a year on professional learning and further education. Half of that time is their personal time. By doing that, Finland invests 30 times more funds in the professional development of teachers and administrators than in evaluating the performance of students and schools, including national assessments. In standardised testing-intensive education systems, like Australia where AUD100 million a year is spent on NAPLAN alone, this ratio is often the other way around.

Strong emphasis on equity in schooling gives a different meaning to *school performance* and how it is measured. Standardised testing has become the most common way in the United States, England, and Australia, for example, to measure schools' performance. Test-based accountability in many parts of the world relies on data from these tests. Teachers and school leaders are held accountable for their students' tested learning using these data. This does not happen in Finland. Absence of standardised tests in Finland leaves schools responsible for assessing student achievement and freedom to focus more on equity and wellbeing as main outcomes of school. A high-performing school in Finland is one where *all* students perform beyond expectations. In other words, the greater the equity, the better the school is regarded in Finland.

Fixing equity: flipping the system

An educational system that is equitable and where students learn well is able to redress the effect of broader social and economic inequalities. This is particularly noteworthy in Australia, a country that has much greater income inequalities and social disparities than in Finland. When I speak to Australians about Finnish educational reforms and how they foster high overall levels of student achievement, while limiting the influence of student backgrounds on learning outcomes and attaining a high level of equity, some ask me why Finnish people see that as being so important. I reply by pointing out that inequity in educational systems within Finland is problematic, since it demonstrates a failure to fully utilise students' cognitive potential. As a small nation, we cannot leave any child behind. We also know from evidence that strengthening equity in education can be cost-beneficial. The OECD, examining the six cycles of PISA data, recently concluded that the highest-performing education systems across OECD nations are those that combine quality with equity (OECD 2012). Other research demonstrates that investing as early as possible in high-quality education for all students and directing additional resources towards the most disadvantaged students as early as possible, is a cost-effective strategy that will produce the greatest impact on improving overall academic performance.

What can Australia learn from those with more inclusive school systems to enhance equity in its schools? Reviews and research about the state of Australian education often refer to declining PISA scores and, as a result, a widening achievement gap between Australia and Singapore and other better performing countries. This 'performance slippage' narrative that relies on statistical data from international and national standardised assessments of reading literacy and mathematics often fail to see educational system performance as broader issue that would include general knowledge, social skills, character, wellbeing, and aspirations and commitment to lifelong learning after school. Another commonly ignored aspect of educational performance is equity of outcomes. While it seems evident in international data that Australian school system has had declining equity of its school system during the past decade and half, there is now reliable evidence that Australian children would lag behind or lead the pack in other academic domains or general outcomes of schooling. Figure 18.2 shows how strongly students' school performance in science is linked to their parents' education in Australia and in other countries.

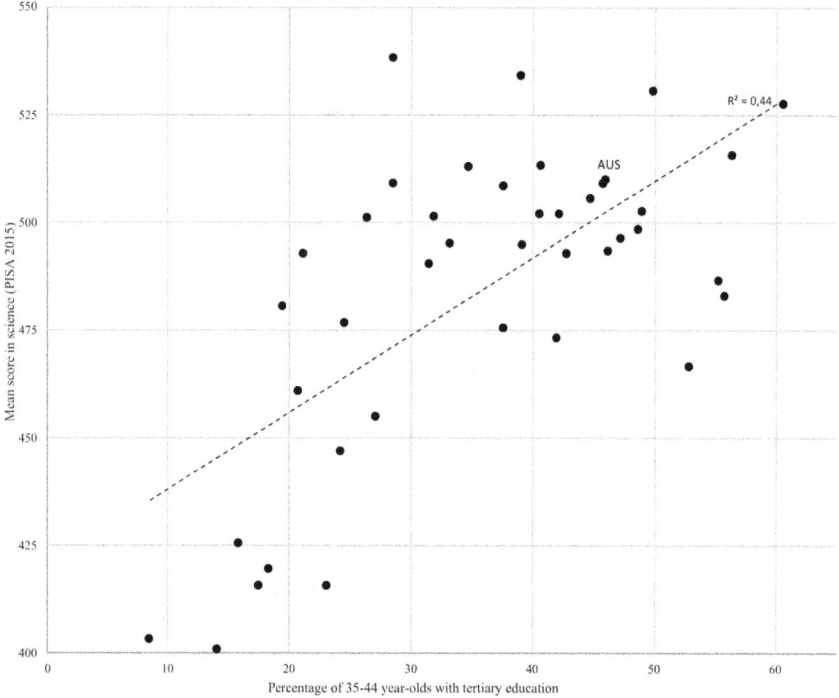

Figure 18.2 Science performance score in PISA 2015 and parents' level of education in 2015
Source: OECD (2016), Figure I.2.9

Let's consider an alternative theory of change to improve Australian education. Rather than assuming that the problem is a 'teacher deficit' or underperforming schools, let's rely on international evidence and assume that the main obstacle holding Australian school system from getting better is in chronic and wide-spread social inequality and unfairness of funding schools and that more equitable education system would also perform better overall. In other words, let's try to fix equity instead. David Gonski's panel stated clearly in its report *Review of Funding for Schooling* (Australian Government 2011) that the fundamental underlying deficit in Australia is unequal allocation of resources in a country where personal wealth and position in the society determines much of the educational opportunity and social mobility in life. This alternative theory of change would be based on a premise that the best way to improve education system performance would be to invest more strategically in helping those children to succeed who otherwise would face too many challenges to meet the expectations in school. This is the same strategy that lies behind celebrated educational success in Canada and Finland, for example. Fixing equity as a driving theory of action leads to very different rhetoric and practices than thriving for excellence that is commonly used in education system with lower-than-desired levels of educational performance, including Australia.

In current global educational reform discourse the dominant question that policymakers ask as a point of entry is: How can we make sure that teachers and principals do what they are expected to do in schools? This leads to practices that have appeared to be ineffective, namely stronger top-down bureaucracy, tougher consequential accountability to control the work of schools, and blaming teachers and children for not working hard enough. NAPLAN and other national assessment and inspection systems are concrete manifestations of this paradigm. In a flipped system the primary question that guides leaders' and authorities' thinking and decision making should be: How can we best empower everybody in schools to do their very best? In advanced systems, that have built teacher and leader professionalism in schools, Hargreaves and Fullan (2012) argue, this paradigm requires deeper collaboration, broader responsibility, and trust in one another so that schools can set their own expectations, choose optimal ways to try to meet them, and critically evaluate their journey towards the goals.

The global education race is on. Schools are required to focus on 'raising the bar' for 'educational excellence' and are held accountable for doing so. National tests and international assessments make sure that teachers and schools stay on course (Sellar, Thompson, and Rutkowski 2017). Externally prescribed curriculum, frequent testing whether curriculum standards are met, and students' maximised learning growth each year are common elements in state-led school systems taking part in the global education race. Flipping that system to shift from accountability and control to trust and empowerment requires different education policy logic. The following three transformations could be considered.

1. From state-led to school-based curriculum practice

State-level curricula and standards are the key instruments that governments have to steer and control what schools do and what teachers teach (Priestley and Biesta 2013). In the system where schools are expected to pursue predetermined education excellence (as measured by standardised tests), the state-led approach is a natural theory of action. Central administration makes sure that curriculum is 'strong' and that it focuses on 'preparing young people for future job markets'. Careful control of inputs is assumed to deliver expected outputs. This is, indeed, the standardised "industrial model school education that reflects a 20th century aspiration to deliver mass education to all children" referred to in the revised Gonski panel review report (The Department of Education and Training 2018).

Centrally mandated standardisation and one-size-fits-all are poor approaches to build equitable in inclusive education systems. Equity in education, as defined in this chapter, requires understanding individuals' needs and responding to these needs without delay. When teachers have authority and responsibility to craft their own curriculum, individualised practices will flourish. In school-led curriculum systems, schools have the freedom and collective obligation to design curriculum according to a wider state framework. If this framework adequately addresses equity, social justice, and inclusion as desired principles of school education, teachers, and principals are much better placed to find the best ways to help all children to succeed than standardised directives. State-level is good at system-level regulations and coherence for quality and excellence (Sahlberg 2018). School-level expertise is better at making school education to meet the needs of each and every child.

Many teachers, principals, and education authorities in Finland believe that the school is the place where the decisions regarding teaching and learning should be made. They also think that the strength of the Finnish education system to provide good education to all children is due to trusting and allowing schools collectively to decide what works for them. Every municipality uses school-based curriculum as an important means to engage all teachers in planning the work of their school. Experiences from schools since the mid-1990s show that engaging in designing your own school curriculum has been, in most schools, a perfect way to empower teachers and principals to collaborate and do their very best.

2. From standardised teaching to individualised learning

Inclusion of children with special educational needs into mainstream schooling is an important guiding principle for equitable and high-quality education. All schools must have adequate resources to employ special education teachers and classroom assistants who can help children with special needs. Special education should be defined so that it addresses difficulties related to learning, behaviour, and wellbeing and should not be limited only to variety of disabling conditions, such as sensory and speech-language impairments, intellectual disabilities, and behavioural difficulties. Furthermore, special education needs should be identified and individualised as early as possible.

Many believe that Finland's special education system is one of those key factors that explain world-class results in achievement and equity of Finland's school system in recent international studies. My personal experience is that most schools in Finland pay very particular attention to those children who need more help in becoming successful, compared to other students. This was my impression of Hesperia School; it is a good example of a Finnish school with a strong focus on equity. Many Australian teachers and principals whom I know think the same way but are often stuck in the middle of *excellence vs equity* quandaries due to external demands and regulations. Standardised testing that compares individuals to statistical averages, unhealthy competition that segregates children based on wealth, power or race, and unfair funding of public schools all jeopardise teachers' efforts to enhance equity, in my view. None of these factors currently exists in the Finnish education system.

3. From funding equally to investing in equity

Education budgeting is next to rocket science in many education systems. Formulas and coefficients determine how money flows from state or local offices to schools. In many countries weightings and indexes are used to allocate resources equally throughout the education system. However, in most cases that I know, a logical, consistent and publicly transparent approach to funding schooling is missing. As a consequence, resource allocations follow more a principle of equality (i.e. everybody gets the same) rather than fairness (more resources for those who have different needs).

In 2011, Gonski's first review panel (Australian Government 2011) concluded that

> there is an imbalance in the provision of funding to government and non-government schools by the Australian and state and territory governments. In particular, the Australian Government could play a greater role in supporting state and territory governments to meet the needs of disadvantaged students in both government and non-government schools.

Therefore, allocation of public funding to schools should reflect the nature of the educational challenges faced by schools taking into consideration its characteristics and student population. In Finland this is called a 'positive discrimination' policy that guarantees public funding to schools follows the values of fairness and aims enhancing equity of education in schools. It is, therefore, considered to be an investment in education rather than simply spending more money on something that is not considered essential for achieving excellence in education.

Closing thoughts

School choice advocates often argue that the introduction of market mechanisms allows equal access to high-quality schooling for all. These same people maintain that when there is enough competition between schools due to parental choice, most schools will eventually get better. This is a popular argument in England, the United States, the Russian Federation, and in Australia, too. However, evidence does not support these views, as the Grattan Institute in Australia and OECD globally have reported. School choice and associated market mechanisms often enhance segregation of schools. Sweden and Chile are good test laboratories to realise the impact of placing school choice ahead of equity in education policy. We have learned that quality remains stagnated and inequity within the education system increases.

Education policies in Finland have for a long time now intended to make all public schools good places for children to learn and teachers to teach. Finland has no private schools and there are only about 80 publicly funded independent schools in Finland. International experience has shown that it is difficult to have an equitable education system by employing liberal school choice policies that encourage the expansion of non-public schools because choice invariably increases school segregation. The basic questions for flipping the system in Australia are: *How should public funds be spent to enhance equity and quality in education? Who should decide what all children need in school to succeed? What is the absolute minimum amount of data needed to provide confidence and trust in education system?* Answers to these questions should be figured out in open dialogue between authorities, teachers, parents and scholars. If this is done professionally, conclusions of these dialogues would lead to needs-based funding of schools, growing professional teacher autonomy, and increasing school responsibility to craft their own curriculum, and diminishing role of census-based standardised national assessments.

Australia should flip the system by empowering schools to lead the way towards more equitable education. The question is not whether the government should or shouldn't recommit itself to full funding of the Gonski 2011 panel's recommendations. It rather is: Can Australia afford to continue to fund inequity in its school system as it seeks to bring its overall educational performance to desired level that requires that all children will learn well? I believe that Australia has many advantages to build great schools for all of its children. Phenomenal cultural richness and substantial national wealth create a unique platform for improvement that places Australia far ahead of many nations. The widely accepted idea of Educational Goals for Young Australians in the Melbourne Declaration that proclaimed that "the Australian governments must ensure that socioeconomic disadvantage ceases to be a significant determinant of educational outcomes" provides a basis for transformation that other countries can only dream of. The importance of Gonski's suggestion for fairer funding of Australian schools is that it would be the best way to accomplish this important national goal. Another shift of focus would be to move from 'evidence-based' to value-based education policy.

Australia has another unique aspect in its school system that calls for elevating equity of education to the policy priority—or flipping the system. It has one of the largest proportions of children studying in non-government schools among the OECD countries. Public schools educate over 80% of students in the lowest quartile of socioeconomic status, indigenous students, students in remote and rural areas, students with a funded disability, and the vast majority of students with English as second language. As a consequence of these characteristics, in vastly segregated education systems public schools continue to suffer from the unfair social stigma of serving these disadvantaged children, rather than carrying the inspiring connotation of providing a unifying, high-quality education for all. Without being able to cope better with these underlying forces that drive inequity in education, it is unlikely that Australia will anytime soon meet the moral commitments and human development imperatives that are regularly heard conditions for a sustainable and prosperous future of Australia.

References

ACARA, 2017. National Assessment Program—Literacy and Numeracy. *Achievement in reading, writing, language conventions and numeracy: National report for 2017*. Sydney: Australian Curriculum, Assessment and Reporting Authority.

Australian Government, 2011. *Review of funding for schooling*. Final report. Canberra: Department of Education, Employment and Workplace Relations.

Hammerness, K., Ahtiainen, R., and Sahlberg, P., 2017. *Empowered educators in Finland: How high-performing systems shape teaching quality*. San Francisco, CA: Jossey-Bass.

Hargreaves, A. and Fullan, M., 2012. *Professional capital: Transforming teaching in every school*. New York: Teachers College Press.

National Board of Education (NBE), 2014. *National core curriculum for basic education 2014*. Helsinki: National Board of Education.

OECD, 2012. *Equity and quality in education. Supporting disadvantaged students and schools*. Paris: OECD Publishing.

OECD, 2016. *PISA 2015 results. Excellence and equity in education*. Paris: OECD Publishing.

Priestley, M. and Biesta, G., eds., 2013. *Reinventing curriculum. New trends in curriculum policy and practice*. London: Bloomsbury.

Sahlberg, P., 2015. *Finnish lessons 2.0: What can the world learn from educational change in Finland*. New York: Teachers College Press.

Sahlberg, P., 2018. *FinnishED leadership. Four big, inexpensive ideas to transform education*. Thousand Oaks, CA: Corwin.

Sellar, S., Thompson, G., and Rutkowski, D., 2017. *The global education race: Taking the measure of PISA and international testing*. Edmonton, Alberta, Canada: Brush Education Inc.

The Department of Education and Training, 2018. *Through growth to achievement*. Report of the Review to Achieve Educational Excellence in Australian Schools. Canberra: The Commonwealth of Australia.

UNESCO, 2018. *Handbook on measuring equity in education*. Quebec: UNESCO Institute for Statistics.

Part IV

Professional learning for a flipped system

This section arranges some clear possible directions for the professional learning of educators in Australia. All five authors advocate building teacher capacity in order to engage with the transformative and developmental challenges of the present, a far cry from yesteryear's en masse informational PD trainings. One size does not fit all. These authors show that today's adult learning opportunities challenge teachers and encourage them to question what they take for granted, in a collegial environment of support and follow-up. Coaching, focusing on the complexities of practice, and action research models are the methods advocated to achieve these aims. The common theme through these chapters, flipping the system means reconsidering and reconfiguring who has power and control over what and how teachers learn.

Jon Andrews and **Chris Munro** are critical of education policy that turns teachers into technocrats, at the expense of opportunities to reflect and engage in genuine professional dialogue. Teacher agency is at the core of their mission to promote coaching as means to a more generative and fulfilling professional culture.

Rachel Lofthouse is critical of the demands policymakers impose on teachers and the constant waves of supposedly transformative pedagogies and curriculum strategies. She argues that there has to be more to professional learning than clocking up hours or ticking boxes. Underpinning her practice development-led model is the recognition of the complexity of effective practice and that developing these complex practices is where the time and energy should be spent.

Ryan Gill and **Carla Gagliano** work to cultivate and promote rich cultures of thinking in their own school and with other educators across Australia. Their aim is to create safe, supportive and thoughtful environments for teachers to explore, inquire, reflect, and wonder. They share their insights into their school's journey, where action research is at the heart of the professional learning culture.

19 Coaching for agency

The power of professionally respectful dialogue

Jon Andrews and Chris Munro

In this chapter, we propose that coaching offers an opportunity for teachers and school leaders to support the dual aims of working towards continual development and refinement of practice, whilst positioning the experience, perspective, and voices of teachers in a place of respect and non-judgement. We argue that the goal of teacher coaching should be teacher *agency*. Drawing on the "ecological approach" to agency proposed by Priestley, Biesta and Robinson (2015), we consider how coaching can facilitate and sustain teacher agency over time, ultimately resulting in a mindful and critically engaged profession enjoying the satisfaction that is derived from exercising agency in response to the complex needs of our students and school communities.

We locate coaching in a contemporary context by first presenting the current backdrop to the work of schools and the teachers therein. In doing so, we explore the influence of unprecedented levels of scrutiny, accountability and prescription on approaches to teacher development and school improvement. Further, we consider the effects of the application of national standards on teacher learning and development. It is against this backdrop that we have developed our own experience in and knowledge of coaching in education, and our unrelenting commitment to enabling professionally respectful and empowering conversations between educators.

This chapter is not intended to be a 'how to' of coaching in education but we will finish by outlining some challenges to be confronted in moving to increase teacher agency through coaching in schools. In keeping with the rationale of the Flip the System series, our chapter seeks to challenge the status quo, in this case, of teacher learning and development, by suggesting an antidote to the erosion of teacher agency.

Teaching against a backdrop of performativity

In an era of hyper-accountability for schools and teachers, locating a dimension of teacher work that is not subject to some form of surveillance, performance rating or judgement is problematic. Usually connected to some larger system or school-level process of improving aspects of schooling or outcomes, these demands call into question the perceived value placed on professional agency and trust in teachers by all levels of leadership. Moreover, in a time where the pursuit of a secure relationship between input and output seemingly dominates the educational debate, teachers' thinking and work is at risk of being reduced to applying 'interventions' and 'treatments' and extracting any risk of deviation from 'what works'. Meanwhile, the growing emphasis on teacher learning and development has simultaneously shifted to align with these systemic and school-level improvement agendas. In an effort to align a workforce's knowledge, skills and experience with organisational goals for improvement, schools have turned to a variety of means to bring about progress. Programs or interventions such as teacher appraisal, performance management, targeted professional development, and even some manifestations of mentoring and coaching, seek to manoeuvre teacher learning and development closer towards collective compliance rather than individual growth and flourishing. These approaches, whilst effective by some measures, fall into the realms of performativity (Ball 2003). Performativity, according to Ball, "... requires individual practitioners to organise themselves as a response to targets, indicators and evaluations, set aside personal beliefs and commitments and live an existence of calculation". Teacher appraisal and training programs aligned with these aims only serve to compound cultures of performance and compliance (Ball 2003, 2015) and can stymy rich dialogue and action that robustly explores practice developments and engages with educational research.

What place is there then for teacher conversations and work around researching and responsibly trialling practices that aren't directly or indirectly mandated? Who gets to judge if teachers are fit to make judgements or decisions about practice? At what point does the responsibility get snatched from teachers only to be supplanted by micro-management and a rhetoric of performance with terms such as 'effect' and 'impact' calling for, and valuing exclusively, the "calculable, describable and comparable" (Mockler 2013, p.118). It may be possible to trace a worrying linear progression from the teacher quality rhetoric; to the enforcement of professional standards; to the prescription of what works; to professional development programs that show teachers *the* way; to 'fixed' teachers. The outcome of such a professionally disrespectful and disempowering approach could be described as *mindless compliance*. Sadly, some practices that have been mislabelled or misconceived as coaching can be found to share these same ends and may rightly be seen as manipulative devices.

The unintended and constraining consequences of 'Standards'

Narratives of progress and improvement place teachers on the frontline of efforts to transform the fortunes of young people. This 'responsibilisation' of teacher work gives the appearance of justifying the detailed mapping and scrutiny of our work, characterised by government intervention into teaching in the form of the Australian Professional Standards for Teachers. Clarke and Moore (2013) point out that the Standards are projected as "a public statement of what constitutes teacher quality. They define and make explicit the elements of high-quality, effective teaching in 21st century schools that will improve educational outcomes for students" (AITSL 2011). More recently, with the addition of 'illustrations of practice' (videos depicting teaching 'effectiveness'), further rhetorical packaging around the role and responsibility of teachers shapes dialogue and expectations around teaching in Australian schools. For example, it includes:

> As a teacher, it's your role to grow and develop the minds in your classroom. That's where the Australian Professional Standards for Teachers comes in. The Standards let you know what you should be aiming to achieve at every stage of your career. So you can improve your practice inside and outside of the classroom.
>
> (AITSL 2018)

Teachers are also reminded on the website of the need to work within the Standards and document their progress towards 'career stages' in order to accomplish a place within a publicly understood hierarchy of competency: "You'll need to evidence certain requirements of the Standards in order to become a registered teacher, or achieve Highly Accomplished and Lead certification."

The introduction of teacher certification in some Australian states and the need to achieve progressive graduation through the career stages appears to be a logical addition to bolster the quality narrative. However, as Mockler (2013, p. 37) cautions us and notes, she and Judyth Sachs

> have argued ... regulatory and measurement-oriented performance cultures, often operationalised in the application of professional teaching standards, have had a damaging effect on teacher autonomy and professional identity. In England, the United States and Australia, these standards have formed the basis for accreditation processes with the dual purposes of providing a level of 'quality assurance' and positioning teachers in some way alongside those 'real' professions such as medicine and law.

While the term 'quality' is contestable, what is not contestable is that in many cases this has translated into intensification of workload, heightened scrutiny and the circulation of abstracted notions of 'what works'. This rhetoric can have the added effect of reducing the thinking and work of teachers further still to an array of practices and methods that are drawn from specific research evidence and seeks to identify, compensate for, or extract variance of effect in an inherently imprecise and variable social setting such as a school or class. At a recent education conference in Denmark, Gert Biesta (2017) suggested that 'logic' of research is not the 'logic' of teaching. The aim of research is to *know*; the aim of teaching is to *educate*. He challenges us to reflect on where and how the 'logic' of research is replacing the 'logic' of teaching and what the cost of this is in terms of arriving at a resolution about how teachers can grow in professional knowledge and practice.

The challenge of how to lift the quality and performance of teachers' work has resulted in a raft of approaches ubiquitously labelled as 'professional development'. We have known for decades that the sustained influence of these formulaic and standardised teacher learning opportunities is questionable. As Fullan and Stiegelbauer (1991) point out: "Nothing has promised so much and has been so frustratingly wasteful as the thousands of workshops and conferences that led to no significant change in practice when teachers returned to their classrooms" (p. 315).

While the intentions of such approaches may be marketed as supportive and efficacious, more often than not the aim is corrective, interventionist or remedial. In contrast, the nuances of one's own practice, classroom circumstances and student diversity are challenging to adjust for in this sense and the fidelity to the original aims diminish with each and every application. Elmore (2016) highlights that in this age of hyper-accountability, schools can often become congeries of confusing administrative structures and strategies with competing priorities for improvement data "clotted with multiple levels of cross-functional relationships" (p. 530). These draw teachers' attention in multiple directions, elevate anxiety to perform and reduce agency.

The existence of professional standards is not the problem. Professional standards *can* be defended as a way of meeting external accountability requirements and instilling public confidence in the profession. At their most useful, standards statements can provide *one* point of reference for contextually based conversations about teaching practice. However, the ways in which these are wielded by government, utilised by regulatory bodies, and enacted by schools can all too easily result in processes of 'hoop-jumping' and 'box-ticking' and ultimately, the erosion of individual professional judgement.

The proposition: coaching that builds agency

Coaching in education is defined by van Nieuwerburgh (2012) as:

> a one-to-one conversation that focuses on the enhancement of learning and development through increasing self-awareness and a sense of personal responsibility, where the coach facilitates the self-directed learning of the coachee through questioning, active listening, and appropriate challenge in a supportive and encouraging climate (p. 17).

There are many definitions of coaching but this particular one is helpful in that it highlights the intent of coaching—self-directed learning and development— and two key outcomes of coaching—self-awareness and responsibility. This definition also raises the notion of 'supportive challenge' and alludes to the importance of the relationship. Philosophically, coaching should be based on "relationships rooted in mutual respect, where the participants are equals, and there is a genuine willingness to share practice. Trust and rapport can thus effect positive change for both the teacher, the pupils and the school as a whole" (Whiteside 2017, p. 5). Coaching emphasises the primacy of trust, but not the abandonment of responsibility. Done well, it promotes learning and reflection to support continual growth irrespective of what priority or initiative the focus of the dialogue, research and action is geared towards.

Research into coaching has for some time shown that it is effective in supporting teacher professional growth (Cornett and Knight 2009, Lofthouse 2016, van Nieuwerburgh 2012, van Nieuwerburgh and Barr 2017) and can bring about gains in student outcomes as a consequence of participants examining their practice, spending time in reflection, engaging with generative data and implementing adjustments to achieve negotiated goals (Kraft, Blazar and Hogan 2018, Kraft and Blazar 2017). Common across the research is the identification of core ingredients of any successful coaching approach; coaching is an organisational priority, coaching has public advocacy, there is a strategic allocation of resources (including time) to offer people equitable opportunities to engage with a trusted and experienced colleague, coaching is a dialogic and action-oriented partnership organised around goals, and there is the gradual creation of a non-judgmental and trust-fostering climate of work and learning. Here we witness the concept of agency being brought into the heart of coaching as a simultaneous phenomenon at play in transforming teaching.

If we are looking for a professionally empowering and contextually respectful approach to teacher growth, then coaching is a positive proposition. Being contextually respectful is about seeing each teacher as the expert in their own context—their classroom with their students. By encouraging and allowing teachers to do the thinking, coaching builds a strong sense of self-efficacy and enables *agency* (Munro 2017).

Here, agency is not something that people *possess* but something that they *achieve* (Priestley 2015). According the 'ecological' view posited by Biesta, Priestley and Robinson (2015), agency emerges dependent on the quality of the engagement of individuals with "temporal-relational contexts-for-action" (p. 23) rather than as a quality of the individuals themselves. Effective coaching can enable the achievement of agency for teachers by facilitating thoughtful and deliberate engagement with their own contexts-for-action.

Agency doesn't come from nowhere; it is something we volunteer; it builds on the past (experience and professional narrative) and is acted on in the present as we notice patterns of what is making a difference in both our practice and consequently student outcomes. This acknowledgement of personal narrative and practice iteration as a result of multiple influences on our beliefs, values and knowledge over time, conjoins coaching and agency and legitimises the self-directed learning of teachers.

Coaching, like agency, is ecologically sensitive in that as systemic or interpersonal circumstances change, the partnership can respond accordingly. The 'terrain' of coaching is akin to Biesta, Priestley and Robinson's (2015) model for understanding the achievement of agency. Their model outlines cultural, structural and material factors that influence agency, suggesting that agency is a configuration of influences from the past, orientations towards the future and engagement with the present. Each individual teacher's identity has been sculpted by their life and professional histories, 'iterated' as the ecology around them or across settings have changed. The knowledge and skills obtained in this professional history are of value if recognised, applied, built-upon and challenged. Through a coaching partnership, honouring these histories becomes a cornerstone for dialogue and a platform for trust. Teachers also experience different 'projections' of their efforts and work across the short and long terms. These projections see teachers encounter periods of high intensity (deadlines, testing, marking, assessment, day-to-day teaching) and more strategic and long-term work such as professional development, further study, project work or development planning.

Coaching works on notions of time in how it reacts to current situations but also plans forward through goal setting. Finally, teachers encounter multiple 'practical-evaluative' forces, which enhance or limit their thinking and work. They have to make sense of their identity within existing cultural norms and organisational values, the way school structures affect whether relationships can form and thrive or not, and how materials (space, resources and environment) can support work. By situating agency (and coaching) within the flow of time, the thinking and actions that are taken at any given time are dynamic. Coaching creates a safe space for self-reflection and examination of these factors in relation to our imperative for growth. Understanding how these factors impact our agency allows us to make sense of why on some occasions we have no agency but in others we do. Coaching seeks to create insight but insight alone will not necessarily lead to change. Change occurs through coaching when insight and action are brought together through the positive tension of accountability created when awareness is raised, possibilities are explored and next steps articulated.

The challenge: ecological growth against mechanistic improvement

Schools have to make decisions about how they wish to support their teachers to grow and develop and balance this against expectations and benchmarks that exist both internally and externally. En masse interventions such as whole-staff professional development might seem attractive in terms of cost-effectiveness and confidence of capturing all staff in the project of bringing about progress. However, for the reasons we have already cited, such approaches, on their own at least, do little to enable the achievement of teacher agency. Korthagen (2016) supports our assertions here, describing what he calls the 'inconvenient truths about teacher learning':

> Teaching is a profession in which feelings and motivation play an essential role, but until recently 'the more unpredictable passionate aspects of

learning, teaching and leading [...] are usually left out of the change picture' (Hargreaves, 1998, p. 558). Hence, if we wish to promote teacher learning, we will have to take their thinking, feeling and wanting into account. ... it is impossible to promote change through a pre-planned, fixed curriculum. In other words, we need a shift in focus from the curriculum to the learner.

(Korthagen 2016, p. 391)

Coaching as a proposition may at first appear costlier in terms of outright expense due to release time for coaches to coach, observations to occur, feedback to be conducted, shared reading to take place, analysis of data and the partnership to form, but the potential for sustained development and trust to flourish are high. As Bryk and Schneider (2002) attest, there are four key elements that help us discern the intentions of others in schools; respect, competence, integrity and personal regard for others. Coaching sets out to respect the dignity of others, seeks out and celebrates the ability of others to formally carry out their responsibilities, aligns actions with values to demonstrate integrity and extends care both in and beyond roles. In these ways we see coaching as a valuable means of supporting the achievement of agency as well as fostering trust.

Coaching may be seen by some as the artificial means of achieving agency and perhaps the enemy of authentic professional formation. However, if coaching can lay the groundwork to developing agency and the means for self-sustained growth, then it is something to strive for. In addition, if coaching can be utilised to link theories/concepts of professional growth to actualities, then it also allows us to describe the activity of the partnership, what artefacts of growth/progress are and the various forms of 'results' such as personal, professional, or student-centred. The deployment of professional standards and certification processes can fall short of documenting the development of agency and sustained growth beyond a moment-in-time classification. Further, they can fall victim to questions of validity of assessment within an abstracted notion of 'quality', one that cannot compensate entirely for contextual obstacles and challenges which influence the work of teachers in so many ways.

As Dutaut and Rycroft-Smith (2018) strongly argue, agency alone cannot be the ultimate goal for solitary educators, it should be a collective endeavour. This requires support, advocacy and activism by and on behalf of teachers by leaders one classroom at a time, school by school, system by system. The act of working closely alongside someone to support ongoing reflection and evaluation, goal creation, research and practice trialling, is a privilege. Like many other learning and development approaches which have far-reaching and deeply consequential orientations, we do need to be cautious that we don't replace one language and system of expectation, performance and workload with another, and we should be required to provide evidence of the transformative potential of coaching. This is still a relatively young field in terms of producing evidence, but the evidence of positive effect is emerging from large and small studies with both short and long-term implementations.

One challenge to the coaching community is how we prevent it becoming just as pernicious and pervasive as meta-analyses and toolkits, the work of psychometricians, platform capitalism and even debunked theories such as learning styles. Coaching is an intricate agency-building process that cuts to the heart of being a professional, feeling valued and heard, and worthy of trust and respect. It needs to be placed in responsible and capable hands, the same mantra we use to describe the responsibility teachers have for student learning and prospects. The role of coach comes with privilege and responsibility. The privilege lies in the deep connection, insight and reciprocal learning that comes from being invited into another's personal professional world, a world that in teaching often remains private. The responsibility is to be faithful to the underpinning principles of coaching and to maintain its integrity as an authentic agency-enabling process. There can be no more professionally respectful and empowering gift for a teacher than agency.

References

Australian Institute for Teaching and School Leadership (AITSL). *Understanding the Standards*. Available from: www.aitsl.edu.au/teach/understand-the-teacher-standards [Accessed 29 April 2018].

Australian Institute for Teaching and School Leadership (AITSL), 2011. *Australian professional standards for teachers*. Available from: www.aitsl.edu.au/docs/default-source/apst-resources/australian_professional_standard_for_teachers_final.pdf [Accessed 29 April 2018].

Ball, S.J., 2003. The teacher's soul and the terrors of performativity. *Journal of Education Policy*, 18 (2), 215–228.

Ball, S.J., 2015. Education, governance and the tyranny of numbers, *Journal of Education Policy*, 30 (3), 299–301, DOI: 10.1080/02680939.2015.1013271.

Biesta, G., 2017. Education is existential. Paper presented at *From pedagogy to empirical education research*, Vingsted Hotel and Konferencecenter, 22–23 March 2018 Bredsted, Denmark.

Biesta, G., Priestley, M., and Robinson, S., 2015. *Teacher agency: An ecological approach*. London: Bloomsbury Academic.

Bryk, A.S. and Schneider, B., 2002. *Trust in schools: A core resource for improvement*. New York: Russell Sage Foundation.

Clarke, M. and Moore, A., 2013. Professional standards, teacher identities and an ethics of singularity, *Cambridge Journal of Education*, 43 (4), 487–500, DOI: 10.1080/0305764X.2013.819070.

Cornett, J. and Knight, J., 2009. Research on coaching. In J. Knight, ed., *Coaching: approaches & perspectives*. Thousand Oaks, CA: Corwin Press, 192–216.

Dutaut, J.L. and Rycroft-Smith, L., 2018. From supply agency to demand agency: Taking back control. *In*: L. Rycroft-Smith and J.L. Dutaut, eds., *Flip the System UK: A teachers' manifesto*. London: Routledge, 1–5.

Elmore, R., 2016. "Getting to scale…" it seemed like a good idea at the time. *Journal of Educational Change*, 17, 529–537.

Fullan, M., and Stiegelbauer, S., 1991. *The new meaning of educational change*. New York: Teachers College Press.

Hargreaves, A., 1998. The emotions of teaching and educational change. *In*: A. Hargreaves, A. Lieberman, M. Fullan, and D. Hopkins, eds., *International handbook of educational change*. Dordrecht: Kluwer, 558–575.

Korthagen, F., 2016. Inconvenient truths about teacher learning: Towards professional development 3.0. *Teachers and Teaching*, 23 (4), 387–405, DOI: 10.1080/13540602.2016.1211523.

Kraft, M.A. and Blazar, D.L., 2017. Individualised coaching to improve teacher practice across grades and subjects: New experimental evidence. *Educational Policy* [online], 31 (7), 1033–1068.

Kraft, M.A., Blazar, D.L., and Hogan, D., 2018. The effect of teaching coaching on instruction and achievement: A meta-analysis of the causal evidence. *Review of Educational Research*. DOI: 10.3102/0034654318759268.

Lofthouse, R., 2016. Teacher coaching; A collection of think-pieces about professional development and leadership through teacher coaching. *Research Centre for Learning and Teaching*, Newcastle University.

Mockler, N., 2013. Teacher Professional Learning in a Neoliberal Age: Audit, Professionalism and Identity. *Australian Journal of Teacher Education*, 38 (10), 35-47.

Mockler, N., 2015. From surveillance to formation? A generative approach to teacher 'performance and development' in Australian schools. *Australian Journal of Teacher Education*, 40, 117–131

Munro, C., 2017. Context, context, context: Implementing coaching in schools. *Education Today*, Term 4—2017, 38–40.

Priestley, M., 2015. Teacher agency: What is it and why does it matter? *The BERA Blog Research Matters*. British Educational Research Association. Available from: www.bera.ac.uk/blog/teacher-agency-what-is-it-and-why-does-it-matter [Accessed 29 April 2018].

Tschannen-Moran, B. and Tschannen-Moran, M., 2010. *Evocative coaching: Transforming schools one conversation at a time*. San Francisco, CA: Jossey-Bass.

van Nieuwerburgh, C., 2012. Coaching in education: An overview. In C. van Nieuwerburgh, ed., *Coaching in education: Getting better results for students, educators, and parents*. London: Karnac, 3–23.

van Nieuwerburgh, C. and Barr, M., eds., 2017. *Resources for coaching in education: Useful research and references*. Sydney: Growth Coaching International.

Whiteside, R., 2017. Is coaching for transformation possible in a culture of performativity? *CollectivED* (1), 5–9. Carnegie School of Education, Leeds Beckett University. Available from: http://educationdocbox.com/Homework_and_Study_Tips/77182178-Collected-working-papers-from-collected-the-hub-for-mentoring-and-coaching-a-research-and-practice-centre-at-carnegie-school-of-education.html [Accessed 19 August 2018].

20 Changing the landscape through professional learning

Rachel Lofthouse

Keeping teachers busy and taking stock of CPD

Teachers are kept endlessly busy, not only in teaching classes, assessing work and reporting outcomes, but also in the time allocated to their own continual professional development (CPD). It seems that those who are positioned as educational experts and policymakers are tireless in their desire to come up with new ways to occupy teachers' professional development time. Teachers and school leaders are exposed to fads and fashions that are claimed to be the next best way that *they* will learn, almost as often as they are directed to new pedagogical and curriculum strategies that will supposedly transform their teaching and their students' learning. Waves of coaching, action research, online training, lesson study and the ubiquitous high profile conferences ebb and flow across the professional landscape. The things we are supposed to know about, or know how to implement come at us thick and fast. Our classrooms can become a whirl of constantly-tweaked activity.

Twitter can both accelerate this onslaught of CPD approaches and ideas and can also distract us by new shiny things, making us anxious if we are not actively teacher-researching, reflecting or testing out new social media or digital platforms to learn from. Who amongst us hasn't felt that moment of excitement when a new idea emerges and seems to gain traction amongst 'tweachers'? But, what if you get left behind on cognitive load theory, memorisation techniques as the new learning silver bullet in knowledge-rich curriculum, or seeing yourself (as every teacher surely should) as a leader. It doesn't take many years in the profession before teachers can become weary of this endless busy-ness and also to start to recognise that despite being kept busy, or being routinely exposed to new ideas, there is not always much to write home about in terms of changing teaching and learning practices, or indeed not always sufficient time and resource to translate ideas into adapted practice. We end up doing what we have no choice to ignore; following the latest expectation from senior leaders, who want to see us demonstrating it the next time they call into our classroom or implementing the latest version of the curriculum as driven by the latest top-down changes in assessment regimes. It may not all be bad, but it may feel like we are chasing too many tails.

In this chapter I want to take stock of CPD, and to propose a way of making sure that our exposure to it can go beyond the episodic and do more than top up the teacher, clock up the hours or tick some-one else's boxes. Although I am no longer a 'teacher', having moved in to teacher education and research in the UK 20 years ago, I will use 'we' and 'our' frequently to describe and discuss the experiences of teachers. I do this out of solidarity; not a romantic yearning to be seen as an insider, but with a sense of teaching as an extended profession, one in which the interdependence between practising teachers, school leaders, educational policymakers and the associated academic community should not be overlooked, and indeed should be seen as the collective capital from which we all improve. I argue that as professionals we need to design CPD that can be engaged with differently so that it is a critical means through which we can 'flip the system'. As Rycroft-Smith and Dutaut (2018) argue, teachers' cognitive agency can only be achieved if teachers are "empowered to develop their professional knowledge, continuously and according to their own priorities, in collaboration with their colleagues" (p. 4).

To explore my proposition that we need 'less busy' and 'more sustained and embedded' CPD I will share a *practice development led model for individual professional learning and institutional growth*, developed through my recent research (Lofthouse 2015), and use this model to explore the opportunities to create a successful and sustainable professional learning ecology from which both teachers and their school communities benefit. I will write from an English perspective because this is my territory, but I am aware that many of the themes that emerge will have an international relevance. This was demonstrated during my work with teachers and school leaders in Australia in 2017. Leading CPD sessions on coaching during both a conference and in schools in Sydney reinforced that, despite each school and its community being a unique place, we face universal professional challenges and opportunities, as evidenced by Kriedemann and Paterson (2018).

Performativity, practice and professionalism

I am conscious of the conditions within which teachers work, and that phrases such as 'making more than expected progress', 'closing the gap', and 'good to outstanding' abound. Schools in England are structured but frenetically busy places; teachers and school leaders undertake specific roles, they are heavily line managed and much of their work is represented as data that can be tracked and monitored. Inevitably, this has implications at both institutional and individual levels. Nearly two decades ago Hargreaves (2000) suggested that teachers' work and recognition had become itemised and categorised into 'checklists of performance standards or competencies' (Hargreaves 2000, p. 152). Ball (2003, 2013) termed this *performativity*. Pupil progress data is generated as a result of assessment. Teachers are held to account for the outcomes, being judged, observed and performance managed by school leaders and by the inspectorate. As a teacher educator I am exposing my student teachers to a process that mirrors their future work. Put at its most crude, the role of teacher educator is to be trainer and assessor within a culture of performativity. What is deemed essential is that we create and then manage a system through which new teachers are provided with the requisite knowledge and skills to teach at a level judged at least 'good'. School teachers and teacher educators alike create spreadsheets, crunch data and place value on being able to demonstrate the right numbers at the right time. Given this culture of target-setting and performance monitoring, it is inevitable that teachers' professional learning (both at career entry and career development stages) is affected. My research has demonstrated that both coaching and mentoring, for example, are workplace learning processes that can get entangled in workplace cultures making them liable to be squeezed under time pressures and potentially distorted by the performativity agenda (Lofthouse and Leat 2013, Lofthouse and Thomas 2014). In researching mentoring of student teachers in primary settings, Wilson (2014) found similar contradictions created when educational activity systems are not well aligned.

One way that I have made sense of this is to consider what is meant by educational practice and practitioners, because I have a hunch that performativity tends to privilege procedures rather than practice. I am defining each as follows:

> Procedures are mechanisms that help individuals or organisations to undertake their work or function; procedures are relatively readily managed, can be monitored and are definable components of a larger system. Procedures can be accomplished by people, and some by conventional and digital technology. Procedures can be replaced, over-hauled or fine-tuned when their part in the system is deemed to be inefficient, or leading to divergence.
>
> Practices are actions that sustain human activities. I take a socio-cultural historical view of practice; that practice is conducted by individuals and groups as a response to evolving contexts and situations. Practices (noun) are influenced by an individual's beliefs, decisions, experience and expertise. They are actions embodying language, relationships and physicality. They can stagnate, but they can also be altered through practising (verb), allowing them to be understood and refined with intent.

However, it is not as simple as that. Procedure and practice intertwine; one is not always good and the other bad; they occur concurrently and are interdependent. My concern is that performativity results in procedure-heavy routines, which tend to lead to be either cautious (safe) or new imported practice. The latter represents an attempt to kick-start or interrupt systems by implementing new interventions often parachuted in to existing cultures from where it is deemed to be 'what works'. My experience and research suggests that performativity typically leads practitioners to demonstrate outcomes based on criteria for success created by 'others', and for this it depends heavily on procedures managed by, and for, the system. Performativity does rely on teachers becoming self-evaluative and self-regulating (even imposing what Ball regards as *self-surveillance*), but the evaluations are essentially accountability-based judgments of the extent to which the externally imposed expectations have been met.

There is a link here to concepts of professionalism; Sachs (2001), for example, contrasts managerial professionalism with democratic professionalism. The former prioritises accountability and thus encourages efficiency and compliance, while the latter promotes teachers as agents of change. Performative cultures open up limited spaces for democratic professionalism, instead heightening the role of managers to direct and validate the work of those they manage, leaving less room for professional discretion and perhaps creating an argument for training rather than learning. Managerial professionalism relies on routines and procedures. Democratic professionalism creates opportunities for more nuanced development of practices, and as such intersects with the values we hold as educators. As I turn my attention to CPD and professional learning it is with an ambition that it takes the form of, and contributes to, democratic professionalism.

CPD as professional intent

No school deploys CPD without intent, but understanding the potential of CPD and designing it purposefully is not straightforward. This is well illustrated through a case study of a designated Teaching School based at East SILC John Jamieson School & Technology College, Leeds, England. The Teaching School has responsibility for developing and securing CPD provision for both the staff within their own alliance and more widely in the local area. As the Teaching School is based in a generic, all age Special School, which caters for pupils with a learning difficulty, the majority of their CPD provision is targeted for teachers to learn how to improve their practices to enhance learning and wellbeing for children with Special Educational Needs and/or Disability (SEND). The CPD itself follows a very recognisable format. The session leaders have expertise to share; they have been given additional facilitation training to enhance their abilities to teach adults and to design and run sessions that are engaging and valued. The CPD is programmed as twilight sessions and the school staff are expected to sign up for six sessions during the year. Some SEND coordinators from other schools also attend courses that interest them. Typically, there are 12–15 professionals in each training session. Some courses, for example in Makaton (a language programme using signs and symbols to help people to communicate), require multiple sessions to complete and others are delivered as stand-alone training events. Some courses introduce new approaches (such as Lego Therapy) and others ensure that knowledge supporting quality teaching for all children is constantly being shared and updated (such as those which focus on speech and language development).

Recently, I worked with Jan Linsley, an experienced consultant who plays a lead role in developing the teacher training work of the Teaching School, to support a practice-based research project to review the impact of this specific CPD provision (Linsley 2018). The research was based on gathering the views of the teachers in relation to value of the CPD through focus groups, questionnaires and interviews, with an aim of gathering evidence on the impact of the CPD on teachers' confidence, knowledge and skills, with a particular concern that they developed a wider repertoire of appropriate classroom approaches. There was also a desire to look at the consequent impact on the children, and at this stage of the work this is being achieved through teachers reporting on the impact they can perceive.

Using Kennedy's (2014) model of the CPD Spectrum the CPD approach designed by the Teaching School would be perhaps best defined as a transmissive training model, although this is not to imply that the sessions are purely transmission based, and indeed the feedback from the participants suggests that the facilitation training has ensured that where possible they take the form of a blend of 'show and tell' and participatory activities. As indicated above, there is an imperative on the senior leaders of the Teaching School to construct an appropriate CPD provision as it is one of the Key Performance Indicators of their designation, and as such the programme can be seen through the 'managerial perspective on professionalism' in terms of its design. There is a focus on learning, in that participants are expected to develop 'technical, role-focused knowledge and skills' (Kennedy 2014, p. 695) and to some extent this is based on concerns about individual's capacities to meet the needs of a diverse SEND cohort, and to ensure that the school can demonstrate to parents and the inspectorate that it meets the expected standard of performance. This is not a cynical intent, it holds the particular needs of the children at the centre, but there is a degree to which demonstrating CPD provision and the appropriate participation of staff is a managerial goal.

The research evidence shows very little criticism by CPD participants of the content provision, indeed in the questionnaires the most significant reasons that teachers gave for choosing specific sessions was 'career development' and 'personal interest', followed with mid-level significance the 'CPD entitlement' and 'performance management'. The format had largely been well-received with comments such as "Really enjoy the intensive interacting meetings that take place on site" being offered, although a number of participants did ask for less use of after school sessions, and others offered suggestions including other content areas that would be helpful, and other formats (such as TeachMeets). Two-thirds of the respondents strongly agreed that the sessions they had attended had 'enhanced their knowledge and understanding of the topics', with almost all the remaining agreeing with this. Their comments included:

> I can deliver some Attention Autism sessions in my sensory classes with a better knowledge and understanding of student needs.
>
> Lego Therapy and Attention Autism—I had no idea what was included or how carried out, but now I would be able to set up and lead sessions independently.

> Using visual supports has helped coming from a mainstream background. Intensive Interaction—now try to incorporate this into all aspects of my involvement with the pupils I work with.

So, there is evidence that the managerial imperative has been met, and also that the outcomes can be seen as 'developmental (enhancing specific strengths and interests)' (Kennedy 2014, p. 695), and might thus be considered to be contributing to what Kennedy refers to as the 'democratic perspective on professionalism'. One of the most interesting questionnaire responses hinted at what else might be possible, with one teacher asking for "The ability to request a topic of training before [the programme] is finalised. Being able to use/ observe expertise already within school. More training that leads to accreditation". This indicates a potential shift further towards CPD as a form of democratic professionalism, and a perceived gap in the current provision. The two focus groups offered more insight, when participants were asked to use a diamond nine ranking exercise to indicate what features of CPD they believed would make it most effective. Their responses were very similar and indicated that 'sustained collaboration with professional colleagues', 'structured support for embedded learning' and 'focusing on refining teaching and learning' were considered most valuable. It could be suggested that the CPD programme had achieved this, bringing colleagues together to focus on specific teaching and learning techniques, but perhaps opportunities to embed and sustain this are being missed. Some of the interviewees indicated that this might be the case. There seemed to be an appreciation of the occasional informal opportunities to follow up training with a colleague, when a specific relevant situation arose, but this was serendipitous rather than by design. Indeed, one interviewee reflected that they would like: "More team building types of CPD, helping us to understand each other—getting help from other teachers learning from each other in a focus group setting. We have to work very closely together sometimes so that really helps." These could be seen as a yearning for further features of democratic professionalism, with greater sense of the 'collective' over the individual, and of the recognition that teacher learning might be based on 'social constructivism' (Kennedy ibid.), for example.

Changing the landscape: re-thinking professional learning

The experiences of teachers in the Teaching School above are not unique, indeed they are quite common. They are also not wholly problematic, with appropriate content being delivered close to practice, which is deemed to meet the needs of staff who are able to identify tangible positive outcomes for children and learning. What's not to like? Well I guess that's the wrong question in my mind. With a crisis in teacher recruitment, retention, workload and stress in England, I also have to ask whether CPD might be able to change the fortunes of the profession. Time and money is invested in it, even during periods of austerity, and even if it is the best possible training, if a growing

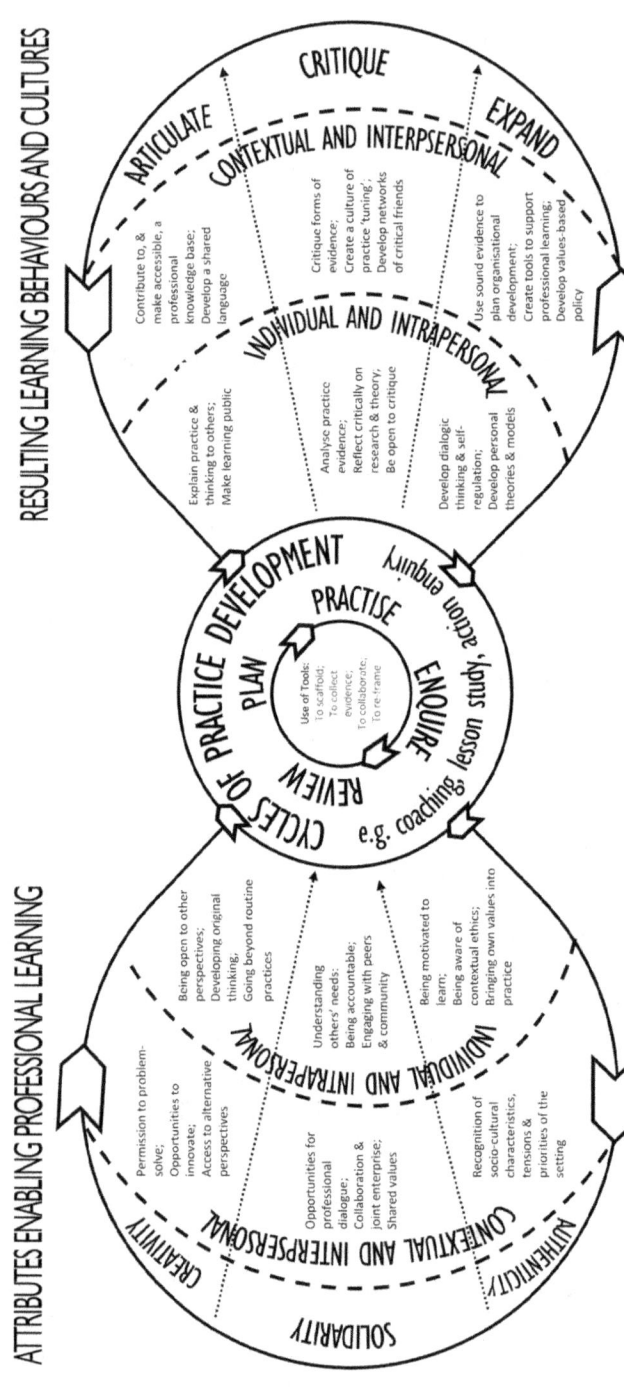

Figure 20.1 Metamorphosis: a practice development led model for individual professional learning and institutional growth

The professional learning ecology shown in the model is complex and interrelated. Both cultural conditions and personal attributes can enable professional learning as well and the outcomes can be at individual and institutional levels. Through the cycles of practice development there can be cumulative effects and renewed opportunities for professional learning. Physical, analytical or conceptual tools (e.g. video, coaching dimensions) can be used to trigger and refine the development of professional practices. The model proposes that focusing on developing educational practices should be cental to both professional and institutional development. (Lofthouse, 2015) proportion of teachers leave the profession each year it starts to look like a lot of the potential benefit to children gained through CPD might have a short life span.

My research, related to both initial and continuing teacher education has led me to develop a model, called 'Metamorphosis: a practice development led model for individual professional learning and institutional growth' to help me to articulate features of CPD that I see as particularly important. The title itself is significant. There is clear reference to three features; first, that it is possible that at least some CPD occurs in a way that deliberately builds in real-time opportunities to develop practice; secondly that the capacity for the development of individual's practice is enhanced through professional learning; and finally that there should be reciprocal relationship between the how the institution (in our case the school, as well as the profession) adapts and improves over time and how the individuals within it adapt too. It is worth reiterating here my distinction between educational practices and procedures. While I acknowledge that we may need to be trained to undertake certain appropriate procedures as teachers, it is values-based practice, enacted through considered and respectful relationships, creating deliberate and nuanced educational actions that I am concerned with.

The model is shaped like a butterfly; with two wings articulating organisational and individual attributes that support professional learning on one side, and the learning and cultural behaviours that might result on the other. Linking these wings is a representation of practice development based on cyclical actions. These actions include CPD approaches that can be adopted at any level that includes two or more professionals, but may be school-wide. They include strategies such as lesson study, coaching or collaborative action research. The problem with any of these is that they can be just imposed activities that involve teachers and keep them busy. They can be subject to fads; if it was coaching last year, it must be action research hubs this year. They can be conducted in a superficial fashion, lacking vim and vigour, as well as efficacy and rigour. They can be badly managed, low quality and undertaken to tick a box on a school improvement plan, or as a crude response to performance management. Or they can be transformative. The model, its subsections, arrows and text imply indicate how this might occur. At its heart is the claim that both the vehicle and objective for professional learning can be practice development; a deliberate focus on the details, characteristics and outcomes of practice through engagement in cycles of action, preferably in some form of collaboration with others. The informed use of appropriate tools is also part of the cycle of development. Video-recording of teaching (for example) may be in vogue, but it is important to question why and how we use it, and what function of professional learning it elicits.

The next proposition on the model is that to enable desirable professional learning outcomes key social-cultural characteristics need to be in place, which complement the personal capacities and motivations of the professional in the workplace. In other words, the people matter; who they are, what they know and value, and how their working and social relationships are facilitated to support them to develop. I also suggest that as individuals learn there is potential for institutional growth, that this is not automatic, but results from a conscious integration of the individual's growth with the organisation's supporting infrastructure. Too often a teacher's learning leaves them isolated or out of step with their school; rather than forming the basis of collegial curiosity, discussion and adaptation. To counter this, I suggest that professional learning through and for practice development has a basis in articulated values and critical enquiry; and allows professionals to relate their practice to their values rather than expect them to uncritically adopt new workplace procedures. This ecology recognises the significance of authenticity, creativity and solidarity as cultural conditions and personal attributes that enable professional learning; and of articulation, critique and expansion as the outcomes of that learning at individual and institutional levels, all of which are unpacked in the model. As such professional learning for practice development is compatible with the concept of democratic professionalism in that it supports teachers in developing agency, and goes beyond compliance expected through managerial professionalism. It is worth noting the flow implied by the model suggesting that professional learning, from foundations to outcomes is reciprocal and cumulative, in that as professional learning is generated and the conditions supporting it are enhanced more professional learning can be sustained for wider and deeper impact on practice.

Thus to change the landscape of professional learning we might orientate ourselves towards practice as both the basis *for* and focus *of* individual and institutional professional learning and growth. Lampert (2010) outlines four typical conceptions of practice, all connected by its focus on what people 'do'. She outlines how it is contrasted with theory, how it is used to describe a collection of habitual or routine actions, how as a verb it describes the discipline of working on something to improve future performance, and how in global terms it is used as a short-hand to indicate the way that professionals conduct themselves in their role. In teaching, too often practice is either dismissed as just a matter of a simple application of learned skills, or is set in primacy above theory and research, as the only genuine concern of practitioners. The professional practice of educators is neither of these things, but nor is it automatically as nuanced and sophisticated as the complexity of the contexts and needs of learners demands it to be.

References

Ball, S.J., 2003. The teacher's soul and the terrors of performativity, *Journal of Education Policy*, 18 (2), 215–228.

Ball, S.J., 2013. *The education debate*. Bristol: Policy Press.

Hargreaves, A., 2000. Four ages of professionalism and professional learning. *Teachers and Teaching: History and Practice*, 6 (2), 151–182.

Kennedy, A., 2014. Understanding continuing professional development: The need for theory to impact on policy and practice. *Professional Development in Education*, 40 (5), 688–697.

Kriedemann, B. and Paterson, C., 2018. Coaching: An emerging school culture. *CollectivED* [online], 3, 5–9. Available from: http://leedsbeckett.ac.uk/-/media/files/research/collectived-apr-2018–issue-31.pdf?la=en.

Lampert, M., 2010. Learning teaching in, from, and for practice: What do we mean? *Journal of Teacher Education*, 61 (1–2), 21–34.

Linsley, J., 2018. Developing enhanced specialist CPD as a teaching school, *Carey Philpott Research Partnership Research Reports* [online], 1, 6–17. Available from: www.leedsbeckett.ac.uk/-/media/files/research/cp-working-papers-issue-1–march-2018.pdf?la=en.

Lofthouse, R., 2015. *Metamorphosis, model-making & meaning; developing exemplary knowledge for teacher education*. PhD thesis, University of Newcastle. Available from: https://theses.ncl.ac.uk/dspace/handle/10443/2822.

Lofthouse, R. and Leat, D., 2013. An activity theory perspective on peer coaching. *International Journal of Mentoring and Coaching in Education*, 2 (1), 8–20.

Lofthouse, R. and Thomas, U., 2014. Mentoring student teachers; a vulnerable workplace learning practice, *International Journal of Mentoring and Coaching in Education* 3 (3), 201–218.

Rycroft-Smith, L. and Dutaut, J.L., 2018. *Flip the System UK: A teachers' manifesto*. Abingon: Routledge.

Sachs, J., 2001. Teacher professional identity: Competing discourses, competing outcomes. *Journal of Education Policy*, 16 (2), 149–161.

Wilson, V., 2014. Examining teacher education through cultural-historical activity theory *Tean Journal*, 6 (1), 20–29.

21 From silo to Study Group
Subverting teacher learning

Ryan Gill and Carla Gagliano

This vignette outlines one school's approach to flipping professional learning from that which was silo and passive to that which is inclusive and personalised. Subverting professional learning here does not mean simply doing things differently, but reconsidering who has power and control over what and how teachers learn. In this picture of practice, we share our insights into the journey of our teachers over the last decade, where an action research stance has been adopted and placed at the heart of our professional learning culture. We present a case study of Masada College, a co-educational, independent Jewish school on Sydney's North Shore at which we are the co-Heads of Teaching and Learning.

Over the last decade, the Executive team at Masada College have worked to cultivate and promote rich cultures of thinking (Ritchhart 2015) and make thinking visible (Ritchhart, Church, and Morrison 2011), guided by Project Zero researchers from the Harvard University Graduate School of Education, notably Mark Church and Ron Ritchhart. Soon after exploring practices to build a culture of thinking, such as using thinking routines, it was realised that it was not enough to achieve the school-wide cultural change that was desired. Professional learning prior to this time was very much done *to* our colleagues. They were passive receivers of practice, some of which landed in their classroom toolbox. But essentially, they deferred to departmental talk which concerned the logistics and management within the day-to-day busyness of the school. We had allowed entrenched and comfortable silos to operate alongside one another, with little or no interaction between teachers in adjacent silos. It made us wonder: What else might we do to create an atmosphere that was hospitable to good thinking and learning—not just for our students, but for our teachers too? How might we create opportunities for rich, valued and meaningful conversations to move our culture of thinking to the next stage? What if the focus of our professional learning was devolved to our educators themselves?

Study groups

For several years, we had been experimenting with professional learning groups, where conversations could be anchored by examples of student learning to enhance teacher practice and unpack the type of thinking present. Inspired by the work of David Allen and Tina Blythe (Allen and Blythe 2004), we aimed to create an environment for our teachers to converse, which valued a culture of thinking, unlike conversations they may have in other environments. "At the heart of most teacher collaboration is a conversation, or better, an ongoing series of conversations. Of course, conversations among teachers are not unusual. Think of a faculty or staff meeting. But the conversations we focus on are different. Unlike either informal faculty conversations that tend to move naturally and quickly from topic to topic ... or that serve mainly to transmit information, the conversations are opportunities for colleagues to reflect together on key questions about their practice and their students' learning" (Allen and Blythe 2004).

Generating and refining a puzzle of practice

Beginning with a volunteer group of teachers, our aim was to establish a supportive, safe and thought-provoking space where we could commune around a puzzle of practice (an action research question) that had been personally generated by our teachers themselves. There were four simple criteria: the puzzles are personally important to them, they are relevant to other educators, they are related to student learning and they seem about the right size. For some, this was the most challenging stage of the process. There were so many puzzles generated when in an initial brainstorm mode. As we sorted them, however, using the Visible Thinking routine 'Questions Sorts' (Ritchhart, Church, and Morrison 2011), it was apparent that some puzzles were too specific, required large-scale institutional change or would not be relevant when sharing and discussing with other educators beyond the particular class or year level. So, they were discarded in the initial phase. Some others evolved, some remained but essentially what came out of the process was inspiring. Our teachers began to consider how they could foster a greater culture of curiosity in their learners, develop critical friends and questioners, nurture a growth mindset for our kindergarteners or to create opportunities for independent learning for our Higher School Certificate students. In doing so, our teachers began to shift their understanding of what nurturing a culture of thinking might be.

Establishing our Study Groups and facilitating the learning

Generating and refining the puzzle was just the beginning. What was needed was ongoing and generative discussion of ways forward with their inquiry questions, with something real on the table to anchor the conversation. We had the substance, we just needed the form: a Study Group. In Study Groups, facilitators assist participants to brainstorm through dilemmas, tune 'plans in the making' and reflect on classroom practice (in the form of student work samples) to help them develop their understanding and next steps towards their inquiry question, using corresponding protocols for these purposes such as the Descriptive Consultancy, Tuning and Looking at Students' Thinking (LAST) to guide the conversation (McDonald, Mohr, Dichter, and McDonald 2013, Allen and Blythe 2004, School Reform Initiative 2018a). Regardless of what was on the table—even when a Kindy teacher was sharing their classroom experiences with a group of Year 9 teachers, there were opportunities to learn, reflect and apply to their own context and inquiry. Whilst Study Groups involved a single teacher's puzzle of practice being explored, it provided a reflective moment for all participants, keeping the business of teaching and learning firmly on the table. It was a real and substantive conversation in a non-confrontational, non-judgmental space. Whilst some were familiar with sharing student learning and work samples with colleagues, sharing a dilemma was a welcomed move we made. It removed the sense that we always share the polished piece with colleagues. In Study Groups, problems were just as welcomed as solutions. Coaching a group of facilitators to guide our Study Groups was the next and simultaneous step and acted to distribute the leadership from the Executive team to those passionate educators amongst the school who could shepherd a small group of fellow educators.

As a result of this flipping of power and control within the school, there were some very real moments of concern for colleagues that arose in our early Study Group conversations. Are we *really* going to be able to change this? What can I do when I'm *just* a Year 9 English teacher? What if parents don't agree with what we're doing? How can I do this when I'm trying to get through the fully packed syllabus? Whilst pertinent, we were careful that these concerns did not leave our colleagues feeling paralysed. By engaging in a Realm of Concern/Realm of Influence protocol (School Reform Initiative 2018b), colleagues became more empowered when they laid out all of their roadblocks and identified which of the concerns were actually in their realm of influence and in doing so they began seeing breakthroughs and actions forward.

Celebration and reflection

With a palpable engagement and connection to their professional learning throughout the year, it was inevitable that a celebration was in sight. Our final gathering for the year was a reflection and celebration of learning session, a culmination of our insights and new questions that had been generated as a result of the areas of inquiry. Colleagues shared artefacts of students' thinking, quotations from students and teacher colleagues and anything else they felt was worthy of sharing with others. There was no glitter, lamination or formal presentations. Rather an honest, genuine representation of learning as everyone participated in a gallery walk and conversation of what was on display.

An evolving process

Fast-forward several years and as we tweak and evolve the process, the puzzle of practice remains at the heart of our professional learning, with an ongoing opportunity to share and commune with others. Our teachers observe their peers in action in their classrooms—stopping by for an unannounced visit in relation to the observed teacher's puzzle of practice. In this way they work in service of the teacher they observe—noticing and describing what they see, with no evaluation of the practice. Once collated, this can be shared and discussions can commence as to how we might bump up that practice. In this sense, we provide further opportunities to model practice and importantly, anchor the conversation in evidence which has been collated by peers and discussed with peers.

Deepening and enriching our culture of thinking

Deepening an understanding of what it was to *become* a culture of thinking rather than to *do* a culture of thinking was at the heart of our goal for initiating this practice (Ritchhart 2015). Masada College has been able to build a culture of teacher thinking, reflecting, planning, and collaborating. Colleagues began to see beyond thinking routines, beyond considering a faithfully enacted set of practices to an opportunity for refinement of our teaching as we strove to make thinking valued, visible and actively promoted in our classrooms. This shifted the goal posts, even the ballpark for some. By looking at a broader range of interactive cultural forces, such as language, time and expectations, whilst simultaneously deepening their understanding of how routines could be used to support these endeavours. When our colleagues were able to see that they were in control of their own professional learning, we moved from a top-down approach to something that was fundamentally different. We flipped the locus of control into the hands of those that needed it most—those that knew their students and classroom context best: the passionate educators within our school.

References

Allen, D. and Blythe, T., 2004. *The facilitators book of questions: Tools for looking together at student and teacher work*, New York: Teachers College Press.
McDonald, J.P., Mohr, N., Dichter, A., and McDonald, E.C., 2013. *The power of protocols: An educator's guide to better practice*. New York: Teachers College Press.
Ritchhart, R., Church, M., and Morrison, K., 2011. *Making thinking visible: How to promote engagement, understanding, and independence for all learners*. San Francisco, CA: Jossey-Bass.
Ritchhart, R., 2015. *Creating cultures of thinking: The 8 forces we must master to truly transform our schools*, San Francisco, CA: Jossey-Bass.
School Reform Initiative. 2018a. *Protocols—School reform initiative*. [online] Available from: www.schoolreforminitiative.org/protocols/ [Accessed 27 April 2018].
School Reform Initiative. 2018b. *Realms of concern and influence—School reform initiative*. [online] Available at: www.schoolreforminitiative.org/download/realms-of-concern-and-influence/ [Accessed 27 April 2018].

Part V

Leadership for a flipped system

This final section addresses the complex notion of education leadership in a swiftly changing world. As trust in enduring institutions fades, educational leaders require the ability to see the world through multiple lenses and in different contexts. Key concepts in this section include: empowering other educators, placing the agenda-setting in the hands of educators, and the importance of listening to and sharing the voices of students. A key notion is the adoption of a more distributed notion of leadership in order to address the intricate web of influences that schools and leaders face in the twenty-first century.

Scott Eacott argues that for too long educators have allowed others to set the agenda. His response to the one-size-fits-all approach is a three-point strategy of clarity, coherence, and narrative. His aim is to empower educators to build a version of education that acts in the best interests of students.

School principal **Rebecca Cody** asks educators to abandon binary thinking as she challenges school leaders and systems to ride two wild education 'horses' at the same time. She points out that academic success measures such as NAPLAN and tertiary entrance requirements are complex but essential, and that these are not oppositional to the aims of holistic education.

Paul Browning shows how, over the past two decades, Australia's concept of respect has been eroded. Paul draws a direct correlation between the decline of trust in western society and a decline in educational standards, showing a clear link between trust and student outcomes. He presents ten leadership practices to engender and grow trust.

Susan Bradbeer examines the rich stories of women in educational leadership in rural schools, showing how they do leadership differently, and challenge current models of leadership and professional learning. She contends that the 'what works' strategies on offer do not adequately prepare and train leaders for the complexities of different contexts.

Primary school principal **Ray Trotter** describes his school's determination to reject prevailing educational thinking and undergo a paradigm shift focusing on best and next practice pedagogy. He argues for the importance of listening to and sharing the voices of students.

Project Zero practitioners **Flossie S. G. Chua, David N. Perkins**, and **Daniel G. Wilson** demonstrate what becomes possible when school leaders invite teachers into the discourse on what matters most to learn and values them as drivers of change. This concluding chapter offers a window into what learning that matters looks like and presents leadership for the twenty-first century as a complex ecology of influences that requires leaders to adopt a more distributed notion of leadership.

22 Empowering educators through flipped school leadership?

Scott Eacott

Educating is political. Decisions regarding what is taught, how it is taught, and how students are assessed reflect a version of what makes an effective school. In the case of contemporary Australia, in the absence of any broader definition of education quality, apparently objective measures such as National Assessment Program—Literacy And Numeracy (NAPLAN) and Higher School Certificate (HSC) outcomes are used as proxies for quality. Well-rehearsed arguments, however, stress that what can be counted and compared is not the whole story of schooling. However, while what is judged as an effective education is contested by many in society, do we as educators actively engage in this contestation? This is not just an education issue, but a broader Australian cultural matter. As commentator Marr (2007) observes, "[w]e aren't the larrikins of our imagination. Australians are an orderly people who love authority. We grumble instead of challenging it" (p. 26). Smyth (2008) builds on Marr's work, to argue that at the heart of democracy is a contest of conversation and the nature of contemporary dialogue and debate has had a profound effect on schooling leading to the "bastard educational leadership" Australia had to have. Originally coined by Wright (2001), bastard leadership refers to "leadership which is animated by the changing policy concerns on government, and the vicissitudes of the educational marketplace, rather than any commitment to substantive and situated values or principles" (p. 275).

In the spirit of flipping the system, in this chapter I work through a *relational* approach (Eacott 2018) I have been developing to propose a flipped approached to school leadership. Significantly, what I am arguing for is an approach where educators set the agenda for discussions about schooling and in doing so establish the criteria by which they will be held accountable. The *relational* approach facilitates this argument by offering a methodology built on recognising our own complicity with the status quo, problematising language, contextualising, going beyond binaries, and productively contributing. While I have written about this in greater theoretical depth elsewhere (e.g. Eacott 2018), this chapter is deliberately applied and seeks to demonstrate how the *relational* approach can productively contribute to schooling, and specifically, flipping the system. In speaking directly to the reader, my argument in this chapter is built on three consistent messages: i) effectiveness begins with clarity of purpose; ii) you are judged on your level of coherence against that purpose; and iii) you construct the narrative for your school. The result is a call for school leadership based on a broad principle that recognises there is no one size fits all approach to education, an embracing of professionalism in the justification of practices, and flipping the criteria for effectiveness to educators and not those outside of schools. Working with the key *relational* concepts of *organising activity, auctor* and *spatio-temporal conditions* (explained as they are introduced), this argument is about empowering educators to build a vision for educating and enacting that vision in the interests of students.

Articulating with clarity

What do we mean when we say "effective school", "successful school", "improving school", or "turnaround school"? And what does this mean for school leaders and teachers? All of these labels are value laden. Our usage of them reflects what we see as the purpose of schooling. That is, for the most part, what we see as most important in educating is what guides our judgement on effectiveness. Many factors come into play in making these judgement including the thoughts and opinions of those around us (e.g., family, friends, workmates, and neighbours) and broader discourses (e.g., employers, universities, and the media). In short, rather than purely independent, our judgements are relational. Importantly, this means that often without realising it, we are complicit with advancing the status quo. Rarely do we call into question the generally accepted norms of what is considered effective. What we start to recognise as effective or improving are those schools and educators who play the game well. As Thomson (2010) argues in relation to headteachers in England (or principals in Australia), in focusing on playing the game better, the rules of the game or its formula for success are usually left unchallenged.

To provide some clarity, what do I mean when I say effective schools—if I ever use such a label—or seek to pass judgement on some form of educating? This is a matter that I have written about previously (Eacott 2011) and spend a lot of time thinking about courtesy of having taught a course entitled "effective schools" for the last three years. Following Oakeshott (1967) via Bates (2006), I believe that to be educated is to "join the conversation of the world" (Eacott 2011, p. 43). Therefore, an effective education is one that introduces and/or continues students' engagement with the conversation of the world—something that is beyond what they would get without an education. This is not simply about setting up a low benchmark based on the simple measure that an effective school is anything better than no school. Rather, it is a broad principle to which I subscribe. Where to be educated is to be aware of broader conversations, limitations of what we know, and the pursuit of understanding. This is my normative position on schooling and the basis from which I pass judgement and advocate.

In taking such a position, I am not denying the significance and relevance of contemporary measures such as NAPLAN, HSC outcomes, and the like, but rather than privilege them I see these as by-products of schooling and not the sole purpose. I am not naïve to the power-laden discourses that shape the content of NAPLAN, the HSC, and so on, and their role in how schooling and individual schools are perceived in contemporary Australia. While there is some argument as to the high-stakes of NAPLAN and HSC, we do not as yet have a system of special measures and failing schools such as in England, but this is not to say that poor student outcomes in these tests does not have an impact on schools (e.g., enrolment, recruitment of quality staff) and the careers of individual educators (e.g., principals, deputy/assistant principals). However, the logic of my argument is that if you take care of educating, in the sense of joining the conversation of the world, performance in standardised tests/assessments will be catered for and advanced. The reverse, focusing primarily on performance in standardised tests, I believe, does not guarantee an education.

This is not to reduce discussions of schools and schooling to effective/ineffective. Such binary thinking is unhelpful as it relies on a universal, stable, and external measure of effectiveness. Instead, what I want to call for is a focus on *organising activity*. Not any one school, classroom, system, but a broader view of educating and how we generate knowledge through the organising of activity. A more holistic approach to thinking about educating that goes beyond any one school or educator and looks at how we come to organise ourselves relationally. This is neither universal nor particular. It does not buy into the "a school is a school" irrespective of location argument or the "every school is unique" claim. Importantly, to go beyond binary thinking is to remove the much used arguments of structure and agency in school leadership. If schools are not entirely bound by structural determinants (e.g., the system, systemic policies) but also lack absolute agency (e.g., the freedom to do whatever they want), then this requires a way of thinking about education that orthodox approaches cannot meet. Herein lays the value of *auctor*—meaning s/he who generates—and how we as educators are not passive recipients of external demands and simultaneously not agentic and capable of overcoming all obstacles if we just try hard enough/do the right things. Rather through our own activity, that which we do and do not, explicitly shapes *spatio-temporal conditions* (the coming together of time and space) and this is why clarity is a key starting point for flipping the system.

Why does clarity here matter? Put simply, if you do not set up a narrative for educating in your context (e.g., classroom, department, school, system) then someone else will do it for you. By not engaging, the passivity that Marr and Smyth noted, educators are complicit in the status quo. This is not about being acted upon or exercising agency, it is about generating the conditions in which we work. It is why *auctor* is a more appropriate way of thinking about our work rather than actor or agent. If we aspire to flip the system, we need to recognise that we are both shaped by and shaping of *spatio-temporal conditions*.

To flip the system in the favour of educators, we need to more actively articulate what is important and put in place the conditions to achieve this.

Whether in public policy debates or private lounge rooms, conversations about education quickly turn to what is wanted from schools and current performance levels. As Ladwig (2010) notes, we hold a perceived normative social need and translate this into desired student outcomes. In the absence of any universal measure, the external version of effectiveness most often called upon is the simplest and most readily available source—numerical data on NAPLAN and/or HSC outcomes. If as Ladwig, and many others argue, schools are considered to be about more than academic outcomes, how do educators flip the current narrative? This was best demonstrated to me during a past project on school leadership where a principal stated:

> We are a really good school. We are effective. We say we will educate the kids in a holistic manner, and that is what we do. Although we are answerable to our political masters, at the same time you have to be true to yourself and enact what we see as a good education.
> (Eacott 2013, p. 27)

This statement has stuck with me ever since. The project itself was targeting primary schools that were not high or low achieving in NAPLAN data. The participating school were statistically, average schools, the types of school that do not attract attention for any particular reason. Yet, the school that this principal worked at was considered desirable. It had a waiting list to try and get in—it has a landlocked site and is single stream—and teachers from other schools, including those in the project, were sent to observe and meet with staff at the school based on its reputation for doing great things. Sending staff to visit the school was regularly mentioned to me by other participating schools in the project without provocation or query. What I have taken away from this is the importance of clarity of purpose and explicitly stating what it is you seek to do. It was not NAPLAN results that were the basis of these visits, it was a reputation built on understanding and articulating what the school is about and delivering on that promise.

Demonstrating coherence

Clarity only matters if it can be demonstrated through coherent practice. Arguably the greatest cause of concern with schooling, from educators, parents/caregivers, politicians, and the like, is when the articulated version of events or goals does not match with actions. I recall attending a parent information evening for my eldest child when he was going into year three (the first round of NAPLAN, then again in years five, seven, and nine). The teacher explicitly stated that year three was not all about NAPLAN before going on to spend the next 45 minutes (of a planned one-hour meeting) explaining how the structure of in-class work and homework was to support

NAPLAN preparation and the schedule of NAPLAN preparation and practice tests the class would be doing. My querying of the lack of coherence was not well-received. Some other staff in the room did smile and acknowledge the contradiction but at the same time in failing to intervene, were equally complicit. Although only a personal anecdote, it highlights the ways in which many parents pass judgements on schools and teachers—coherence between what is said (or written) and done. In explicitly articulating what education was about for the year, or more specifically what it was not about, my child's teacher had established the criteria from which she sought to be judged. This was more strategic than not saying anything and leaving those in the room to establish the criteria based on their own normative positions. But in stating a position, you articulate that to which you are willing to be held accountable for. This is the key take-away in the quote from the principal I cited earlier. To build my argument and demonstrate my own coherence I am going to focus on three aspects of schooling that flipping education to privilege joining the conversation of the world impacts on: leadership; recruitment; and teaching and learning.

Leadership

An important starting point for school leadership is what does this all mean for the orthodox practice of establishing a shared vision. What does it actually mean to have a shared vision? How does a shared vision actually work? There are many ways in which educators seek to organise their work. A shared vision is one form of *organising activity* designed to bring alignment to an organisation. But depending on how recruitment and the supervision of teaching and learning are enacted, a shared vision can lead to groupthink and a centralisation of practices. Embracing the idea of joining the conversation of the world, organising education needs to bring people together without narrowing thought and opinion. Rather than a single shared vision, a broad touchstone serves this purpose. If we must, this is a shared vision of contestation and that there is no one way to do education. The purpose of leadership as an *organising activity* is to ensure diversity among staff (hence the importance of recruitment) and facilitating ways of exposing staff to different approaches. Melding different approaches is how educators as *auctors* generate the *spatio-temporal conditions* of the school and expose students to a rich conversation of the world. Arguably one of the most effective means of achieving this is through meetings.

A focus on joining the conversation of the world has an impact on the nature of meetings. For many, meetings are the most frustrating aspect of school work. First there is the volume of meetings, then their duration, but most significantly their content. To demonstrate coherence with conversation, meetings need to be based on dialogue and debate. If simply disseminating information, or worse still presenting a monologue, then meetings are really adding no value and arguably costly as educators could be doing more productive activities. Therefore, if you are not doing work at meetings, it is possible that the meeting was not needed. The benefit of the meeting is the diversity of knowledges and experiences in the room. In expanding the professional repertoire of educators, meetings need to provide opportunities for staff to work together and hear different ways of approaching matters. This is not about providing another platform for the dominant voices, it is about ensuring all staff have the opportunity to contribute and this raises interesting questions for recruitment.

Recruitment

Substantial discussion on education policy has focused on the recruitment (e.g., university entry requirements), training, and early career supports for teachers. There is a genuine push to only recruit the "best and brightest" into education (Gore *et al.* 2016), even if that requires fast tracking high performing graduates from other areas into the classroom (e.g., Teach for Australia). What is less discussed is recruitment of teachers at the school level. Such a discussion is complicated by systemic differences, where government schools still retain a primarily centralised systemic approach, and Catholic and independent schools have more localised control over staffing appointments. Rarely mentioned in matters of staffing in schools is fit. That said, the everyday language of fit frequently perpetuates the status quo (see Tooms *et al.* 2010). As with the idea of a shared vision, fit is often mobilised to mean alignment with the current practices of the school. In shifting from a shared vision to an overarching principle, we need to think relationally, and not about more of the same, but how one contributes to the whole. It requires taking a big picture view of the *organising activity* that is schooling but simultaneously not forgetting the contribution of individuals. Recognising that a school is constituted by its many members (past and present) and material resources (e.g., buildings) but not reducible to them.

Taking a *relational* approach to thinking about recruitment means to privilege diversity in the staffing profile. Not just in the sense of demographic markers (e.g., age, gender, race, ethnicity) but pedagogical contribution. If we aspire to educate based on joining the conversation of the world then we need faculty that represent the many conversations of the world. Grounding recruitment in pedagogy diversity means we do not require all teachers to adopt similar approaches to teaching. To join the conversation of the world means that we should expect, if not demand, that our staff demonstrate a multitude of classroom-based approaches. A challenge that emerges, and remains enduring, in such a stance is that it is important to remain respectful in recognising that others may go about their work in ways very different to your own. Not all teachers need to engage with the latest edtech or have the walls removed and funky furniture to be quality. But this is not to discredit those who do either. Similarly, working in rows quietly is not necessarily bad or working in small collaborative groups beneficial. Rather, to engage in *organising activity* focused on joining the conversation of the world means that it requires teachers and students of all types. As *auctors* we generate these conditions through our actions. In recruiting teachers we need not more of the same, but those that can contribute to broaden the conversation of the world for our students, fellow staff, and community members. The more diverse voices and contributors there are in the school the richer the dialogue and debate. Recruitment is therefore less concerned with alignment with the status quo and more concerned with introducing new and different voices to the educating of the entire school community.

Teaching and learning

Instructional leadership is once again popular among educational leadership literatures, preparation and development programs, and systemic/school interventions. Building on the work of Robinson *et al.* (2008) and recently Hattie (e.g., Hattie 2009, Eacott 2017), the supervision of teachers has focused very much of effect sizes and what practices work best. If, however, we seek to join the conversation of the world, a key question is who gets to decide what is best and for what purposes.

In flipping the system we shift not only the burden of evidence to the educator, but also the criteria from which they are judged. Rather than an external list of what works, teachers articulate what educating means to them and how their practice is coherent with that version. Professional conversations disrupt traditional supervisory/line-management reviews and focuses on how is you work coherent. In short, teachers need to be able to justify their practice in line with their articulated purpose of education and defend it in the face of criticism. For example, if I claim that educating is about joining the conversation of the world, it is coherent to have the classroom set up to facilitate dialogue and debate among participants. Activities and assessments should be based on engaging with a diverse range of stimulus materials—including the contributions of others in the group. Teaching and learning is an *organising activity* where *auctors* (e.g., teacher, students) generate the *spatio-temporal conditions* of knowledge. This is not a progressive content free version of teaching, as there remains unequal distribution of knowledge among participants, but what remains central is the exposure to differing points of view and knowledges and mobilising these to expand both individual and collective understanding. As an approach this works irrespective of disciplinary area.

Leading the narrative

In this chapter I have sought to explicitly articulate my position on what it means to be education—joining the conversation of the world. To make this case, I have framed the chapter around a three-point strategy of clarity, coherence, and narrative. In explicitly naming my stance on education I have flipped the narrative of schooling. Instead of allowing others to dictate what counts and how I and others are to be judged, I have sought to generate the conditions of my work. Judgement is reserved for the ability to deliver on the promise and a broad coherence to what was articulated. In doing so, as educators we lead the narrative of schooling.

How is this position both possible and dare I say desirable? First, in explicitly articulating my normative position there is a common ground on which we can engage. There is no secret or hidden agenda, and instead a basis from which I can have dialogue and debates about the merits of choices made. As a professional, to think relationally as I have argued means that our actions can be justified and defended on the basis of an explicitly articulated vision for education. Through clarity and coherence educators can establish the narrative to which they are held accountable. To that end, this is not a critique of status quo. A critique merely overlays a novel vocabulary on an existing terrain and the conditions remain intact. What I have sought to offer is a productive contribution for how school leaders can flip the dialogue and debate on educating and schooling. I have no doubts that schools are good at what they prioritise, but for too long in Australia (as with elsewhere), educators have allowed others to set the agenda. The time is now to articulate an alternate vision for educating and through coherent actions lead the narrative of schooling.

References

Bates, R.J., 2006. Presidential address: Public education, social justice and teacher education. *Asia-Pacific Journal of Teacher Education*, 34 (3), 275–286.

Eacott, S., 2011. Preparing 'educational' leaders in managerialist times: An Australian story. *Journal of Educational Administration and History*, 43 (1), 43–59.

Eacott, S., 2013. Asking questions of leadership: Using social theory for more than critique. *Leading & Managing*, 19 (1), 18–31.

Eacott, S., 2017. School leadership and the cult of the guru: The neo-Taylorism of Hattie. *School Leadership & Management*, 37 (4), 413–426.

Eacott, S. 2018. *Beyond leadership: A relational approach to organisational theory in education.* Singapore: Springer.

Gore, J., Smith, M. and Holmes, K., 2016. Who says we are not attracting the best and brightest? Teacher selection and the aspirations of Australian school students. *The Australian Educational Researcher*, 43 (5), 527–549.

Hattie, J.A.C., 2009. *Visible learning: A synthesis of over 800 meta-analyses relating to achievement.* London: Routledge.

Ladwig, J.G., 2010. Beyond academic outcomes. *Review of Research in Education*, 34, 113–141.

Marr, D., 2007. His master's voice: The corruption of public debate under Howard. *Quarterly Essay*, 26, 1–84.

Oakeshott, M. 1967. Learning and teaching. *In*: R. S. Peters, eds. *The concept of education.* London: Routledge & Kegan Paul, 156–175.

Robinson, V.M.J., Lloyd, C.A., and Rowe, K.J., 2008. The impact of leadership on student outcomes: an analysis of the differential effects of leadership types. *Educational Administration Quarterly*, 44 (5), 635–674.

Smyth, J., 2008. Australia's great disengagement with public education and social justice in educational leadership. *Journal of Educational Administration and History*, 40 (3), 221–233.

Thomson, P., 2010. Headteacher autonomy: A sketch of a Bourdieuian field analysis of position and practice. *Critical Studies in Education*, 51 (1), 5–20.

Tooms, A.K., Lugg, C.A. and Bogotch, I., 2010. Rethinking the politics of fit and educational leadership. *Educational Administration Quarterly*, 46 (1), 96–131.

Wright, N., 2001. Leadership, 'bastard leadership' and managerialism: Confronting twin paradoxes in the Blair education project. *Educational Administration and Management*, 29 (3), 275–290.

23 Riding two wild horses

Leading Australian schools in an era of accountability

Rebecca Cody

Two wild horses: holistic education and rigorous academic achievement

> If you can't ride two wild horses at once, you shouldn't be in the circus.

This native Scottish proverb has been referenced most enthusiastically by politicians—such as James Maxton in 1931 and Bob Hawke in 2014—to explain why they were trying to hold two simultaneous and seemingly contradictory positions. Across two decades of leadership experience in schools, I have formed the position that this pithy phrase also resonates cogently for Australian educators. Indeed, the principles of holistic education are often represented as being opposed or entirely different to the requirements of academic success measures, such as Australia's national standardised testing of numeracy and literacy, NAPLAN, and tertiary entrance results. Whilst each aspiration brings with it inherent complexities, both must be pursued simultaneously. For the benefit of all learners, Australian educators can and must ride two wild horses: that of holistic education and that of rigorous academic achievement.

Intrinsically connected to this rationale are the differences and complementarity of schooling and education. As an educational leader, I perceive the wild horse of exceptional education linked to human flourishing, whilst the wild horse of stellar schooling addresses fundamental skills. So often, resourcing in schools can be hijacked by the belief that these are different entities serving a conflicting purpose. Teachers, leaders and parents can jostle for which entity they subscribe to and waste time ignoring what the other offers. Such tension can emerge in early years' education. I have mediated debates about why young children should play and not be stressed by the formalities of schooling, in which parents argue that "we just want our children to have fun and be happy—there's plenty of time to learn that other stuff later". This argument leads me to wonder: At what stage of human development do we inculcate the mindset that learning, fun and happiness are mutually exclusive? Similarly, why do we apologise for the difficulty of learning, instead of celebrating that through toil comes great reward? A toddler beginning to walk personifies such a reward; while there may have been frustration resulting from the trial and error strategies employed, nothing can surpass the sensation of those steps towards a parent and ultimately, the satisfaction of positive accomplishment.

Positive accomplishment is the fifth and final component of Seligman's (2011) PERMA theory of wellbeing. In part, it calls attention to grit and self-discipline being as twice as important for success than IQ or talent. Co-researcher Duckworth's work (Duckworth and Seligman 2005) around this points to the "other stuff" or the "formalities" of learning being fertile ground to develop tenacity and that such development aligns with the concept of happiness; developing fundamental skills brings with it the joy of engagement and the opportunity to embark on further learning adventures. Helping stakeholders to recognise the importance of this for our youngest learners is generally an amicable task; however, when it comes to the nationalised standardised testing in Year 3 (in Australia, the commencement of NAPLAN) or the final marks attained at the end of schooling (the ultimate ATAR or university entrance score), conversations frequently intensify.

There is no denying that the accountability associated with national testing and tertiary entrance processes is demanding for teachers and school leaders, let alone our learners, but we should not shy away from what is demanding. With age-appropriate preparation and scaffolding, assessments administered expertly can build, not deter from, self-efficacy and student agency. Effect size data regarding feedback and its impact on student learning (Hattie and Timperley 2007) suggests that the most critical aspect of testing is effectively unpacking and productively utilising measures of achievement. What this *doesn't* look like is: "Here's your ranking"; "This is your score"; "Your potential is defined by this number/this grade". I'm certainly not the first to argue that class rankings and league tables are the antithesis to the widespread aspiration of personalised learning and collaborative pedagogy. To compete within and between schools breeds silo thinking and practice. It generates ambitions of individual conquering, as opposed to cooperating for the benefit of all.

A 'fair go' for students and support for teachers

The benefit I seek is one that nurtures progress for learners and schools, one that celebrates educators' mastery in diagnosis, intervention and evaluation. The phraseology of this model includes questions such as, "How do we bridge this child's learning gaps?" and "Where to next for this learner?" The pursuit of answering these questions is precisely why national testing and tertiary entrance processes should exist. Surely, as a country whose identity is carved around rugged resourcefulness and giving everyone a 'fair go', we should want a schooling system that thrives on effective diagnostic tools, not for pigeonholing learners and shaming school communities, but for identifying where and how support needs to be applied. This approach not only promotes equity, it is ingenuity in action; you can't offer a 'fair go' unless every learner, through their schooling and education, is equipped to have choices in their lives. Choices are enabled through preparedness: namely, being willing and able to select pathways beyond secondary schooling, ones that cannot be predicted by family postcodes but are available because as a country we prioritise the professional learning and ongoing development of teachers.

Strengthening teachers' capacity to prescribe the next learning opportunity is an art and a science that must be informed by evidence (such as testing). Central to both stellar schooling and exceptional education is the cultivation of teachers' abilities to source the evidence and have differentiated prescriptions at hand. This focus isn't just about literacy and numeracy; it is about gifting children and adolescents the opportunity to develop mastery across twenty-first century capabilities. Without repeated skills training (the wild horse of schooling), capabilities cannot be born. The continuum from knowledge to skills to capabilities and competence (the wild horse of schooling) cannot take place without teaching. A competence emerges once skills are transferred successfully to diverse contexts. This transference, wrapped in a values framework, enables purposeful choices to be made, which in turn give rise to human flourishing. Indeed, we cannot optimise our capacity to thrive by giving all our attention to the conventions of schooling; there must be an equal player (or another horse) that encourages meaning making. Competencies must be supported by the parallel development of beliefs which lead to attitudes and predilections; these combine to give meaning to education.

Education is meaning making

Human beings are meaning makers. We crave to make sense of ourselves, each other and the world at large, especially during times of struggle. Attending any Australian school should give rise to such exploration. With curiosity as a universal character strength and a value that helped found our nation, discovering who I am, where I belong and why I exist is a familiar odyssey. A learner's expression of this search may take many forms and be prompted by uncertainty. There is, of course, the age old and ubiquitous uncertainty that arises from general disappointments and difficulties, including those associated with schooling. Then there are the exponential technological, political and economic changes that breed unpredictability, perhaps none more troubling than the mercurial phenomena of the Middle East, Brexit, Trump and North Korea. Young Australians are not immune to the shocking impact of such phenomena and in my experience, are hungry to unpack each scenario with sage mentors. These mentors are the same professionals who prepare learners for NAPLAN and ATAR examinations. In a flipped system, teachers are moral agents, not just experts in a field of inquiry or course of study. In an environment of ubiquitous information, the skills of discernment and critical thinking must be developed in our students.

As schooling involves an intense socialisation process, during which students become increasingly aware of the perspectives of classmates, teachers and their community, the role and role-modelling of educators is a dominant influence in shaping identity, reasoned thought and ethics. This shaping ultimately leads to a new generation of entrepreneurs, scientists, artists, politicians, and philosophers who will work collaboratively to lessen the aforementioned uncertainties. I want these citizens to have optimised their literacy and numeracy skills at school, and to have been nurtured artistically, athletically, emotionally, intellectually, morally, socially and spiritually; all within the context of a curriculum augmented by challenge and choice, and individuals' progress tracked through measures that keep the village raising children deeply accountable. This is a uniquely complex endeavour that aspires to engage a young person's head (thinking), heart (feeling) and hands (doing). Such experiences provide for skills to become part of more comprehensive capabilities. For me, this is the landscape of holistic education: an environment where both wild horses are ridden freely. There is nothing 'soft' or 'non-academic' about holistic learning. It is a profoundly rigorous pursuit, demanding skills to be taught and capabilities to emerge. Accordingly, a holistic education is responsive to diverse learning styles and the expansive needs of human beings.

To accommodate such styles and needs the education of Australia's children needs to evolve from a predominantly knowledge and subject based system to a skills and values base system. This evolution would, over time, become palatable to teachers and inspirational for our students, as schooling begins to prioritise connected relevance of experiences rather than silos of subjects, soon to be forgotten. Piaget's learning theory of constructivism (Piaget 2013) supports this; humans construct knowledge and meaning from their experiences. Vygotsky's theory of proximal development and creativity (Vygotsky 1966) also supports the idea of the power of relevance in education: "Learning is more than the acquisition of the ability to think; it is the acquisition of many specialised abilities for thinking about a variety of things" (Vygotsky 1978, p. 83). These theories are the seeds for what is now known as holistic education, where sense of purpose intersects with perceived relevance of skills acquisition.

Holistic education began to emerge as a coherent philosophy in the mid-1980s. Integrating effective theory and practices from diverse educational alternatives, Miller's writing (1991) synthesises the work of pioneers influencing holistic learning, including: humanitarians (Pestalozzi 1980); transcendentalists Alcott, Emerson and Thoreau (see Gura 2007); founders of progressive education (Dewey 1916); and trailblazers Montessori and Steiner (see Nielsen 2006). Aspects of these thinkers' views also resonate strongly with current positive psychology theories mentioned earlier (Seligman 2011); in particular, the notion that people find identity, meaning and purpose in life through connections with one another, the natural world and spiritual values such as compassion and service. On the now unavailable Paths of Learning website, Miller wrote that:

> a holistic perspective asserts that education must start by nourishing the unique potentials of every child, within overlapping contexts of family,

community, society, humanity, and the natural world. Holistic education is not a fixed ideology but an open-ended attempt to embrace the complexity and wholeness of human life.
(Paths of Learning website cited in Martusewicz, Edmundson, and Lupinacci, p.16)

Perhaps we should hold holistic education to an even higher account. The quintessential test is the quality of characters this nation produces.

Abandoning binary thinking in education

In and of itself accountability is not harming Australian schools. The damage comes from the inordinate amount of energy that can be spent lamenting the motivations of policymakers and being outraged by politicians using the education agenda to feed media hype. The kind of hype that lusts after exposing deficits and publishing ill-informed school comparisons deters would be great educators from embracing the profession and wearies those sharing their expertise every day because they believe in a better world. Given we lack the maturity as a nation to adopt a completely bipartisan approach to education, the least teachers and school leaders can do going forward is to accept that we are riding two wild horses and make the most of both experiences.

Flipping the education system does not mean rejecting testing, academic rigour, measurement and accountability; these can be productive forces that work in harmony with holistic education. Abandoning binary thinking and riding the horses together can showcase the brightest outcomes for learning and teaching. If, for example, we object to national testing and the ATAR, a mental shift can be embraced to release the agitation and serve our utopian ideals. This is where imagination can lift our eyes and keep us focused on what really matters. When struggling to implement yet other mandated initiative, I imagine that government decision making always centres on what would be most effective for the people in our schools. I imagine national testing and the like as missions to collect evidence for applying intervention strategies that keep our youth motivated to learn. I imagine the most remarkable hearts and minds in the country being compelled to school and to educate. This imagining isn't delusion. It is a wholehearted yearning for every child who has the extraordinary fortune to be born in Australia.

With a proactive mindset, the accountabilities of stellar schooling can elevate the outcomes of exceptional education. Undoubtedly, all learners are better placed for an evolving and increasingly uncertain world if society recognises that "the whole is greater than the sum of its parts" (Aristotle 1933, 1045a10). This is about valuing the ride of both wild horses and honouring the tenets of holistic education as a philosophy and practice that uplifts human capacity and in doing so, builds a stronger, more adaptable nation.

References

Aristotle, M., 1933. *Aristotle in 23 volumes*, Vols.17, 18, translated by Hugh Tredennick. London: William Heinemann Ltd. Available from: www.perseus.tufts.edu/hopper/text?doc=Perseus%3Atext%3A1999.01.0052%3Abook%3D8%3Asection%3D1045a [Accessed 28 May 2018].

Dewey, J. 1916. *Democracy and education*. New York: Macmillan.

Duckworth, A.L. and Seligman, M.E.P., 2005. Self-discipline outdoes IQ in predicting academic performance of adolescents. *Psychological Science*, 16, 939–944.

Gura, P.F., 2007. *American transcendentalism: A history*. New York: Hill and Wang.

Hattie, J. and Timperley, H., 2007. The power of feedback. *Review of Educational Research*, 77 (1), 81–112.

Martusewicz, R.A., Edmundson, J. and Lupinacci, J., 2014. *Ecojustice education: Toward diverse, democratic, and sustainable communities*. Routledge.

Miller, R., 1991. Educating the true self: Spiritual roots of the holistic worldview. *Journal of Humanistic Psychology*, 31(4),53–67.

Nielsen, T.W., 2006. Towards a pedagogy of imagination: A phenomenological case study of holistic education. *Ethnography and Education*, 1, 247–264.

Pestalozzi, J.E., 1980. Cómo Gertrudis enseña a sus hijos: Cartas sobre la educación de los niños. *Libros de educación elemental* (prólogos). México: Porrúa.

Piaget, J., 2013. *The construction of reality in the child*. Abingdon: Routledge.

Seligman, M.E., 2011. *Flourish: A visionary new understanding of happiness and well-being*. New York: Free Press.

Vygotsky, L.S., 1966. Igra i ee rol'v psikhicheskom razvitii rebenka. *Voprosy psikhologii*, 6, 62–76.

Vygotsky, L.S., 1978. *Mind in society: The development of higher psychological processes*. Cambridge, MA: Harvard University Press.

24 A culture of trust

Key practices of compelling leadership

Paul Browning

Currently, the world looks to Finland, Singapore and Shanghai for the answer to an excellent education system. In ten years' time it will be another three countries, but for now politicians, and even some educators, blindly believe that these jurisdictions have the solution. Each proudly accepts visitors and enjoys the world's attention, but the solution is beyond simplistic answers such as a back-to-basics approach, funding, visible learning, or better teacher education.

My hypothesis: A country's educational performance is not a reflection of the quality of its education system but a reflection of its values and culture. I have had the opportunity to visit the big three in educational standings: Finland, Shanghai and Singapore. I have listened to their students, their teachers and parents; visited schools and observed their societies (albeit briefly). My hypothesis is a deeply reflective hunch and would need considerable research to prove but I suspect I could be right. All three countries have vastly different cultures to our own here in Australia.

Shanghai and Singapore are not too dissimilar from one another. Shanghai classrooms are packed with students sitting in rows, reciting in unison instructions from the teacher. There is little sign of creativity, differentiation or individualisation. Classrooms are sparse; resources are limited. So why does Shanghai perform so well?: A culture of sheer hard work. As a country China demands a work ethic second to none. Students and their families know that the only way to a better life, the only way to lift themselves out of poverty is to work as hard as they can. In Singapore, the classrooms are less sparse and less densely populated but they still achieve the results they do through hard work. One Year 6 student in Singapore told me that she starts school at 8am and finishes at 3:30pm. She then goes to tutoring for another three to four hours, every day. She has homework from school and her tutor. Study doesn't finish until late at night. The children know that if their grades aren't good enough they will be taken out of the academic stream and put into a vocational program.

Finland's culture is very different, but again vastly different to our own in Australia (and at this point you could insert the UK or the USA). Their schools are surprisingly poorly resourced by our standards. Students actually receive far less instructional time and have less homework. So how is it that they have an educational system that outperformed most other developed nations at the beginning of the twenty-first century? The country has a culture that respects teachers and values children and learning, and more importantly, a culture of trust.

The teaching profession in Finland has a high status, and it's not because of the money, but because of the value the Finnish people put on raising their children. Teacher preparation is good but even Pasi Sahlberg states that the quality of an education system can exceed the quality of teachers. Sahlberg goes on to say:

> The Finnish experience shows that a consistent focus on equity and cooperation—not choice and competition—can lead to an education system where all children learn well. Paying teachers based on students' test scores ... have no place in the Finnish repertoire for educational improvement.
>
> (Sahlberg 2010, p. 9)

Finland is a country with high levels of trust in its people. For example, to the unaccustomed visitor it appears that the public transport runs on an honesty system. You need to buy a ticket to travel but there are no electronic gates you put your ticket into before going on the subway, no one on the trains checking if you have paid, and no security as you disembark. From my fifth-floor hotel room I spent time watching a busker. When he wanted a break he left his tin money out in the open and went to buy lunch. No one stole from him. The same level of trust is afforded to schools and teachers in Finland. There are no inspections of schools, no evaluation of teachers and no standardised tests with publicised results. Finland knows that people perform better when they are trusted, for as a result they feel empowered, valued and in control of their own life choices and consequences.

Contrast these three countries cultures with Australia. In 2003, when PISA was first administered Australia performed near the top of the OECD countries. However, since then its standing has taken a remarkable turn. Politicians and the media speak of our education system as though somehow it's the schools' or teachers' fault that standards have taken a plunge. But since 2003 not a lot has changed in our schools but in contrast, Australian society has. Nine Eleven and the Bali bombings in 2002 were turning points. Since those tragic events we have become less trusting and more suspicious and fearful.

There have been other significant changes since the turn of the millennia. Technology has become ubiquitous, transforming every facet of our lives. Mobile technology has reached saturation point and the conversations have shifted from excitement about the power of technology to concern about its influence on young people's mental health and development. Questions about screen time, cyber-bullying, and impacts on social and emotional development have not been answered, indeed; rates of anxiety and depression amongst young people have risen and tenuous links have been made with technology.

In the last two decades Australia's concept of respect has been eroded, influenced by the media who cruelly attack our leaders and public figures at every turn under the guise of freedom of speech. No sooner do we vote in governments then we want them ousted. In the last ten years Australia has had no fewer than five prime ministers (including two rounds of Rudd); there were only three prime ministers in the previous 24 years. I would also argue that the 'golden' economic years in Australia built on the back of the mining boom (2001–2007) created a spoilt generation who have a materialistic and entitlement belief rather than a hard work ethic and an inner peace and happiness for what they do have. As an educator, I have seen this attitude pervade our students as they carry around the latest iPhone and want to be spoon feed the information they need to pass the assessment rather than expressing a sheer joy and privilege for learning.

It appears that the political leaders of Australia value economic growth above all else, even above our children. Education is no longer about enriching our humanity, but about ensuring our long-term economic viability as a nation. Public policy has commodified the heart of education (the relationships that make schools work) by increasing the accountability and scrutiny of schools and as a result, has undermined trust and done damage to the key relationships between teachers and students. The MySchool website is one such policy example, where the results of the National Assessment Program for Literacy and Numeracy (NAPLAN) are published and school's data is compared to create 'league tables'. The intention of this policy was to offer a transparency for parents as they sort to choose a school for their children, but the result has been the temptation on the part of individual schools to manipulate the data to give the appearance that they are better than another and stay off the 'shame' list.

What is certainly evident in the data (if you measure the quality of a schooling system on the performance of NAPLAN and PISA) is that Australian schools aren't getting better, and in fact, many would suggest the system is in decline. However, what hasn't been recognised is the significant influences that have reshaped our culture and values, which in turn, have impacted on the education of young people. No matter the effort placed on policy, no matter the money injected into the system, I doubt that Australia will see an improvement. You can keep hitting the dog, but in the end, it will just become more obedient and not a better and more loving pet. The current public approach to education in Australia needs to be challenged, indeed, the system needs to be flipped. Rather than placing the education of our nation in the hands non-educators, it needs to be put back into the hands of the professionals.

The importance of a culture of trust

It is our culture that has caused the demise of our academic standards, or more specifically, the demise of trust. Does this mean that we shouldn't bother with working to lift the quality of teaching and our schools: of course not. But as Peter Drucker's adage goes, we need to recognise that 'culture eats strategy for breakfast'. Society's problems, issues, norms, and values (i.e. culture) are our responsibility. We are all responsible for what society is like, and for raising and educating the next generation. It is no coincidence that there is a correlation between a decline in trust in our western society and a decline in educational standards. According to the OECD, trust in government is deteriorating in many of the OECD countries. Only 40% of citizens, on average, trust their government. According to the Edelman (2012) Trust Barometer trust in the UK fell five points between 2011 and 2012 from 43% to 38%.

The link between trust and student outcomes has been made in a longitudinal study in the United States of America. In their seminal work, *Trust in Schools*, Bryk and Schneider (2002) found that it is trust that makes a significant difference to student learning and outcomes, not policy, curriculum, standardisation, or accountability. Their study found that where there were strong positive trust reports in a school their students were three times more likely to be improving in reading and mathematics compared with schools with weak trust reports. In fact, Bryk and Schneider found that schools with low levels of trust (amongst their faculty, between teachers and students, teachers and parents), had virtually no chance of showing improvement in either reading or mathematics. This was a profound finding. So how is it that this simple social phenomenon called trust, that only exists when people are in relationship, can have such a profound effect on learning?

Bennis and Nanus (1985) consider trust to be the lubricant that makes it possible for organisations to work. When trust is low or missing in schools, staff may be evasive, dishonest, and inconsiderate in their communications. When teachers or students feel unsafe, energy that could be devoted to teaching and learning is diverted to self-preservation. In the absence of trust people are increasingly unwilling to take risks and demand greater protections to defend their interests (Tyler and Kramer 1996); issues are seldom discussed and never resolved; a school cannot improve and grow into the rich, nurturing micro-society needed by children and adults alike; and people are likely to say only those things they expect others want to hear (Lovell and Wiles 1983).

A low-trust culture invariably can be the result of, or results in, a withdrawal of the leader to a traditional hierarchical and authoritarian form leadership (Duignan 2006). Without trust leaders lose credibility (Reina and Reina 2006). This loss poses difficulty to leaders as they seek to call people to respond to their responsibilities. The painful alternative is to be punitive, seeking to control people through manipulation or coercion. This in turn can become an endless cycle of distrust, broken only by the removal of the leader.

Conversely, the reward of a trusting school environment is immeasurable (Blase and Blase 2001). Sergiovanni (2005) espouses the importance and value of trust in school leadership, particularly in relation to school improvement agendas. He states that school leaders should be trustworthy. The building of trust is an organisational quality. Once trust exists it becomes the norm that sets the standard for how teachers behave toward each other and their students. Once part of the culture of the school, trust works "to liberate people to be their best, to give others their best, and to take risks: All of these behaviours help schools to become better places for students" (Sergiovanni 2005, p. 90).

Sergiovanni states that trust is so important in a school that it is vital to firstly build trust before anything else, even before a leader develops a vision. To build trust after setting a vision and developing strategy is nowhere near as effective. The responsibility of the creation of a vision to bring about school improvement rests on the shoulders of effective school leaders (Leithwood and Riehl 2003, Mahoney 1990). When staff members view their leader as trustworthy the vision, when well communicated, becomes collective and inspires and creates commitment on behalf of the school members to take the necessary risks and innovative steps required to see their school improve.

Hargreaves (2006, 2009) has supported Sergiovanni's assertions, suggesting that to embrace new and exciting ways of operating, schools need to develop and maintain professional cultures of trust, cooperation and responsibility. He identified trust as one of three key human resources in educational change; the other two were confidence and emotion. There is a level of predictability for people when others react and behave in a trusting way; assumptions of acting in good faith abound. Hargreaves concluded that trust improves schools, increases achievement, and boosts energy and morale.

Trust not only plays an important role in taking schools forward toward strategic improvement, but also in the development, and capacity building of teachers. Blase and Blase (2001) investigated the construct of shared governance—the development of cooperative relationships in order to reach collaboratively agreed goals. While Blase and Blase did not set about to examine trust, one of the key conclusions they drew was that in a shared governance context, a key challenge of the principal was to build a trusting environment. They suggested that principals can do this by: encouraging openness, facilitating effective communication, and modelling understanding. Their data indicated that principals built trust by working to create school cultures free of intimidation, fear, coercion and criticism. They claimed that the effect of a high-trust environment is likely to manifest in motivated, satisfied and confident teachers. Due to an atmosphere of trust, teachers are more likely to work harder, be optimistic and feel a sense of professionalism.

So if trust is the key resource for school improvement, the resource that unlocks the potential of every teacher and student, how is it achieved?

Investigating how to achieve a culture of trust in schools

After experiencing first-hand the impact of low levels of trust on organisational culture, staff moral and outcomes, I undertook a doctoral research project through the Queensland University of Technology. The work aimed to identify practices that engender trust.

The project was undertaken in two parts. Part one was the identification of four highly trusted transformational school leaders in large school settings, i.e. with staff more than 130. Trust is typically relational, and easier to establish when there is the opportunity to get to know people, but much harder when we are 'removed' from everyday social interaction. The project was about finding leadership practices that can be learned by any person in a leadership role, regardless of their personality.

Using two reliable tools that measure transformation leadership (Transformational Leadership Measurement tool or TLM) and trust (the Organisational Trust Inventory or OTI) four highly trusted leaders were found. Two were female, two male. Two were introverts and two were extroverts. Interestingly, one said, "trust isn't about being nice, because I am certainly not nice". The data revealed another fascinating finding—trust was not connected to tenure. We often think that trust grows over time. That isn't the case. One of the identified leaders had been in role at their new school for one year, another for 17 years. The data for all participants in the first phase of the study showed a range of tenure and levels of trust. The leader with the lowest level of trust had been in role for 16 years. The data showed that it all came down to the behaviour, or practice of the leader. There is also no such thing as a 'trust' bank. You can't make deposits into that bank and then a massive withdrawal. The data also showed that it isn't a question of whether you are trusted or not, but a question of how much you are trusted.

The data also showed a very strong correlation between trust in the leader and trust in the culture of the school, that is, between teachers. These high levels of trust were unlocking potential through increased collaboration and peer-to-peer learning which in turn, was having a significant impact on student learning and achievement. Neuroscientist Paul Zak (2017) has found that organisations with high levels of trust are 50 per cent more productive and their staff report 74% less stress, 106% more energy at work which in turn leads to a 13% reduction in sick days. The benefits of trust are not only for learning and wellbeing, but also economic. There is little evidence against the value of trust.

The second phase of the study was to go into the four schools, interview staff and shadow the head. This work revealed 21 practices, but when a cross-case analysis was done, ten practices were found to be common between all four of the leaders.

Ten leadership practices to engender and grow trust

It is important to understand that trust is a socially constructed phenomenon; it means different things for different people. For this reason, you cannot have a commonly agreed definition for trust. For the person who has been through a traumatic marriage break up, discovering that their spouse was having an affair, trust is closely associated with its opposite: betrayal. For the person who has had their personal story shared without their permission by someone they were willing to be vulnerable with, trust is about keeping confidences. For others it is associated with decision-making and the opportunity to have a say in the things that will impact them. No single trust building practice is more important than other. When you led a diverse group of people, each with their own life story and experiences all ten leadership practices are equally important.

1. Admit your mistakes

Leaders are not infallible; they are human. How leaders deal with the mistakes they make sets the tone for the rest of the organisation and is a practice in the creation of trust. A leader's willingness to display his/her vulnerabilities, both personally and professionally engenders a staff's admiration and trust. Staff members view this practice not as a weakness but as a key strength of leadership, connecting them to their leader on a very human level.

The willingness to be vulnerable, to have the ability to be self-reflective and recognise one's own strengths and weaknesses, to apologise when an error had been made or to reverse a poor decision portrays the leader's *humility*.

2. Offer trust

No one likes to be micro-managed. One of the most powerful actions for gaining the trust of others is to firstly give it. For leaders this means taking a risk and trusting in others first.

The benefits of offering trust go beyond the empowerment of staff to perform their roles; it encouraged many staff members to extend themselves and grow professionally. As a result, for those staff members, self-doubt gave way to self-belief and career progression.

3. Actively listen

Listening is often a mere mechanical process whereby a person is simply waiting for their turn to speak, usually motivated by the desire to impart their own view point. Highly trusted leaders practise what is defined as *empathic listening*, or active listening. This type of listening is about opening oneself to the talker, seeking to identify what they are truly trying to say, to the point where one can actually feel what they are feeling.

4. Provide affirmation

We all have an innate desire to be appreciated and valued. Research has shown that organisations that excel at employee recognition are 12 times more likely to generate strong results than those that do not.

Highly trusted leaders employ a range of appreciation strategies including publicly thanking a member of staff at a staff meeting, sending an email or a handwritten thank-you note, or simply speaking to the person privately to affirm them. Staff find affirmation very motivating, leading to a strengthening of trust because it leaves them with the impression that their leader knows them and the work they do.

5. Be consultative in decision-making

Highly trusted leaders made informed and consultative decisions. Some decisions have to be made promptly. Staff members often need an answer straight away; invariably a good decision maker is able to do that if the issue warrants it. However, for larger decisions, or decisions that will potentially impact others, trusted leaders use a consultative process, ensuring that the views of all stakeholders are valued and taken into account.

6. Be visible

The administrative load of a CEO can easily keep them confined to their office. Being visible to the organisation is an effective strategy for building trust between a leader and his/her staff.

For many staff visibility is linked to the accessibility of the leader. Staff of trusted leaders not only *see* the CEO but know that they are accessible to them. Leaders who are inaccessible cannot possibly expect to be trusted just because they have a title.

7. Keep a consistent demeanour

A consistent, predictable manner and approach to situations engenders the trust of staff. People by nature want to know what they are going to get. If their leader acts in a reasonable and predictable way people will respect and trust them.

Each of the leaders participating in the study of trusted leadership possessed the ability to control their emotions and remain calm and level-headed. Knowing that a leader's behaviour will be respectful and focused on the agenda of the staff member rather than themselves, gives staff confidence and provides them with a feeling of safety.

8. Coach and mentor staff

"The real power of effective leadership", writes Brigadier Jim Wallace, former Head of Australian Special Forces, "is maximising other people's potential" (Dickson 2009, p. 36).

When you reflect on the notion of trust and how to increase leadership credibility few would imagine that the practice of coaching and mentoring would be linked. Perhaps too few leaders take the time to develop individual staff members, leaving the profession with only a handful of people applying for leadership positions. But as a result of this practice staff members become empowered to manage difficult situations themselves.

9. Offer care and concern

Staff members are naturally inclined to put their trust in a person who is interested in them as a person rather than just an employee appointed to perform a role. Effective leaders care enough to want to learn about their staff so they can act with compassion and empathy towards them.

10. Keep confidences

The final trust engendering practice identified by the study was an obvious one. In any kind of relationship, confidentiality is essential to maintaining trust. When others have entrusted a person with private or sensitive information they have a moral obligation to honour that trust; the breach of confidentiality may cost that relationship. Trust for individual staff members comes from knowing that they can share personal information with their leader, safe in the knowledge that unless they grant permission, it will not go any further.

Conclusion

Each of these ten practices can be learned and developed by any leader regardless of their personality and position. If you are a leader ask yourself, "Am I having a positive impact on the organisation I serve? Are my leadership behaviours and practices inspiring, building and sustaining trust? If not, where can I do better?" Every student and teacher deserves a school where learning can flourish.

To an educator working at the coal-face in a school, the solution to improving our education system is obvious: flipping the system by giving those working in schools trust and support, rather than accountabilities. Every professional understands the need for accountability, but they also value respect and want to be trusted to do their job. Rather than placing the education of our nation in the hands of non-educators, it needs to be put back into the hands of the professionals. Trust is the key.

References

Bennis, W. and Nanus, B., 1985. *Leaders: Strategies for taking charge*. New York: Harper and Row.
Blase, J. and Blase, J., 2001. *Empowering teachers: What successful principals do* (2nd ed.). Thousand Oaks, CA: Corwin Press.
Bryk, A. and Schneider, B., 2002. *Trust in schools*. New York: Russell Sage.
Dickson, J., 2009. *Humilitas*. Grand Rapids, MI: Zondervan.

Edelman., 2012. *Trust barometer: Business can earn the license to lead.* Available from www.scribd.com/document/79026497/2012-Edelman-Trust-Barometer-Executive-Summary [Accessed 6 March 2018].

Duignan, P., 2006. *Educational leadership: Key challenges and ethical tensions.* Melbourne: Cambridge University Press.

Hargreaves, A. and Fink, D., 2006. *Sustainable leadership.* San Francisco, CA: Jossey-Bass.

Hargreaves, A. and Shirley, D., 2009. *The fourth way: The inspiring future for educational change.* Thousand Oaks, CA: Corwin Press.

Leithwood, K. and Riehl, C., 2003. *What we know about successful school leadership.* Philadelphia: Temple University.

Lovell, L. and Wiles, K., 1983. *Supervision for better school* (5th ed.). Englewood Cliffs, NJ: Prentice Hall.

Mahoney, J., 1990. Do you have what it takes to be a super superintendent? *The Executive Educator*, 12 (4), 26–28.

Reina, D., and Reina, M., 2006. *Trust and betrayal in the workplace* (2nd ed.). San Francisco, CA: Berrett-Koehler.

Sahlberg, P., 2010. *Finnish lessons.* New York: Teachers College Press.

Sergiovanni, T., 2005. *Strengthening the heartbeat.* San Francisco, CA: Jossey-Bass.

Tyler, T. and Kramer, R., 1996. Whither trust? *In*: R. Kramer and T. Tyler (Eds.), *Trust in organisations.* Thousand Oaks, CA: Sage, 1–15.

Zak, P., 2017. *Trust Factor: The science of creating high-performing companies.* New York: AMACOM.

25 Context matters

Women leading in rural schools

Susan Bradbeer

In education, leadership has increasingly become the 'magic bullet', the catalyst for radical change and large-scale school reform (Leithwood *et al.* 2008, Pont *et al.* 2008). Research in Australian Educational Leadership reveals that perceptions of work intensification, pressures of greater accountability, including evaluation, differences related to student achievement and the unique demands of the local context have all impacted the recruitment of leaders in Australian schools (Mulford 2007). Ongoing supply deficit and the imminent retirement of principals—many of them post war 'baby boomers'—have culminated in a leadership 'crisis' in both an Australian and international context. Government and policymakers now have a warrant to actively build the capacity of candidates aspiring to become school leaders (Watterston 2015).

The Australian Institute of Training for School Leadership (AITSL 2015) recognises the need to train and prepare leaders. There has been increased attention to the delivery of professional leadership training evidenced in the range of training programs on offer across all sectors. The urgent need for a reliable and effective leadership model has seen schools adopt a reductionist 'what works' approach to leadership development, evident in professional learning offerings. Watterston's (2015) environmental scan of current principal preparation programs in Australia highlights a lack of funding, collaboration, and rigour around identifying and developing leaders in general and a lack of tools to measure the effectiveness of training. Accordingly, it can be concluded that the narrow minded 'what works' approach to leadership is perhaps a limiting masculine construct that ignores the nuanced requirements of women leaders and more specifically, women leaders in rural schools. To address the inevitable leadership crisis in Australian schools, a better understanding of the complex challenges faced by women in leadership in rural schools is required.

This chapter critiques the current *'what works'* leadership discourse and examines the role of the 'rural' as a space and place that impacts leadership, professional learning and professional identity in education. My doctoral research that included semi-structured interviews and email exchanges with 12 women in leadership in rural schools in Victoria, contributes to what I argue is a gap in the research. It confirms that women want to make a difference in education, but they are often overlooked for leadership opportunities in rural schools and there is little encouragement to consider stepping up, due to the persistent more immediate demands of the school. I begin the discussion with some of the recent approaches to understanding the rural in the current Australian education climate and then subsequently explore leadership, professional learning and identity formation through this rural lens. Having focused on these interconnected ideas relating to the rural and women and leadership, the chapter elaborates on the current challenges for women leaders in rural schools by illustrating these issues from my own research data. The narrative accounts elevate the voices of women in leadership working in rural schools and challenge the way the 'rural' in policy and decision making is embraced, so that we flip the system.

The rural context

The rural context remains difficult to define (Halfacree 1993). Terms such as 'rural', 'regional', 'country', 'remote' and 'isolated' are all used to describe the experience of educators, but each have different connotations. From conjuring up idyllic settings to propagating a deficit view of the rural, each term hints at the impact of isolation, access, limited population sizes and reinforces common perception of rural as a binary term (Schulte and Walker-Gibbs 2016). However, the notion of rurality is fundamental to shaping identity and developing a place-based consciousness (Perumal 2015, Gruenewald 2003, Halsey 2011, Starr and White 2008).

Pini, Moletsane, and Mills (2014) advocate that the "rural itself is considered largely irrelevant, little more than a pre-modern backwater increasingly peripheral and inconsequential to the urbanised cosmopolitan twenty-first century world" (p. 453). Historically, little attention has been paid to rural education and leadership, but in the last five years there has been emerging interest in the intersection between the rural context and teacher identity, often with reference to gender (Blackmore 2015, Pini *et al.* 2014, White and Corbett 2014). In this chapter the term 'rural' will be used to refer to a space and place a significant distance from an urban centre.

Context matters (Bush 2018). Interest around contexts for leadership has previously included organisational and environmental settings (Hallinger 2018). The more nuanced features of the rural are now gaining scholarly attention. The Australian Department of Education and Training commissioned an *Independent Review into Regional, Rural and Remote Education* (Halsey 2017) to consider the challenges and barriers to student learning outcomes. This student-focused review does not adequately address teacher support and training or leadership development. In this chapter, I argue that gendered experiences of leadership and professional identity formation take on a particular form in the rural that is complex and not readily understood in simple terms. The following sections focus on leadership, professional learning and identity and align both recent scholarship and the 'voices' that emerge from the data.

Being a leader in a rural school

Spurred on by education reform and the drive for school improvement, leadership in Australia has been the focus of programs promoted by AITSL, Bastow Institute of Educational Leadership and the new national principal certification. But as Watterston (2015) reported, fundamental to addressing the need for quality leadership is research and investment in the identifications of leaders, rigorous selection process for programs, collaboration and partnership between sectors and an evidence base to target areas of need. I argue that my research indicates that such areas of need include women leaders in the rural context.

Leadership in schools has preoccupied researchers and has been dominated by different approaches, styles, models that demonstrate effective leadership (Bush and Glover 2003). Trait-based, distributed, situational, instructional and transformational theories of how to lead have all gained some degree of traction. Simkins (2005) argues that there is both a traditional and an emerging conception of leadership, and this perspective is helpful if we are to make sense of leadership. The rapid growth of a '*what works*' approach fails to address a broader need for theoretical framework in educational leadership (Moller 2017). The diversity inherent in the research includes everything from Gronn's (1999) thesis on the formation of leaders, to the practice of leadership in schools in the work of Leithwood, Jantzi and Steinbach (1999). An alternative approach to leadership in education starts to uncover some of the inherent ambiguities and this can be seen in the work emerging from Thompson (2017) and Gunter (2001). These researchers challenge the dominant thinking that leadership can be prescribed and replicated and argue for a more disruptive, dialogic approach. There is limited space here to elaborate on the various iterations of these debates in leadership, but I argue that whilst a '*what works*', checklist approach might appear to be a practical and attractive option for school leadership in theory and practice, it is not mindful of context. There is a notable absence of engagement with rural space and the role of gender in identity formation. This approach to leadership development fails to acknowledge the needs of women in leadership in rural schools. As can be seen from the following excerpt from my research, women leaders in rural schools don't just lead from the top. Principals, both men and women, in small schools often juggle classroom responsibilities with administration demands, without the support of permanent staff or assistants. Jillian, a principal in the research study bemoans that:

> in these small schools we don't have the money to appoint a leading teacher and put them in charge of an area ... we still have to do things bigger schools do. We have to do the policies, the annual implementation plans, annual reports, schools strategic plans ... I have had a few debates with the department and said this doesn't work for our size school and a few times they have agreed. But I have had to do it anyway.

There is constant tension that arises from applying the mandates from Government departments and this is evident as school leaders work hard to attract and retain students as changing enrolments from year to year threatens the school's viability and reputation. School principal, Grace says "we have a decreasing school age population and ... economic climate" so it is difficult coping with the "changing dynamics ... as it puts pressure on staffing and how we structure programs".

Women in leadership have shared their frustration of being in a role without trusted colleagues to mentor them, without effective orientation to the job, without resources or release to leave school to access professional learning. Grace's appointment into a head of school role meant that "I suddenly found myself 330 km away from my support network, my family and friends". The autonomy and freedom that came with the role was overshadowed by feeling as though she had to "muddle your way through". This sense of leading in isolation is reiterated by Harriet, who describes feeling 'insignificant' as a head of department. She describes being "just in role, I am just a piece of paper whereas elsewhere I have felt that I am a leader". Harriet discovered that she had no 'voice' in her organisation and her school was: "missing leadership, someone steering the ship. I think we are out at sea and getting through it and that is not how a place should be, it should be on a road somewhere".

Some teachers are appointed to leadership roles in a rural context as part of a career pathway to moving into a new leadership role in an urban school. One research participant, a leading teacher, spoke at length about the exhaustive support she had to offer a young man in his early thirties who had landed the principal role via an alternative teaching preparation program. In contrast, others have moved from urban to rural schools, pre-empting retirement. Carla, a principal in her early fifties, noted that she knew she was taking on a challenging rural school. She says it was "badly damaged and I knew I could turn it around ... the change has been phenomenal". Despite the quiet success she sees in learning outcomes, school attendance and the gradual strengthening of the school community, Carla feels like an outsider to the impenetrable clique of established leaders. The data revealed that a lack of collegiality between leaders is exacerbated in rural schools and often reinforced by students and the school community. Ella's experience of living and working as a leader in a rural school is that it is "competitive and that goes against the level of trust you can have with people. We live in little silos".

An additional finding in the research study uncovered the voices of women who were reluctant leaders and in spite of being experienced, did not see themselves as a leader. Annabelle makes the distinction between leaders and managers suggesting she would "prefer to be allowed to get into the classroom and get on with what I am good at". Women in leadership roles in rural schools struggle with a multitude of challenges highlighted by the small numbers of students and teachers, the interconnectedness of the local community, the struggle to belong and the distance from 'home' or a larger urban centre. Annabelle sums up many of the voices heard in this research project when she says, "as a leader in a rural school like this you are isolated, it is that simple". Women in leadership in rural schools have specific needs that often remain ignored by traditional professional learning offerings.

Professional learning in a rural school

Professional learning plays an integral part in the development of leaders in education. Some of the recent programs targeting women in leadership in education in Victoria include Catholic Education Office Melbourne's "Supporting Women in their Leadership Journey" (2009–2011), the Eleanor Davis School Leadership Program (1997–2012) offered by Bastow Institute of Educational Leadership in Victoria, and the National Excellence in School Leadership Initiative (NESLI) that supports an Advanced Leadership Program for Women. These have not, however, been tailored to the issues and experiences of rural educators which are significantly different issues to their urban counterparts. Watterston's (2015) extensive survey of the programs available to equip aspiring principals affirms that there is professional learning on offer. Furthermore, new modes of professional learning via online programs and the utilisation of professional online learning networks via social media platforms have enlarged the possibilities of an interactive, connected learning space for rural participants. However, there is little data available on whether any of these models have led to real change in opportunity, preparation and support in leadership roles for women specifically, or if it addresses their complex needs of leading in a rural school.

In my research, women spoke openly about their fears and anxiety about taking on higher positions of leadership and the daily stress of being in a principal role. Leah, a Deputy Principal worries how "consuming that might become ... I don't want to lie in bed and worry about the things that might be placed on a principal's shoulders if something goes wrong". She admits that it is fear that is "holding me back". Similarly, Carla knows that "in a small school, where the expectations of a principal of a small school are the same as the expectations of a principal in a large school ... here I am it". Women in leadership in a rural school desire to be heard and understood. But it is often a lack of time, resources and the tyranny of distance that has made it difficult for rural teachers to connect, to access professional learning and therefore build leadership capacity (Stack *et al.* 2011).

The passion with which the participants shared their leadership experiences confirmed the need for mentoring, coaching and professional networks. Beck, a Head of Faculty argued that:

> location certainly impacts our ability to improve, build teacher capacity through study, I certainly believe that. Our location impacts our ability to get people out to the country- it is sometimes not appealing.

In several email exchanges with participants, photographs that reflected their experience in role were submitted. Many of these images highlighted the long distances on country roads travelled by women into work each day, the beauty of the natural environment, open spaces, but also the isolation. Harriet reminded me that where she lived had 'terrible reception' and she was unable to connect with a professional learning network online whilst at home. The ways in which women leaders in rural schools spoke about their own professional learning experiences suggests that being a teacher, being a leader and a woman in a rural school impacts how professional identity is shaped.

Professional identity formation and the rural

In the last 20 years there has been burgeoning interest in the notion of professional teacher identity (Beijaard et al. 2004). Professional identity is a complex, contested and highly organic. Context also influences and shapes teacher identity (Flores and Day 2006). Mockler (2011) argues that there are three domains that are integrally linked to identity: personal experience, professional context and the external political environment. It is in the engagement between political environment and the professional context, the enhancement of reflection and self-knowledge and the openness to change practice that is integral to the complex, dynamic notion of identity. Context plays an integral role in constructing professional identity and how teachers develop professionally determines identity. Therefore, identity is not a fixed, stable notion but it emerges as a relational phenomenon, an ongoing process where the self is being interpreted alongside of and against various social contexts, the image of self, the role which one inhabits and the experience and practice of being a teacher. Being a leader and a woman in the rural has significant impact on how identity is constructed and the role practised. Beck reflected on the demands of her role:

> ... you know I used to look at women and think how do you do that, what you do. How do you work full time, how do you have two children, live out of town and stay sane? I didn't think I was that strong ... but I am.

The underlying assumptions here is the multiplicity of demands of the role is exacerbated by the rural space and place—living out of town, establishing a work life balance and the need to be strong in order to succeed in role as a leader. Similarly, Freda acknowledged that her own mental health and well-being would be at risk if she were to take on higher leadership roles:

> Because I am a self-doubter I think I would be so worried about doing a good job I think I would put too much time in. It would have too much of an impact on your work life balance.

A common theme in the data was not only the fear and anxiety associated with the idea of stepping up into a higher leadership role, but the lack of support women received on the journey into leadership. It was rare that women could say they had both professional and personal support in their role.

Flipping the system for women leading rural schools

Empowering women to share their story and comment on their leadership experiences provides the knowledge and the motivation to develop effective strategies to help other women to lead in the rural. In this chapter, I have argued that leadership, professional learning and professional identity are influenced by context, the rural. The rich and complex stories of women in educational leadership in rural schools depict them doing leadership differently, defying the norm and flipping the narrative of *'what works'*, as they challenge the current models for leadership and professional learning. This research aims to empower women by connecting others to their stories and inviting the education system to 'flip' their perspective and respect the unique *'voice'* and experience of women in leadership in rural schools.

The recent research suggests that Australian educators are responding to an imminent leadership crisis, but the *'what works'* strategies on offer do not adequately prepare and train leaders for the complexities of different contexts. Development of leadership capacity of women wanting to work in a rural school will require effective use of the data already collected on educational leadership in rural contexts and further feedback from key stakeholders. Key questions for future consideration include:

- How do we assess the challenges and issues faced by women in leadership in rural schools in way that allows meaningful, measurable change to occur?
- How do we promote educational research with a rural focus?
- How do we connect women in leadership in rural schools with each other and offer innovative and contextually relevant professional learning?
- Can a singular theoretical framework for educational leadership accommodate the context of women in the rural?

Women in leadership positions in rural schools desire more support. Leadership development opportunities relevant to their context are lacking. These key findings, emerge from my research. They challenge us to better understand how the rural context influences leadership practices and identity formation and respond by supporting current and future women leaders in their rural school context.

References

Australian Institute for Teaching and Learning (AITSL), 2015. *Preparing future leaders: Effective preparation for aspiring school principals.*

Beijaard, D., Meijer, P., and Verloop, N., 2004. Reconsidering research on teachers' professional identity. *Teaching and Teacher Education*, 20, 107–128.

Blackmore, J., 2015. Gender inequality and education: Changing local/global relations in a "post-colonial" world and the implications for feminist research. *In*: Zajda, J., ed., *Second international handbook on globalisation, education and policy research*. Dordrecht: Springer, 485–501.

Bush, T., 2018. Leadership context: Why one-size does not fit all. *Educational Management Leadership & Administration* 46, 3–4.

Bush, T. and Glover, D., 2003. *School leadership: Concepts and evidence.* Available from: dera.ioe.ac.uk/5119/14/dok217-en-School_Leadership_Concepts_and_Evidence_Redacted.pdf [Accessed 9 January 2018].

Flores, F.M., and Day, C., 2006. Contexts which shape and reshape new teachers' identities: A multi-perspective study. *Teaching and Teacher Education* 22, 219–232.

Gronn, P. 1999. *The making of educational leaders.* London: Cassell.

Gruenewald, D., 2003. Foundations of place: A multidisciplinary framework for place-conscious education. *American Educational Research Association* 40, 619–654.

Gunter, H.M., 2001. *Leaders and leadership in education.* Thousand Oaks, CA: Sage.

Halfacree, H.K.H., 1993. Locality and social representation: Space, discourse and alternative definitions of the rural. *Journal of Rural Studies* 9, 23–37.

Hallinger, H.P., 2018. Bringing context out of the shadows of leadership. *Educational Management Administration & Leadership* 1, 5–24.

Halsey, R.J., 2011. Small schools, big future. *Australian Journal of Education* 55, 5–13.

Halsey, J., 2017. *Independent review into regional, rural and remote education: Discussion paper.* Commonwealth of Australia.

Leithwood, K., Harris, A., and Hopkins, D., 2008. Seven strong claims about successful school leadership. *School Leadership and Management* 28, 27–42.

Leithwood, K., Jantzi, D., and Steinbach, R., 1999. *Changing leadership for changing times.* Philadelphia, PA: Open University Press.

Mockler, N., 2011. Beyond "what works": Understanding teacher identity as a practical and political tool. *Teachers and Teaching: Theory and Practice* 17, 517–528.

Moller, J, 2017. Leading education beyond what works. *European Education Research Journal* 16, 374–385.

Mulford, B., 2007. *Overview of research on Australian educational leadership 2001–2005.* Australian Council for Educational Leaders.

Perumal, J., 2015. Critical pedagogies of place: Educator's personal and professional experiences of social (in)justice. *Teaching and Teacher Education* 45, 25–32.

Pini, B., Moletsane, R., and Mills, M., 2014. Education and global rural: Feminist perspectives. *Gender and Education* 26, 453–464.

Pont, B., Nusche, D., and Moorman, H., 2008. *Improving school leadership. Policy and practice volume 1: Policy and practice.* Available from: www.oecd.org/education/school/44374889.pdf [Accessed 8 October 2015].

Schulte, A., and Walker-Gibbs, B. (Eds.), 2016. *Self-studies in rural teacher education, self-study of teaching and teacher education practices.* Dordrecht: Springer.

Simkins, T., 2005. Leadership in education: "What works" or "what makes sense"? *Educational Management, Administration and Leadership* 33, 9–26.

Stack, S., Beswick, K., Brown, N., Bound, H., and Kenny, J., 2011. Putting partnership at the centre of teachers' professional learning in rural and regional contexts: Evidence from case study projects in Tasmania. *Australian Journal of Teacher Education* 36, 1–20.

Starr, K., and White, S., 2008. The small rural school principalship: Key Challenges and cross-school responses. *Journal of Research in Rural Education* 23, 1–12.

Thompson, P., 2017. *Education leadership and Pierre Bourdieu.* Oxford: Routledge.

Watterston, B., 2015. *Environmental scan principal preparation programs prepared for the Australian Institute for Teaching and School Leadership.* Melbourne: AITSL.

White, S., and Corbett, M., eds., 2014. *Doing educational research in rural settings: Methodological issues, international perspectives and practical solutions.* New York: Routledge.

26 One school's journey to create a new education paradigm

Ray Trotter
With the help of Jennie Vine and Janet Whittle,
Assistant Principals, Wooranna Park Primary School

Wooranna Park is a government primary school servicing the community of one of Australia's most diverse urban areas. The school is located in the State of Victoria, on the outskirts of Melbourne, in the suburb of Dandenong North. In total, 20% of students attending Wooranna Park travel from outside the school's local catchment area, due to the school's innovative approaches to teaching and learning. Consistent with this book's theme of 'flipping the education system', the following chapter describes one school's determination to reject the prevailing educational thinking, as typified by the 'Global Education Reform Movement', presently suffocating children's learning in most Western countries.

In 1993, Wooranna Park Primary School was appointed a 'Gifted and Talented Resource Centre' by the Victorian Education Department. In order to facilitate this responsibility, the school initiated a program of workshops for talented students. While the workshops were always over-subscribed, the school realised that even our own students attending the workshops returned to classrooms where little attention was given to differentiating the curriculum, or providing opportunities for students to negotiate their learning. In response, the school established the 'Autonomous Learning Unit for Year 5 & 6 Students' in 1997. Since that time, Wooranna Park Primary School has sought to create a paradigm shift in education for all of our pupils.

In creating this paradigm shift the school has had to address the three fundamental questions of *why*, *what* and *how*. Why do we need to change? What are the underpinning principles of such a change, and how will this be implemented? In addressing these questions, this paper will highlight the blend of best and next practice pedagogy developed by the school.

Why do we need to change?

Today's students are living in a world vastly different from the one in which their parents grew up. The shelf life of education is shorter than it has ever been. Simon Torok and Paul Holper (2016), in their book *Imagining the Future: Invisibility, Immortality and 40 other Incredible Ideas*, write that at the start of the twentieth century the amount of human knowledge doubled every 100 years.

It now doubles every year and by 2020, according to Torok and Holper, could double every day. Despite this ever-increasing explosion in human knowledge, our school curriculum is still primarily based on the same principles typical of days long since passed.

At the same time, our students are facing an uncertain future, as young people around Australia find it increasingly difficult to find work. The 'Foundation for Young Australians' (FYA 2015) tell us that nearly one in three young people in Australia are currently unemployed or underemployed; and on average it takes 4.7 years to transition from full-time education to full-time work. Such difficulties also include university graduates, with only 65% able to obtain a full-time job within four months of graduating.

Research undertaken by Oxford University (Frey and Osborne 2013) tells us that 47% of the world's current jobs are at risk in the future due to global forces. The FYA (2016, 2017) identifies these global forces as Automation, Globalisation and Flexibility. Their research also highlights the need to better prepare our students for the workforce by prioritizing the teaching of STEM subjects and enterprise skills, such as problem solving, creativity, social intelligence, along with digital and financial literacies.

Failing to prepare our students to enter the workforce is not the only problem inherent in our schools today. Underachievement and lack of engagement permeate our schools. Geoff Masters (2016), Chief Executive of the Australian Council for Educational Research, (ACER), lists the 'long tail' of underachieving students who fall behind year level expectations and fail to meet minimum international standards, as a significant problem for Australian schools. While an Australian engagement survey commissioned by the Australian Institute for Teaching and School Leadership (AITSL 2015), for their 'Learning Frontiers' program, shows that a significant number of students fail to feel a sense of belonging at school, or a connection with the learning.

Sir Ken Robinson (2016) is one of many educators arguing for sweeping changes to how we educate our students. He shares a belief with Pasi Sahlberg (2012), the highly acclaimed Finnish educator that the Global Educational Reform Movement, (GERM), presently dominating the educational systems of most western countries, is a virus. A virus that I believe is partially responsible for much of the well-publicised underachievement in Australian schools. Robinson argues that our present system of education is based on a particular conception of conformity, in that it prioritises a certain type of intellectual conformity, inconsistent with the uniqueness and breadth of human intelligence. "Some people are good at it; some are not"! By prioritising a narrow concept of intelligence, Robinson argues, our educational system stops looking for other types of intelligence, resulting in a large group of our students being considered low achievers, despite the fact that their talents lie elsewhere.

Unfortunately, the introduction of 'NAPLAN' and 'My School' for Australian schools has compounded this problem, by highlighting and praising schools and students good at teaching/learning this narrow body of intellectual intelligence. Often at the expense of not focussing on subject areas unfairly judged as less important, or not easily tested, as schools feel pressured to narrow their curriculum in search of higher test scores. For international readers not familiar with the terms, NAPLAN is Australia's 'National Assessment Program' in Literacy and Numeracy for students in Years 3, 5, 7 and 9, and My School is a website that allows parents to assess their child's school NAPLAN results against other schools. Pleasingly, from my point of view, NAPLAN and My School are not without their critics. Radhika Gorur and Stephan Lewis from Deakin University, writing for *The Conversation* in November 2017, comment:

> While it helps us understand schooling at the system level, information gained from NAPLAN about individual students, classrooms and schools is too limited and error prone to be of use.

This may help explain why Geoff Masters (2017) supports changes to NAPLAN in order "to place less emphasis on comparing the performances of schools and more emphasis on supporting student learning" and why a recent article written by Tom Bentley and Glen Savage (2017) titled 'Educating Australia—why our schools aren't improving', includes the following statement:

> NAPLAN and My School have not led to improvements in literacy and numeracy, with 2016 data showing either stagnation or decline.

Powerful statements considering that Tom was a senior advisor to the former Prime Minister and Minister for Education, Julia Gillard, who introduced My School and NAPLAN, and Geoff is the Chief Executive of ACER.

Australia's teaching profession must also accept part of the responsibility for the state of education in our schools. Too many schools have chosen to narrow their curriculum in order to satisfy State and Federal Governments' obsession with NAPLAN results. Too many of our schools have also chosen to adopt teaching practices that research has shown to be enervating to students' perception of themselves as learners.[1] In an article for *The Age* newspaper, on 13 March 2016, Henrietta Cook states that around 98% of Australian secondary schools, according to the OECD, use some form of streaming. While I am not aware of any authoritative figures relevant to Australian primary schools, I think I am on safe ground suggesting that the practice is also extensively used in primary schools. The use of public Data Boards to publicise student achievement levels is also a practice equally damaging to the self-esteem of lower achieving students. In my opinion, the following words of film producer and educator, Lord David Puttnam (n.d.), should be essential reading for all educators:

> ... under-achievement most frequently stems from a lack of expectation as originally perceived in the eyes of others. A lack of expectation we come to accept as our reality, our fate.

What are the underpinning principles of such a change?

Today's Generation Z students, born between 1995 and 2009 make up about 20% of Australia's population. They are characterised as highly individual, entrepreneurial, globally connected, digital natives (McPherson 2017). The digital world is their "playground", providing instant gratification and access to the world at large. Maintaining their interest at school requires a real world, authentic approach to curriculum planning, along with a more personalised and differentiated focus when addressing individual student's needs. Creating such an environment must, I believe, include:

- Student agency as a priority across the school;
- An emphasis on the development of entrepreneurial and enterprise skills;
- A strong focus on innovation to address the ever changing nature of our world;
- The ubiquitous use of ICT;
- Developing appropriate growth mindsets;
- The harnessing of social media as an educational tool;
- A strong focus on collaborative, problem based, enquiry learning;
- The teacher's role expanded to include the roles of mentor, researcher, facilitator, student confidant, co-learner and co-creator of the learning;
- STEM subjects given a prominence in the curriculum;
- A lessening in the use of grouping children according to age;
- Team teaching, where groups of teachers truly share responsibility for students in their care;
- A dramatic increase in the use of mentors to assist young students, particularly from the ranks of our skilled retirees;
- Ongoing professional development for all school personnel;
- An interdisciplinary approach to curriculum development, with a prominence given to the sustainability of our planet, global citizenship, creativity and The Arts; and finally
- An increased focus on 'real world' learning, with a recognition of the importance of Asian Literacy for the future of Australia.

How have our teachers and students implemented these changes?

Our first task, when commencing our journey, was to house all of our Year level students together in Learning Communities under the direction of a team of teachers, with each teacher given the added responsibility for shaping the learning journey of around 20 students. Much of our energy and time initially was devoted to redesigning the learning environment—a focus that continues today. During this time—as we sought to personalise student learning within a collaborative framework, influenced by Reggio Emilia philosophy—student learning was primarily focused around the following four pedagogical practices:

1. Workshops: Traditional large group presentations focused on specific subject areas, or broader interdisciplinary learning themes.
2. Targeted Teaching: Small group teaching sessions designed to address the individual learning needs of selected students.
3. Learning Agreement Time: For younger children LA is about providing small provocations to inspire children's learning and allowing them to explore the various learning centres that comprise their learning community. While for older children, LA is about students increasingly taking responsibility for their learning.
4. Student/Teacher Conferences: Short regular weekly meetings designed to co-plan and differentiate each child's learning.

Early in our journey, the school leadership team recognised that we needed to document our journey for parents and future staff. As a result, our website has a wealth of film explaining our pedagogical practices. In 2014, the school completed a series of 13 videos focused on our approach to Personalising Student Learning. These videos were subsequently translated into Spanish by Sister Monica from the College Montserrat in Barcelona. I mention these videos here, because much of what is described is still pertinent today and provides the thinking from which many of our recent innovations have evolved.

It was around this time I received an email from the American educator, David Thornburg, requesting some photographs of our school to include in a book he was writing, titled *From the Campfire to the Holodeck* (2013).[2] David argues that from primordial times humans have learned in four discrete ways: at the Campfire, at the Watering Hole, in the Cave and from Life—metaphors for direct teaching, collaborative learning, learning from oneself (through reflection and introspection), and building on ones' learning in the course of their daily lives. He was also responsible for creating 50 short videos to excite students' learning, a program he called 'Knights of Knowledge', along with building a Holodeck in Brazil, for older students to experience life on-board a spaceship on route to Mars. As a principal who believes that schools should be as exciting as Disneyland, I was immediately hooked.

In response, we started to prepare our own films to excite our students' learning and challenged our students to undertake 'Enigma Missions' to solve the conundrums and mysteries of life. We also built a new learning space, which we called the Enigma Portal on the recommendation of one of our students. Unfortunately, our plans were hindered, in part, by our inability to produce films quickly, a significant task given the multitude of topics in which students expressed an interest. It was at this point that my assistant principal, in charge of the senior school, Jennie Vine, resolved our problems and laid the foundation for many of our more recent innovations.

Jennie recognised that it was not essential that we prepare films to excite children's learning. She used students' innate curiosity, along with her worldly knowledge and teaching skills, to introduce students to a number of

One school's new education paradigm 227

next-practice pedagogical procedures. Our subsequent involvement in the AITSL 'Learning Frontiers Program', led by Valerie Hannon, along with our inclusion in Michael Fullan's international research project, 'New Pedagogies for Deep Learning', helped solidify these innovations. The following infographic (see Figure 26.1) summarises where we are today relevant to our underpinning practices, pedagogy and student attributes.

The introduction of Enigma Missions as a pedagogical practice was dramatic in its impact. From day one of our journey to transform our school, one of our goals has been to increase student ownership of their learning. But the increased levels of student agency as a result of the introduction of Enigma Missions was beyond our expectations, as was the quality and advanced nature of student learning.

We soon learned that students' interests extended well outside the primary school curriculum. Should we allow our students to explore and impact on social issues they felt strongly about? Should they learn about black holes, DNA, autism, de-extincting animals, the God Particle, or how the brain works? We chose to allow our students to select their own Enigma topics, although some of the students' choices needed to be modified to avoid culturally sensitive issues, or placing them in danger, i.e. exploring homelessness on our city streets.

It is also important to understand that this was not an exercise in exploring surface learning. Nothing could be further from the truth! As a former

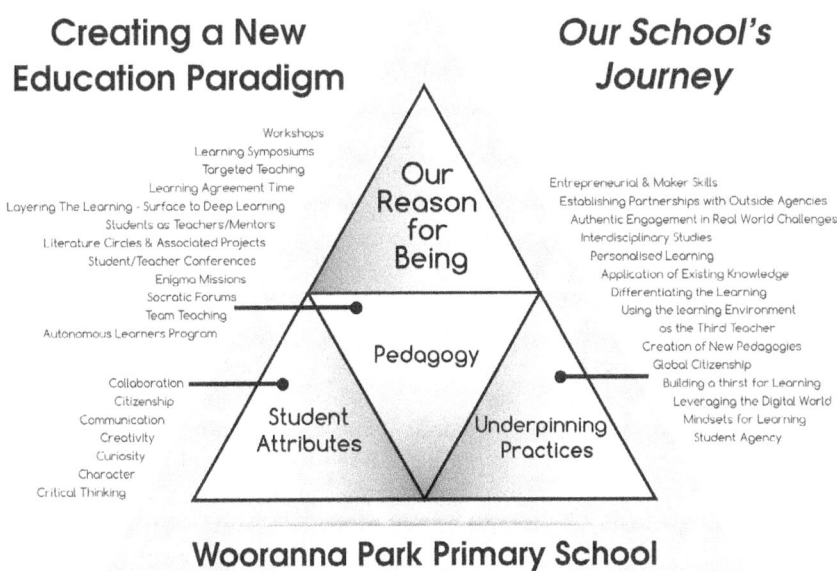

Figure 26.1 Creating a new education paradigm: the Wooranna Park Primary School journey

secondary school teacher, Jennie expected students to provide a bibliography detailing their research sources, contact experts for additional information and be prepared to present their findings to, and answer questions from their peers, teachers and parents. She also recognised that the students' learning needed to be 'layered' in order for students to move from surface to deep learning. This led Jennie to introduce a new pedagogical practice called 'Learning Symposiums'.

Learning symposiums promote student ownership, autonomy and collaboration, shifting student knowledge from short term to long-term memory. With similarities to a Q&A forum, audience members in a learning symposium have a specific task. They must interrogate the student presenter respectfully, identifying the depth of their knowledge throughout their presentation. This process must be carefully layered by teachers prior to the experience, ensuring all members are aware of questioning technique, etiquette, social conduct and level of expectation.

When the presenter has exhausted their knowledge bank, they must record areas of weakness, so that they can be addressed before the next symposium, where they will present once again. This encourages accountability and promotes purpose. Presenting students are also encouraged to share their research without the use of cue cards.

One of the most successful pedagogical practices introduced has been the 'Autonomous Learners Card'. This program is about encouraging all students to recognise themselves as autonomous learners. The card allows Year 5 and 6 students to work outside the confines of their Learning Community. To obtain an AL Card students have to write a formal application addressing a list of questions relevant to their ability to work and learn unsupervised. They are also required to attend an interview with a panel comprised of students and teachers in order to discuss their application. If successful, they are given a two-month trial. On the successful completion of the trial, applicants are formally recognised as Autonomous Learners at a meeting of the Student Parliament.

The adoption of the simple pedagogical practice of encouraging all students to see themselves as teachers and mentors, passing on their expertise and wisdom to other students, has also proven extremely beneficial. Jessica Langer (2016) writing for 'Usable Knowledge', Harvard Graduate School of Education, comments that allowing her high school students to teach their peers sends a powerful message to her students, "You have knowledge worth sharing, you have a teacher's trust, and you have an opportunity to support your friend's learning". For Wooranna Park the program has also proven beneficial in other ways. First, it can be adapted for use at all year levels, with our Prep Professors Program proving a wonderful success and secondly it has been used very successfully to socialise some of our high functioning autistic students. Seth, one of the children in question, is Singaporean and as such started his schooling in Singapore, where he was unable to adjust to the highly compliant nature of the learning environment. His father searched the web for a more appropriate setting and Seth was enrolled subsequently at Wooranna

Park, where his talent with all things digital, proved the ideal "vehicle" to assist him to socialise with other students.

Wooranna Park also places an emphasis on the development of entrepreneurial skills and students' ability to leverage the digital world. Students are encouraged to apply for loans from the Student Bank to establish start-up businesses. The bank is managed solely by the student leadership and financed via a grant from the school council. Profits raised after repayment of the loans are split evenly between worthy social causes and the Year 6 Graduation Class. This allows our exiting students to purchase a gift for the remaining students to commemorate their association with the school.

In embracing the digital world, the school has discovered students whose skills in this area are more advanced than ever expected. Areas of study, previously the domain of universities, have become problems for primary school-aged children to solve! Students have developed everything from virtual reality games, custom built computers, to fully functioning virtual and physical CISCO Networks and recently started work on creating a life-sized, 3D printed, open source robot. Wherever possible Wooranna Park has sought to introduce cutting-edge advancements into our digital programs, as highlighted by students' exploration of the following: virtual and augmented reality; coding; computer building; Cisco routing and switching; Blockchain technology; crypto-currencies; robotics and 3D printing. Students have become the driving force behind these programs, as they traverse a multitude of digital terrains without fear of failure! We also hope to open our newly built STEAM Centre early next year, housed in four shipping containers. There are numerous videos on our website featuring the school's approach to digital learning.

I would like to finish this chapter with the thoughts of one of my students when asked to write a short statement about how her learning was progressing. I do this because as I read back over the chapter I realise that I have not captured the voices of my students and surely, it is their judgement, in the final analysis, which decides our success or failure as educators. It is by listening to and sharing the voices of students that we can truly flip the education system to one that is based on the voices that most count.

> So far, this year has been so different from last year. It feels like the world has just changed itself, just like that!
>
> I believe that the whole idea of Wooranna Park Primary School is to lift us and our capabilities. The way the staff treat us is as if we're adults and not students. Wooranna Park is to make us feel complete, like we have finally achieved something as students. To tell us that all our sins are in the past, like they were never even there.
>
> I have felt dark days, like a shadow has been cast upon me, but Wooranna has helped me to overcome that and that's what makes me, me. Wooranna is my home. The teachers are our role models, leaders. All of us are connected in some possibility.

I have done a lot this year. Enigmas for example. This is to help us with our knowledge, passion, education, leadership and our roles in life. I believe that we all have a voice and Wooranna is our guide.

(Extract from a Year 6 student's written response to a request by her teacher to describe her feelings about Wooranna Park Primary School in 2017)

Notes

1 The Pygmalion effect, or Rosenthal effect, is the phenomenon whereby higher expectations lead to an increase in performance (Source: Pygmalion in the classroom, Rosenthal and Jacobson, 1965).
2 The holodeck is a fictional plot device from the television series Star Trek. It is presented as a staging environment in which participants may engage with different virtual reality environments.

References

Australian Institute for Teaching and School Leadership, 2015. Learning frontiers, professional practices to increase student engagement in learning, Issue 2.

Bentley, T. and Savage G.C., February 2, 2017, Educating Australia—why our schools aren't improving. *The Conversation*. Available from: https//theconversation.com/educating-australia-why-our-schools-aren't-improving-72092.

Bryan Bruce Interviews Dr Pasi Sahlberg, Published on YouTube, 24 May 2016. Interview recorded for inclusion in 'World Class? A documentary about the New Zealand Education System'. Available from: www.youtube.com/watch?v=1w7CunvjvdE.

Cook, H., 2016. The downside of separating students into A, B and C classes. *The Age*.

Foundation for Young Australians (FYA), 2015. How are young people faring in the transition from school to work. Available from: https://www.fya.org.au/report/how-are-young-people-faring-report-card-2015/.

Foundation for Young Australians, 2016. The new basics: Big data reveals the skills young people need for the New Work Order. Available from: www.fya.org.au/report/the-new-basics/.

Foundation for Young Australians, 2017, The new work smarts. Available from: www.fya.org.au.

Frey, C.B. and Osborne, M.A., 2013. The future of employment: How susceptible are jobs to computerization? Oxford University.

Gorur, R. and Lewis, S., 2017. Never underestimate the immune system. *The Conversation*. Available from: https://theconversation.com/naplan-has-done-little-to-improve-student-outcomes-86049#.

Langer, J., 2016. Students as teachers. Blog article for Usable Knowledge, Harvard Graduate School of Education. Available from: www.gse.harvard.edu/uk/blog/welcome-usable-knowledge.

Masters, G.N., 2016. Five challenges in Australian school education. *Policy Insights*, Issue 5, Camberwell, Vic, ACER. Available from: research.acer.edu.au/policyinsights/5/.

Masters, G.N., 2017. Shifting the focus of NAPLAN. Teacher Bulletin, ACER. Available from: www.teachermagazine.com.au/columnists/geoff-masters/shifting-the-focus-of-naplan.

McPherson, S., 2017. GEN Z: World wise, digital natives, changemakers, Foundation for Young Australians. Online News. Available from: www.fya.org.au/2017/09/28/gen-z-world-wise-digital-natives-changemakers/.

Puttnam, D., n.d. Voice recording, Included in: Personalised student learning, Video 1, Wooranna Park Primary School. Available from: www.woorannaparkps.vic.gov.au.

Robinson, K., 2016. Keynote speaker, big picture: Big Bang, Orlando Florida. Published on YouTube, 11 August 2016. Available from: www.youtube.com/watch?v=9xCGAVQOUB4.

Rosenthal, R. and Jacobson, L., 1968. Pygmalion in the classroom. *The Urban Review*, 3 (1), 16–20.

Sahlberg, P., 2012. GERM that kills schools, TEDX East New York. Available from: www.youtube.com/watch?v=TdgS–9Zg_0.

Torok, S. and Holper, P., 2016. *Imagining the future: Invisibility, immortality and 40 other incredible ideas*. Melbourne: CSIRO Publishing.

Thornburg, D.D., 2013. *From the Campfire to the Holodeck: Creating Engaging and Powerful 21st Century Learning Environments*. San Francisco, CA: Jossey–Bass.

Wooranna Park P.S. (n.d.), Personalising Student Learning: 13 videos. Available from: www.woorannaparkps.vic.edu.au.

27 Finding our roots in the leaves

An ecology of change in leading learning that matters

Flossie S. G. Chua, David N. Perkins and Daniel G. Wilson

Figure 27.1 Preschoolers Amy, Cathy, Eugene, Rob, and Reena with teacher Lynette George learning to use Blackwood leaves as soap

Preschoolers Amy, Cathy, Eugene, Rob, and Reena dash back to their teacher, Lynette George, eager to show her the leaves they had picked from the Blackwood trees.

Reena: Is this the leaf? This can make soap?
Lynette: Let's test it, shall we? [*She wets her hands, takes some of the leaves and crushes them between her hands.*] First, we crunch the leaves with water in our hands, and then we rub it very hard and fast with our hands. [*The students begin to imitate her actions.*]
Eugene: I'm getting bubbles! Look! I made bubbles!
Rob: Me too! It's really soap!
Lynette: Smells nice, doesn't it?
Cathy: It does! My hands feel all clean and nice now!

Amy:	My leaves are not making any soap!
Lynette:	Try the other leaves. Do they work?
Amy:	No. Where can we find those leaves? [*She points to the leaves that the other students are using.*] I want to get more of those.
Lynette:	Not all the leaves will work. You have to test them. [*She puts some fresh leaves in Amy's hands.*] You need more water. We need to be persistent, don't we? It's hard, isn't it? We've got to practise!
Eugene:	I think I can wash myself every day with these leaves!
Cathy:	Yes! But you need many, many more leaves. Let's pick more!
Lynette:	Remember: we can only take these ones off the trees today because we are making soap. You can't pick them all the time. We only pick what we need, or we won't have more to use next time.
Reena:	What else can we do with the leaves?
Lynette:	Well, the Wurundjeri people soak them in water and use the water for a lot of things, like reducing headaches and sore eyes, and treating insect bites and stings. Many other plants and trees are used for different things. So, you see, the land we live on takes care of us in many ways.
Rob:	Is that why we have to take care of the land too?

+++++++++++++++++++++++++

How can school leaders transform and energise the learning that students experience in the classroom? What becomes possible when relevant and compelling learning lies at the heart of school decisions? This chapter offers a window into what a strong focus on the learning that matters for the lives that learners will live and can look like through the example of Beaconhills College, an independent, open-entry, co-educational Christian school established in 1982 in Melbourne's south-eastern suburbs. The school defines itself through its sense of community, diverse and innovative curriculum, global outlook and emphasis on caring for others both locally and abroad. The Beaconhills example proposes that leading learning that matters for our contemporary world involves tapping a complex ecology of influences and adopting a more distributed notion of leadership. Doing so engages the school community in creating a shared vision, setting directions, developing capacity, and sustaining progress. It also demonstrates how leadership can flip the system by visibly trusting and supporting the professional capacity of teachers to imagine and drive change.

Developments in the last century—the rise of the global economy, increasing uncertainty created by sociotechnical developments, unprecedented population mobility reshaping our world, and more—have challenged educators to shift how they think about what matters most to learn. Traditional systems of learning around the world are being substantially challenged and reshaped, and not only how we teach but *what* we teach has become a critical front of exploration for schools.

Our team at Project Zero of the Harvard Graduate School of Education, an educational research and development group, has been collaborating with

Independent Schools Victoria, a coalition of independent schools in Victoria, Australia, since 2011 on a programme called *Leading Learning that Matters* (LLtM). LLtM is a loosely structured process for individual schools and small coalitions of schools. It invites participating school leaders and their staff and community to engage in a reflective process of rethinking some aspects of what's taught and how it's taught. It encourages them to construct a vision and to make that vision a daily reality in courses and classrooms. Beaconhills College headmaster, Tony Sheumack, was in the pioneer cohort of school principals on the LLtM programme.

Through the LLtM work that we have been doing, we have found that school leaders who seek to prepare learners for today's dynamic and complex society focus on the learning that matters (*what is worth learning*): they open up possibilities beyond more traditional conversations about methods of teaching and reconsider evaluation. These leaders recognise that while instruction and assessment are important, paying attention only to the 'how' of teaching and evaluation can often narrow a school's focus, leading to incremental solutions that do not address deeper problems of education. Schools may get better at delivery and assessment while not facing the more fundamental challenge of remaining relevant to their learners and their communities in a swiftly changing world.

The LLtM programme is now in its second cycle with a new group of school leaders. While we could draw worthwhile stories from most of the settings that both cohorts of school leaders work in, and thank them heartily for their participation and good work, for the sake of sharing a full picture, we have chosen to focus on one school here.

Learning that matters at Beaconhills College

At Beaconhills College, preschoolers like Amy, Cathy, Eugene, Rob, and Reena experience the Aboriginal connection with the land on a regular basis. They explore the bushland area in Beaconhills College's Pakenham Campus, and come to understand how the local Indigenous people have sustainably used natural resources for generations to live a healthy life.

Year 5 students at the College embark on interdisciplinary investigations focused on the local community and the land that they live on, and what it means for the College to be located on the land of the Wurundjeri and Boon Wurrung, traditional custodians of the land. They learn what "landownership" and "custodianship" mean, and develop a sense of who they are vis-à-vis the land.

Instead of camps, Year 9 and 10 students embark on programs including trips to the Northern Territory where they practise Aboriginal traditions of deep reflection, shared learning, and storytelling with the local communities. They collaborate with students from the local schools, meet local Indigenous leaders, and learn age-old methods of living and working.

On the College grounds, a dedicated outdoor space combines a medieval Christian maze with a circle of Aboriginal thinking stones made from local mudstone. Students go there to think, meditate, reflect and pray. The setting also encourages shared learning, reflection and storytelling—important aspects of Aboriginal tradition.

Such experiences are part of Beaconhills College's Indigenous cultural learning programme, designed to support students towards a multi-perspectival understanding of Australia's history. The programme recognises the First People's roles, cultures, and contributions to the country, and constitutes an integral part of the College's LLtM initiative.

The *learning that matters* at Beaconhills College is described in Six Key Pillars—*learning*, the *environment, our world and other cultures, citizenship and service, wellbeing*, and *values and character*—at the heart of the College's vision and mission. They define the elements the College believes are necessary to support the holistic education of students. The Beaconhills curriculum aligns with the Six Key Pillars for a more holistic curriculum that include programs more traditionally considered "extra-curricular". Traditional learning areas at Beaconhills College are inflected via the *learning that matters* lens as teachers identify relevant and meaningful learning outcomes for the students.

When teacher Lynette George first proposed to the leadership team that an authentic understanding of Indigenous culture must be anchored in a collaborative, respectful relationship with local Indigenous communities, she had no idea that it would become a full-scale curricular programme in the College, touching the lives of all students and staff. According to Tony, Lynette's proposal came at an opportune time for the College:

> We tried many different programmes for about 15 years, with no success at all, because there was no shared need with the Indigenous community. The reality is that we cannot impose ourselves on them; it needs to resonate with the community. We need to develop a shared understanding that is built on deep respect and mutual trust.

Today, the College runs regular events that weave Indigenous learning into the fabric of school life: annual Reconciliation events for all levels to celebrate and recognise Indigenous culture; workshops led by the head elder of the Wurundjeri people on Aboriginal history and traditions; classroom lessons that nurture a broader understanding of what being "Australian" means. Non-teaching staff are also heavily involved, for instance, helping to conceptualise and build the reflection circle. The College's Outdoor Education programme has broadened and deepened to offer culturally different experiences for students and staff to "not just 'see' a place ... but to be a part of it, to serve and be out of one's comfort zone, to live the life of the community".

Four key leadership practices

In general, LLtM does not offer "right answers" to what learning matters. Instead, it invites schools to engage questions of *what learning matters* for their context, *for whom and why*, using key questions and other tools. It invites principals into problem finding, experimentation, and developing new practices. More importantly, it emphasises that the enterprise is not a solitary one; often, it is best embarked in collaboration with the school community, making the LLtM initiative unique and responsive to the school's needs and structure. Over several years of documenting school leaders' LLtM initiatives, we have noted four essential leadership practices: *creating shared vision, developing collaborative structures, supporting individual development*, and *sustaining progress*. In what follows, we explain each practice, illustrating it with examples from Beaconhills College.

Creating shared vision

School leaders are crucial change agents for their schools when leading LLtM initiatives. Effective leaders involve stakeholders in crafting and shaping a compelling and shared vision of the learning that matters. By creating spaces for dialogue across the community, they allow answers to emerge over time.

At Beaconhills College, the leadership team used *learning that matters* as a critical lens by which to arrive at what eventually became the College's Six Key Pillars of learning and holistic education. The leadership team created opportunities for staff to reflect on what learning matters using prompts such as: *Who are we as "Beaconhills", and what do we stand for? What's our mission?* Inviting the staff to collaboratively articulate a vision of the learning that matters for the College built momentum for the LLtM initiative, resulting in school-wide support for it because everyone felt ownership of it.

The leadership team also invited staff to rethink the work that they had been doing through the lens of *learning that matters*, prompting curricular review and innovation. Stephen McGinley, Head of Education, describes how *learning that matters* has provided a way for the College to talk about what matters to learn and why, effectively connecting curricular conversations to the College's strategic direction, identity and philosophy.

More importantly, working towards a shared vision has pushed the staff to challenge the status quo and assumptions about what learning really matters. Yvonne Ashmore, Head of Wellbeing, sees the focus on the *learning that matters* as "an invitation to really interrogate what programmes like Wellbeing means from the perspective of Beaconhills. *Learning that matters* is a broad aspirational idea that allows us to define what it means for us".

A shared vision, however, becomes a stumbling block if the community cannot find their way into it, or find themselves in it. Early on, Tony realised that everyone had their own idea of what "holistic learning" meant:

> We had to break down the ideas behind 'holistic learning', to distil what the important aspects are into the Six Key Pillars, and really make sure that we hit those in everything we do. The language of the Pillars resonates because it is accessible, and people can easily unpack it ... yet it is still open to interpretation, so our staff can own it and communicate it in their own words.

Developing collaborative structures

Another key LLtM practice involves putting in place structures that support interdependent learning and experimentation among the staff. These structures create spaces for staff to think together, and develop processes for sharing ideas, encouraging risk taking, learning from mistakes, and giving feedback. Such structures range from redesigning meetings, to including stakeholders' voices in decision making, to using physical spaces to invite and support collaboration.

A key move that Tony made when Lynette proposed her idea for Indigenous cultural learning was to connect her to Sam Maddock, Head of Beacon Explorers. He encouraged them to rethink and, if necessary, retool the existing Outdoor Education programme. In the course of working together, Lynette's perspective on Indigenous cultural learning as an Indigenous person encouraged Sam to deeply reflect on what about outdoor experiences matter:

> I've visited many national parks in Australia, and I've always had this almost spiritual feeling that there's something about this land I'm standing on that I don't know about, and I want to understand who was here before me and why it was important for them. Working with Lynette really pushed me to think about how outdoor experiences should really get the students to ask themselves: *what is this environment I'm in, and why is it important to me and also to my community?* This gets them to bring in the history and culture, and taking these different perspectives builds deeper thinking.
>
> (Sam)

Their collaboration resulted in the embedding of Outdoor Education within the school curriculum, signalling unequivocally that outdoor experiences, in the context of this school, are as important as classroom learning. Now, students participating in the Outdoor Education programme no longer embark on local and overseas trips to learn *about* other communities; instead, they are required to enter into and *participate* in the life and rhythm of the communities. Students on these trips reflect on their responsibility to their fellow human beings, and have begun to raise important questions about their world:

> They start asking questions like: *Who is an Aboriginal person and how do you know?* They see now that it's not a colour distinction, that Aboriginal people are not all a certain colour. And neither do you have to live in the Northern Territory to be Aboriginal. It's so important that they are now asking these difficult questions and grappling with them.
>
> (Sam)

Lynette and Sam regularly tested their ideas for the Outdoor Education programme with the staff, inviting their feedback and suggestions. They also involved more staff in the programme. As the staff began to see the results of

Lynette's and Sam's experiments with the programme, they became bolder about asking questions hitherto deemed risky. Sam describes how teachers now feel confident sharing their vulnerabilities with him: *What is that story we want to tell about the place we are taking the students to? How do I teach it, what do I say?* The teachers have grown more sensitive to the traditions of the Indigenous communities, and deeply cognizant and respectful of the protocols to telling Aboriginal stories.

> They now see and really respect that there are protocols in the Aboriginal oral tradition about who can tell the story, and why ... They are more aware of how the Aboriginal stories are an important way of passing on to the next generation the accumulated knowledge, spirituality, and wisdom of the community. They are asking: *Is it my story to tell? If not, who can help me tell the story?* So, we began collaborating with the Indigenous communities to create a programme that honors the Indigenous voice and perspective.
>
> (Sam)

Tony believes that the current College-wide impetus towards deeper understanding of and greater engagement with local Indigenous and global communities is the result of the right people in the right places at the right time:

> It's about having good people who want to do good things, and giving them enough latitude so that they can explore and experiment and really do good things ... It has to be strategic; we put people to lead each of the Six Key Pillars across the College, and our staff know who is doing what. There's no mystery; everyone knows who to go to with an idea for the learning that matters.

Supporting individual development

Leading an initiative, however compelling, is challenging unless underpinning the endeavour is the human capacity for change. School leaders engaged in LLtM successfully create stimulating conditions for staff to develop capacities for learning and change by tapping into their intrinsic motivation and beliefs to support the change, and supporting agency, experimentation and risk taking.

Lynette's experience is a case in point. Tony recognised early on that her passion for and commitment to her proposal made her an ideal champion for the Indigenous cultural learning programme across the College's two campuses:

> We wanted a programme that involved the local Indigenous community in an authentic way, but we didn't have a champion. So, whatever we had ended up very tokenistic. To complicate things, any programme had to be implemented across our two campuses in synergistic ways. With Lynette,

the programme really took off. She really championed the programme, connecting to people, and working across the campuses on the programme.

Lynette credits the support from Tony and his leadership team for her success in implementing and growing the programme. She remembers how, right from the outset, they had allowed her to make decisions and run with her ideas, and to organise things and "just have a go". She smiles as she remembers how she was told: "If it worked, that's good. If it didn't, let's think about what we could do better next time." One of her fondest memories is the first assembly she organised for Year 4–12 students and staff:

> We had 900 children in the auditorium, several speakers, and the event went on for two hours. Allowing me to run that meant stopping the whole school's usual routine. It was tough for some teachers to give up their teaching time for it, and it wasn't even during the regular assembly time! It was so encouraging that the school would allow that!

Ultimately, it was the leadership's trust in her proposal and her capacity to lead it that gave Lynette the confidence to forge ahead on what was previously uncharted territory for her:

> Just allowing me some of my dreams and aspirations, to go forward, and to educate other people on a topic they didn't know much about—that's just been huge for me ... I was just trusted to do a good job, trusted to get the right people in to talk to the children, to decide how long it was going to be. To be able to have that was very humbling. I was so proud of myself!

Sam similarly attributed his drive to stretch himself to explore new ideas to Tony's trust in his capacity to lead change:

> Just being recognised that you are the expert in your field, so off you go; that same trust, autonomy and opportunity that we are trying to give our students, that's what we've been given as leaders, and we all thrive on that! To allow our passion and trust our expertise and give us that opportunity, that's absolutely been the biggest part of it for me.

Sustaining progress

A critical leadership practice in shepherding an LLtM initiative is embedding processes to sustain the initiative in the everyday work of the school. Often, as an initiative rolls along, and the general feeling is that nothing seems untoward, little thought goes to institutionalising it, making the initiative fragile. Sustaining an LLtM initiative involves allocating time and resources to support staff; protecting staff from distractions; defending the initiative against sceptics; and embedding the initiative in school policies and systems.

At Beaconhills College, a priority is maintaining focus on the LLtM initiative among staff and in curricular experiences. The leadership team recognises that even good initiatives are susceptible to distraction and sprawl when a new trend surfaces. Stephen emphasises that:

> Any idea or proposal is examined through the lens of *learning that matters*. That lens has really helped us focus our efforts and not get distracted by the latest buzzwords or frameworks. We don't use other language so that what we are doing is consistent, and there's no encroaching on our thinking.

Focusing on *learning that matters* also achieves long-term stability through strategically changing the College's leadership structures (e.g. leadership positions created to lead each of the Six Key Pillars across the two campuses), and its strategic plans (e.g. articulating a shared vision for the learning that matters and making it accessible through the Six Key Pillars; developing a map of where and when innovations would be implemented). Structurally, the leadership team and champions of various initiatives lead cross-campus groups, and are empowered to experiment with and implement their ideas. Tony explains that the crux was supporting the good things already going on in the school, and consolidating them under the LLtM banner, so that good work was clearly valued.

Tony and his team were also wary of pushing too much change or pushing change at an untenable pace. As staff became energised by the initiative, many ideas for innovations were floated, especially during the planning stage. Those ideas were put through a consultancy process with teams of staff members, who discussed them using the question, "*Where does that fit with the learning that matters?*" Ideas were tweaked and revised until they turn into well-thought-out proposals. Tony also posed an enabling constraint on the ideas proposed: *All ideas must be implemented with existing resources, so what do we lose to get this new thing?*

Taking the temperature of the staff's capacity for change was critical. Tony advised that "a little bit of success, when it actually sticks, allows you to do a little bit more. Sometimes you have to go slowly because it's not resonating, but at all times, never lose sight of where you are going".

The LLtM initiative has also been institutionalised into the College's planning and hiring systems. Year 4 teacher Sue Collins described the *learning that matters* as a mindset in the College, "It's like a compass for us now; you see it in everything that we do in the classroom, and outside the classroom". Interviews for staff positions require applicants to articulate what the learning that matters for them is, and the College hires those whose aspirations and commitments align with the school's vision.

Looking inward to look outward

Behind each LLtM initiative lies an amazing amount of work done collaboratively by the staff in a singular effort towards a collective vision. At Beaconhills

College, the LLtM initiative might have started out as the headmaster's project, but it's now anything but that:

> Not many people were energised by it initially, especially when it involved a lot of extra work. What's worse, it's seen as the headmaster's project being pushed onto the school ... But it wasn't going away: we kept going, institutionalising it in all our systems, finding champions and supporting their work, finding a consistent way to talk about it. After three years, we had embedded it in the culture, the ethos, the identity of Beaconhills. Any new initiative now has to be incorporated into the learning that matters. It not only drove change, it legitimised it. The first couple of years, the initiative could have died very quickly. But now, it'll be struggling to disappear because it's no longer a project done at ISV and Harvard; it's now just what Beaconhills is and does.

The Beaconhills example underscores the exciting possibilities of educational change when school leaders invite teachers into the discourse on what matters most to learn, and value them as drivers of change. When teachers find their history and ongoing commitments folded into the school's vision of the *learning that matters*, they become powerful partners in the very systems on which the school operates and thrives.

Conclusion
Speaking hope into education discourse

Deborah M. Netolicky, Jon Andrews and Cameron Paterson

In Australia, as in other parts of the Western education world, tacit knowledge—that is, the wisdom of practice and of practitioners—is often devalued. Mechanistic high stakes accountability, standardisation and bureaucratisation, present as strategies of surveillance and serve to control the unwieldy education system. Soundbites of mass-consumed media, in Australia and around the Western world, intensify the narrative of an ailing and failing system at odds with itself, thereby undermining the important work of teachers and schools.

Teachers, middle leaders, senior leaders, and principals, are largely voiceless in the public discourse on schooling. Teachers especially are routinely viewed as grunt workers at the bottom of the pecking order, disempowered and deprofessionalised. It would be highly unusual for a television panel discussing education to feature a teacher involved in the debate. Teachers tend to feel uncomfortable and unprepared for such public limelight, challenged by the prospect of reducing the complexity of education to a media grab. The absence of teacher voices in relation to the dominance of system-wide assessment, the commercialisation of public schooling, and the deprofessionalisation of teachers in an era of hyper-accountability can only be reversed by politicians and reform leaders engaging with the profession, and listening with intent to the voices in everyday educational settings. This book pushes back against destructive aspects of the education system by doing just that: presenting a range of voices and perspectives on what matters in education.

This is a Flip the System *Australia* book, which includes primarily the voices of Australian academics, teachers, school leaders, and those working in education. We have also reached out beyond our national border to include international voices who provide powerful insights and ideas about political, social and economic forces that influence numerous aspects of education in Australia and around the world. These forces manifest themselves at the intermarriage of policy formation and subsequent decisions on what constitutes effective or worthwhile education. Large-scale assessment, the use (and misuse) of big data at all levels of schooling, corporate investment, and new models of governance and technological innovation, are pervasive. They have given rise to 'edupreneur' culture, policy borrowing, and the Silicon Valley innovation agenda which masquerades as 'social justice' but often reinforces structural inequality and submits education to unregulated, self-serving players. In such a system, we should not be isolated in our classrooms or schools. Nor should we be isolated within our national systems or thinking. Our international authors bring an important lens through which Australia can consider itself within a global milieu, and through which educators from other nations might see Australia's contribution.

We acknowledge, however, that there are voices missing from this book, including those of students themselves. The voices and civic agency of the students in the USA who spoke out against gun violence in 2018 are one example of the power of student voice. Our students are not just future or hypothetical citizens, or citizens in training, they are citizens today and they have the right to be listened to and heard and to make meaningful contributions. Students possess agency in a truly flipped education system.

Australia has been nicknamed 'the lucky country' after the title of Donald Horne's 1964 book. Horne's book suggests, however, that Australia is unexceptional and undeserving of its good fortune. It posits that Australia has ridden on fortuity rather than strategy, and has relied on luck rather than good leadership or a desire to achieve (except in sport). Australia is not without poverty, inequality, the marginalisation of Indigenous Australians and the mistreatment of asylum seekers. Australia's more recent desire to become the 'clever country' has not managed to serve all students. For instance, Graham et al. (2015) argue that education policy has compounded social stratification. While Australia is blessed with hard and soft commodities, the Anthropocene era has witnessed it (like other nations) experiencing an over-reliance on natural resources to propel economic strategy. This is an unsustainable economic and geopolitical position. Global and local environmental change has catalysed a spate of managerial activity aimed at buffering the effects of energy insecurity, spatial development stresses and the consequential burgeoning social inequalities. As Jelmer Evers indicates in the Foreword, while the democratic imperative was always central to the notion of a flipped system, he and René Kneyber didn't fully grasp how democracy itself was under threat when they wrote the original Flip the System book. In just a few short years, people have become increasingly alienated from democracy, political parties are now overtly connected to corporations, and economic management is aligned with global capital. Hacking and cyber-surveillance are coupled with a corrosive decline in democracy as sweeping laws stifle press freedom, curb community advocacy, and result in disillusionment with political discourse. Politicians trivialise issues and analysis is replaced by Photoshop. In the face of these threats, a well-informed and engaged population is the best response. As an ethnically diverse nation Australia continues to face deep questions about identity as cultural diversity is a reality at odds with insufficient racial literacy. We have no choice but to activate our moral consciousness to find our own answers to what matters in our world. The path forward in education will not be delivered by someone else, but by those working with students in schools and classrooms. Questioning, exploring and feeling unsettled with colleagues are productive professional practices that can lead to shared understanding and better solutions. Questions give order to the world and it is re-examination, experimentation, cognitive challenge, and shared construction of meaning, that is intended to be the unifying theme of this book.

In some way, all authors herein are engaging with questions of 'What matters?' or 'What *should* matter?' in education. They engage with other questions, too. How might professional trust be developed in our schools and education systems? How might that trust be reciprocated when policies have repeatedly failed to listen to the experience and evidence sitting in our schools, articulated by those doing the work, rather than those who steer from a distance or are seemingly driven by ideological imperatives? How can educators understand and navigate international testing and accountabilities in meaningful ways? What are the effects of commercialisation in the education sector? What are the mechanisms that perpetuate inequality in education and how might we best address or redress these? In what ways can the Australian education system best serve its Indigenous and socially disadvantaged communities? How are Australian schools already harnessing collaborative expertise or community engagement? What professional learning and leadership practices can empower educators and positively transform education? Whose voices are privileged in education policy and practice, and whose voices are silenced or ignored?

This book's contributors grapple with the complexities, the humanity and the possibilities in education. Educators are increasingly sharing their views, voices and wisdom of practice through platforms such as blogs and books. Social media is equalising education discourse to some extent as it brings diverse voices into public conversation. It is important for educators to communicate, interact, be open to challenge, and build places where people with different views can bring their ideas to the table. Educators should be invited, not only to tables within their own schools, but into education policy, reform and research discourses. In 2003 Judyth Sachs famously issued a call to action arguing that an activist teaching profession is an educated and politically astute one. It is now, more than ever, time for the teaching profession to heed her call. To lead is to accept the responsibility of enabling others to achieve purpose in the face of uncertainty. This is what teachers do every day. Ultimately, education is a political act. We are all activists. We have no other choice. With this comes a responsibility to ensure that we are fairly representing the views, needs and aspirations of our communities rather than the prolific and vociferous few having their views exposed to politicians, sculpting the debate that may well be at odds with those who need representation the most.

The process of flipping the system is always in flux. It is iterative. It is an ongoing global conversation between education stakeholders. Like Kneyber and Evers' (2013) pre-Flip-the-System book, *Het alternatief*, this book offers alternative ways of considering, doing and thinking about education to much of what is presented by the current systems across the world. While *Flip the*

System Australia is partly about revealing issues in education, our focus is not on deficit or polarising narratives, but on solutions and alternatives. Some of the contributions within are alarming. Some are inspiring. Many suggest different ways of being, teaching, leading and speaking. We do not claim that the contributions here speak for all Australian educators. Rather, we present these diverse but collective perspectives as part of the iteration of education policy, research, narrative and practice.

As we were editing this book, we were reminded of the lyrics of some iconic Australian songs. The Paul Kelly song 'From little things big things grow' is reminiscent of the way that a few voices or the seed of an idea can grow into something much bigger, in the way that Flip the System is now a burgeoning snowball of a movement. This is the third Flip the System book, but it is not the last. Midnight Oil's 'Beds are burning' paints a picture of the Australian landscape and talks of fairness. It calls Australians to action around the treatment of Indigenous Australians. It tells us we cannot stand by when the system is unjust. The lyrics of another song have also resonated with us: 'You're the voice', a 1986 protest song written by Chris Thompson, Andy Qunta, Maggie Ryder and Keith Reid, and performed by Australian singer John Farnham. It has been called Australia's unofficial national anthem. The song is about people using their voice, speaking up, and standing together, in order to make a difference. As the song suggests, the authors in this book are standing together with a shared purpose. At the essence of this book are a multiplicity of voices from education standing together, not only to challenge the system, but to speak up with the aim of an education system that best serves its students, trusts its leaders, and honours its teachers. This book is our offering to the process of questioning, refining, and being open to change, rather than codifying and replicating what we currently have in education.

This book speaks hope into education discourse through the stories and experiences of those already subverting the system: teachers, leaders and scholars leading change, building a culture of trust, respect, collective strength, and professional dialogue and reflection. Flipping the system is more about creating and nurturing cultures than it is about installing structures. It interrogates what it means to be educated and educator, and the role played by schools, policies and people. Evers and Kneyber (2016) conceptualised flipping the system as turning a hierarchical pyramid on its head. Rycroft-Smith and Dutaut (2018) claimed that flipping the system is about emboldening teachers as networked agents. We argue that flipping the system is about flattening the system, while more tightly interconnecting the members of that system. We argue for a system in which multiple education voices and stakeholders can dialogue constructively, respectfully and representatively. Democratising the system means liquefying top-down power structures and fostering trust and collaboration. It means that those from within and across the education system work together for the good of the students and families being served by the system. This is ultimately a book about the human aspects of education, so often forgotten in our data-obsessed world of numbers and metrics. Flipping the system means focusing on lived experiences, nuances, contexts, and the humanity of education. It means trusting and listening closely to the people within the system. It means co-constructing a system—of distributed, webbed, non-hierarchical and productive networks—from the ground up and the middle out. Flipping the education system is a vision for empowered teachers, supported school leaders, and a world in which the privileged few do not eclipse or speak for those pushed to the margins.

References

Evers, J. and Kneyber, R. eds., 2016. *Flip the system: Changing education from the ground up*. Abingdon: Routledge.

Graham, L.J., Van Bergen, P., and Sweller, N., 2015. 'To educate you to be smart': disaffected students and the purpose of school in the (not so clever) 'lucky country'. *Journal of Education Policy*, 30 (2), 237–257.

Horne, D. 1964. *The lucky country*. Sydney: Penguin Books.

Kneyber, R. and Evers, J., 2013. *Het alternatief: Weg met de afrekencultuur in het onderwijs!* Amsterdam: Boom.

Rycroft-Smith, L. and Dutaut, J.L. eds., 2018. *Flip the System UK: A teachers' manifesto*. Abingdon: Routledge.

Sachs, J., 2003. *The activist teaching profession*. Buckingham: Open University Press.

List of contributors

Teacher and school leader **Jon Andrews** has 20 years' experience of working in a variety of school settings in the UK and Australia. He is currently responsible for leading whole-school professional learning and coaching and supports staff to develop professional knowledge and practice. He tweets as @Obi_Jon and is co-editor of *Flip the System Australia*.

Gert Biesta is Professor of Education in the Department of Education of Brunel University London and Visiting Professor at NLA University College, Bergen, Norway. He holds the NIVOZ Professorship for Education at the University for Humanistic Studies, the Netherlands. He is co-editor of two book-series with Routledge: *New Directions in the Philosophy of Education* and *Theorising Education*.

Susan Bradbeer is a secondary school English teacher and PhD Candidate at Deakin University, living and working in a rural space. Her research interests in rurality, gender, leadership, and teacher identity has led to her online involvement with #womenEd and #womenEdAus, a grassroots movement which connects existing and aspiring women in education. She tweets as @suzbradbeer and blogs at jesterflys.wordpress.com.

Dr Paul Browning has led two large independent schools. His strongly held belief is that it is the head who creates the conditions for learning to flourish. Browning's PhD study examined the importance of trust and how a leader can establish it. He has published numerous articles and spoken across the world on the importance of trust.

Dr Carol Campbell is Associate Professor of Leadership and Educational Change and Co-Director of the Knowledge Network for Applied Education Research Secretariat at the Ontario Institute for Studies in Education, University of Toronto. Carol's recent co-authored books include: *Teacher learning and leadership: Of, by and for teachers*, *Empowering Educators in Canada* and *Empowered educators*.

As an International Senior Associate with the Innovation Unit, **Keren Caple** assists with innovation in education, particularly in the Asia Pacific region. Keren spent the last five years of her career working on improving and innovating teaching and leadership throughout Australia as General Manager of the Australian Institute of Teaching and School Leadership.

Kelly Cheung is a feminist, activist, teacher–researcher who brings working class knowledges to the mainstream in order to confront and disrupt an unequal education system. She holds a BMedia, Grad Dip Ed., MInternational Relations, MResearch, and is a PhD candidate with Macquarie University.

Flossie S. G. Chua is a Senior Research Manager at Project Zero, whose work focuses on nurturing good thinking and the capacity for informed and positive action. Her projects explore emerging practices of progressive pedagogies in schools, the leadership structures that support them, and innovative paradigms for visual artists and the arts.

Rebecca Cody started her teaching career at St Michael's Collegiate School in Tasmania and then PLC Perth, where she rose to Head of Senior School. Her first principalship was at Woodford House, New Zealand, at the age of 31. She was principal of MLC Perth from 2009 to 2017, and in 2018 Rebecca became the 12th principal of Geelong Grammar School.

Benjamin Doxtdator embraces teaching as an act of resistance and care. His days are full of the joy and hard work of teaching middle school students how to read and write more critically at the International School of Brussels. Benjamin has an MA in philosophy from McMaster and BEd from OISE.

Scott Eacott is Director of the Office of Educational Leadership in the School of Education, UNSW Sydney. He is widely published with contributions falling into three areas: relational theorising, strategy in education, and school leadership preparation and development. Find him on Twitter @ScottEacott or at scotteacott.com.

Melissa Fotea has worked with young people for the past 20 years in private practice and with *Youth Off The Streets* for the past nine years. As a naturopath and psychotherapist, her focus is the wellbeing of young people. Melissa has presented to schools and education conferences and is currently a Training Facilitator with *Youth Off The Streets*.

A K-6 educator, **Carla Gagliano** is passionate about teaching for understanding and supporting all learners to become critical and creative thinkers. She is currently a classroom teacher and Head of Teaching and Learning (ELC-Year 6) at Masada College, Sydney. The wonders of young minds and reflecting on those 'ah-ha' moments are what Carla loves most about being part of education.

Ryan Gill is a passionate advocate for critical and creative thinking. Having taught in the UK and Australia, his current role, as Head of Teaching and Learning (7–12) is at Masada College in Sydney. Ryan is a key figure in the development of Cultures of Thinking across Australia and a founding member of the Project Zero Sydney Network.

As director of *Cut Through Coaching & Consulting*, **Dan Haesler** has acted as a consultant on government education projects, corporate business, schools, professional associations, *The Black Dog Institute* and other not-for-profit organisations. Dan is an international keynote speaker and has presented alongside well-known education thought leaders as well as Olympians, Academy Award Winners and His Holiness the Dalai Lama.

Gavin Hays has led pedagogical change in both his current role as Leader of Learning at the Catholic Education, Diocese of Parramatta, as well as in his former role as Assistant Principal at Parramatta Marist (2012-2016), specifically in contemporary learning pedagogies. He is currently undertaking doctoral studies in educational psychology through Erasmus University, Rotterdam.

Andy Hargreaves is Professor at Boston College and the University of Ottawa. He is President of the International Congress for School Effectiveness and Improvement. Andy's books have attracted multiple Outstanding Writing Awards. His most recent book (with Michael O'Connor) is *Collaborative professionalism: When teaching together means learning for all.*

Adam Hendry is the current assistant principal at Parramatta Marist High. Since 2008, he has been involved in the implementation and development of project/problem-based learning at the school. He holds a BA, DipEd, a Master's Degree in Ancient History, and is currently undertaking doctoral studies in educational psychology through Erasmus University, Rotterdam.

Dr Anna Hogan is a lecturer at the University of Queensland, Australia. She is currently researching the commercialisation of education policy and practice and is involved in projects investigating the commercialisation of Australian public schooling, the for-profit delivery of schooling and the commercialisation of student health and wellbeing.

Melitta Hogarth is a Kamilaroi woman who is also the Indigenous Education Lecturer at the University of Southern Queensland. Prior to entering academia, Melitta taught for almost 20 years in all three sectors of the Queensland education system. Melitta's interests are in education, equity and social justice. She is currently a PhD candidate at Queensland University of Technology.

Tomaz Lasic is a Humanities and Design and Technology teacher of 18 years, almost exclusively in the low socio-economic areas of metropolitan Perth, Western Australia. He is interested in the ways in which young people and fellow educators learn and express what they are becoming and how education is shaping them to do so. Tomaz is a blogger, tweeter, and questioner.

Ben Lewis is the Indigenous Program Coordinator at Wesley College, Perth, and a member of staff at the University of Notre Dame Fremantle for their Working with Indigenous Students course. He works closely with local Elders and the Nyoongar community to facilitate authentic and engaging cultural experiences that empower Aboriginal and Torres Strait Islander students.

Dr Bob Lingard is Emeritus Professor at the University of Queensland. His research is located within the sociology of education with a focus on education policy. His most recent books include *Globalising educational accountabilities* and *Politics, policies and pedagogues in education*. He is also editor of the journal *Discourse: Studies in the Cultural Politics of Education*.

Rachel Lofthouse is Professor of Teacher Education in the Carnegie School of Education at Leeds Beckett University. She has a specific research interest in professional learning, exploring how teachers learn and how they can be supported to put that learning into practice. Rachel was previously Senior Lecturer at Newcastle University, and co-director for the Research Centre for Learning and Teaching.

Kevin Lowe, a Gubbi Gubbi man from southeast Queensland, has had extensive educational experience including being a high school teacher, TAFE administrator, University lecturer, and NSW Board of Studies Inspector, Aboriginal Education. He is an Indigenous Post-Doctoral Fellow at Macquarie University undertaking research on working towards the development of sustainable, culturally enhancing model of educational improvement for Aboriginal students.

Cameron Malcher is the producer of the Teachers' Education Review Podcast. Having worked as a teacher, head teacher and curriculum advisor for the NSW Department of Education over 11 years, Cameron is currently the Communications Officer of the NSW Teachers Federation. Cameron holds a Masters in Educational Psychology, and is not averse to the sound of his own voice.

Chris Munro is a Director with Growth Coaching International. In this role he provides coaching, and facilitates coaching training programs, for educators across Victoria and beyond. Chris has extensive experience in supporting and leading the development of teacher professional learning strategy in government and independent schools, and in higher education.

Dr Deborah M. Netolicky has almost 20 years' experience in teaching and school leadership in Australia and the UK. She works to flip the system from the inside out and shift education narratives via the intersections of practice and research around school leadership, professional learning and identity. She blogs at theeduflaneuse.com and tweets as @debsnet.

Michael T. O'Connor PhD, is the assistant director of the Providence Alliance for Catholic Teachers program at Providence College in Providence, Rhode

Island, USA. A former middle school English Language Arts teacher and instructional coach, Michael's research interests include writing, language and literacies, and international designs of collaborative professionalism in education.

Cameron Paterson leads learning and teaching at Shore School in North Sydney. He has taught high school History for more than two decades. He also works for Harvard Project Zero at the Project Zero Classroom institute and as an online course instructor.

David N. Perkins is the Carl H. Pforzheimer, Jr., Research Professor of Teaching and Learning, Emeritus, at the Harvard Graduate School of Education. He has conducted long-term programs of research and development in the areas of teaching and learning for understanding, creativity, problem-solving and reasoning in the arts, sciences, and everyday life.

David Rutkowski is an Associate Professor with a joint appointment in Educational Policy and Educational Inquiry at Indiana University, USA. His interests include how large scale assessments are used within policy debates, the impact of background questionnaire quality on achievement results, and achievement estimation in heterogeneous populations.

Pasi Sahlberg is a Finnish educator and widely published author who has worked as schoolteacher, teacher educator, researcher, and policy advisor in Finland and has studied education systems, analysed education policies, and advised education reforms around the world. He is a Professor of Education Policy at the Gonski Institute for Education at the University of New South Wales.

Sam Sellar is Reader in Education Studies at Manchester Metropolitan University. His current research focuses on large-scale assessments, data infrastructures, commercialisation and new accountabilities in schooling. Sam's recent books include *The global education race: Taking the measure of PISA and international testing* and *Globalising educational accountabilities*.

Yasodai Selvakumaran is a Humanities teacher, Practicum Coordinator and Professional Practice Mentor at Rooty Hill High School. She is a trained classroom observer and has curriculum expertise in History and Society/Culture. In 2017, she was named one of *The Educator's 30 under 35 'Rising Stars'* in Australian Education.

Greg Thompson is Associate Professor of Education Research at Queensland University of Technology. His research focuses on educational theory, education policy, and the philosophy/sociology of education assessment and measurement with a particular emphasis on large-scale testing. Recent books include *The Global Education Race: Taking the Measure of PISA and International Testing, National Testing in Schools: An Australian Assessment* and *The Education Assemblage*.

Ray Trotter has been the principal of Wooranna Park Primary School in Dandenong North, Victoria, since 1987. In 2007 Ray was the co-recipient of Monash University's 'Jeff Northfield Memorial Award for Excellence in Research' and in 2009, Deakin University named their Flexible Learning Centre after him. Ray's qualifications include: FACE, BA, BEd, and Trained Primary Teachers Certificate.

Shaneé Washington, a former middle school teacher, is a PhD candidate and teaching fellow at Boston College and recipient of the Donald J. White Teaching Excellence Award. She also serves as a lecturer at Brandeis University. Her dissertation investigates family-school-community engagement in a New England, USA school district with a specific focus on Indigenous families.

Daniel G. Wilson is the director of Project Zero at the Harvard Graduate School of Education where he is a Principal Investigator, a Lecturer of Education, and the Faculty Chair of its Learning Environments for Tomorrow Institute. His research focuses on collaboration and group learning across a variety of contexts.

Index

Page numbers in italics refer to figures.

Aboriginal and Torres Strait Islander Education Advisory Group (ATSIEAG) 111
Aboriginal and Torres Strait Islander students 125–130, 133–136; discourses of *see* contradictory discourses
Aboriginal community engagement *see* Indigenous and Aboriginal community engagement
Aboriginal Education Consultative Groups (AECG) 129
Aboriginal traditions 234–235, 238
accountability: and binary thinking 202; 'fair go' diagnosis 199–200; hyper- 163, 166, 242; meaning making 200–202; overview 198–199; test-based 152–153
ACER *see* Australian Council for Educational Research (ACER)
active listening/empathic listening 210
Advanced Leadership Program for Women 218
AECG *see* Aboriginal Education Consultative Groups (AECG)
AERA *see* American Educational Research Association (AERA)
AEU *see* Australian Education Union (AEU)
The Age 224
agency, trust and 64–65
AISNSW *see* Association of Independent Schools New South Wales (AISNSW)
AITSL *see* Australian Institute for Teaching and School Leadership (AITSL)
ALL *see* Australian Learning Lecture (ALL)
Allen, David 183

alternative education programs: and 'disengaged' students 139–140; and engagement 137–139; *vs.* mainstream schooling 143–144; overview 137; and SDT *see* Self Determination Theory (SDT)
American Educational Research Association (AERA) 60
American Psychological Association (APA) 60
Anderson, Francis 117
Andrews, Jon 1, 163, 242
APA *see* American Psychological Association (APA)
Ashmore, Yvonne 236
Association of Independent Schools New South Wales (AISNSW) 69
ATAR league tables 2, 100
ATSIEAG *see* Aboriginal and Torres Strait Islander Education Advisory Group (ATSIEAG)
auctors 191, 193, 195
Australia: Capital Territory 58; curriculums 24; Indigenous education policy 109
Australian Council for Educational Research (ACER) 24, 101, 223
Australian Department of Education and Training 215
Australian Education Union (AEU) 19, 21
Australian Educators' Online Network 42
Australian Institute for Teaching and School Leadership (AITSL) 2, 10, 20–21, 28, 70, 214, 216, 223
Australian Learning Lecture (ALL) 90

Australian Principal Health and Wellbeing Survey 4
Australian Professional Standards for Teachers 2, 10, 164, 165
'Autonomous Learners Card' 228
'Autonomous Learning Unit for Year 5 & 6 Students' 222
autonomy: collective 9, 98; SDT 142

baby boomers 214
Ball, Stephen J. 2, 164, 173
Bandura, Albert 86–87
Basic School Reform 150
Bastow Institute of Educational Leadership 216, 218
Bates, Richard 190
Beaconhills College 233–241
The Beautiful Risk of Education (Biesta) 43
Beijaard, Douwe 11
belonging/relatedness 142–143
Bennis, Warren 207
Bentley, Tom 224
BIA *see* Bridge International Academies (BIA)
Biesta, Gert J. J. 43–44, 163, 165, 167
Big Picture learning design 145
binary thinking 202
Birmingham, Simon 55
Blase, Joseph and Jo 208
Bloomfield, Di 25
Blythe, Tina 183
Borat (2016) 55
boundary crossing events 90
boundary-spanning relationships 70
Bourke, Terri 25
Bradbeer, Susan 214
Breidenstein, Angela 67
Bridge International Academies (BIA) 49
British Columbia 65–67
British Columbia Education Plan 65
Browning, Paul 204
Bryk, Anthony 169, 207
Butler, Judith 49

Caldis, Susan 89
Campbell, Carol 74
Campbell, Corinne 39, 41
Campbelltown Performing Arts High School 67–69
Canadian Teachers' Federation (CTF) 77
The Canberra Times 120
Caple, Keren 64
caring costs, of teachers 94

Catching Up: Learning from the Best School Systems in East Asia 56
Chetty, Darren 44
Cheung, Kelly 115
Chua, Flossie S. G. 232
Church, Mark 182
City Connects 100
Clarke, Matthew 164
Closing the Gap: Prime Minister's Report 2016 107, 108
coaching, for teacher agency: description 166–168; ecological growth *vs.* mechanistic improvement 168–170; overview 163; and performativity 163–164; standards for 164–166
Cody, Rebecca 198
Cognitive Coaching 12
Cohen, Sascha Baron 55
coherent practice 192–195
collaborative learning, by design 67–69
collaborative professionalism 79–81, 98–99
collaborative structures, of LLtM 237–238
collective autonomy 98
Collective Teacher Efficacy (CTE) 85–88
College Montserrat 226
Collins, Sue 240
commercialisation: affordances of 22–23; challenges of 23–25; overview 19; teacher deprofessionalisation and diminished wellbeing 25–27; teacher professionalism and system restructuring 20–21
competence, in students 141–142
Connell, Robert W. 121
continual professional development (CPD): overview 172–173; performativity 173–175; as professional intent 175–177; re-thinking 177–180
contradictory discourses: description 108, 111–112; overview 107–108; policy discourses 109–110; political discourses 108–109; representations 110; role of non-Indigenous people 110–111
The Conversation 224
Cook, Henrietta 224
Coolangatta Statement on Indigenous Peoples' Rights in Education 110, 112
Council of Australian Governments 110
CPD *see* continual professional development (CPD)
creative reimagining 71–72
Cronbach, L. J. 60

cross-school teams 71
CTE *see* Collective Teacher Efficacy (CTE)
CTF *see* Canadian Teachers' Federation (CTF)
cultural interface 124
culture of trust: achieving 208–209; importance of 206–208; leadership practices to engender 209–212; overview 204–206
curriculums: Australian 24; practice, state-led 155–156; school-based 151–152, 155–156
custodianship 234

Danielson Framework for Teaching 12, 16n1
Data Boards 224
Deans of Southern Cross University 93
Deci, Edward 140
decisional capital 82
democratic professionalism 175
de-privatisation, of professional practices 78–79
Descriptive Consultancy 184
digital learning 229
'disengaged' students 139–140
Doxdator, Benjamin 43
Doxtator, Honyery 47
Drive (Pink) 140
Drucker, Peter 207
dual operating systems 68
Duckworth, A. L. 199
Dutaut, Jean-Louis 169, 173

Eacott, Scott 189
ecological growth: *vs.* mechanistic improvement 168–170
Edelman 207
Edmondson, Amy C 68
'Educating Australia—why our schools aren't improving' 224
Educational Goals for Young Australians 158
education: alternative, engagement and 137–139; alternative *vs.* mainstream schooling education 143–144; budgeting 157; fairness 149–150; in Kazakhstan 55–56; limit 34; measurement industry, global 30; outcomes of 31; policy, Indigenous education 109; public 78–79; sample-based evaluation systems 151; *see also* alternative education programs; equitable education; new education paradigm; teacher-led educational improvement
'The Education of Girls' 117
educators: meetings 193–194; wellbeing *see* teachers' wellbeing
Eleanor Davis School Leadership Program 218
ELEVATE community 69–70
Elmore, Richard 2, 69, 71, 166
empathic listening/active listening 210
engagement, and alternative education 137–139
Enigma Missions 226–227
Enigma Portal 226
equitable education: in Finland 150–153; fixing 153–157; funding equally to investing in 157; overview 149–150; standardised teaching and individualised learning 156; state-led and school-based curriculum practice 155–156
Escuela Nueva 99
Evers, Jelmer 1, 3, 5, 243–245
Every Student Succeeds Act (2015) 96
evidence-informed professional judgement 76–77

Feniger, Yariv 62
Finland: culture of trust in 204–205; equitable education in 150–153; special education system in 156
First Nations 47
flipped school leadership: articulating with clarity 190–192; coherent practice 192–195; leading narrative 195–196; overview 189–190
Fotea, Melissa 137
'Foundation for Young Australians' (FYA) 223
Friedman, Tom 71
From the Campfire to the Holodeck (Thornburg) 226
Fullan, Michael 48–49, 155, 166, 227
FYA *see* 'Foundation for Young Australians' (FYA)

Gagliano, Carla 182
Gallup Student Poll 137–138, 143
Gardner, Howard 70
Garrett, Peter 102

Generation Z 225
George, Lynette 235, 237–239
GERM *see* Global Educational Reform Movement (GERM)
Gifted and Talented Resource Centre 222
Gill, Ryan 182
Gillard, Julia 56, 224
Global Educational Reform Movement (GERM) 222, 223
global education measurement industry 30
Gonski, David 2, 74, 81, 99, 154–155, 157–158
Gorur, Radhika 224
Graeber, David 48
Grattan Institute 56, 157
Gronn, Peter 216
Grumet, Madeleine R. 116
Gunter, Helen M. 216

Haesler, Dan 137
Hannon, Valerie 227
Hargreaves, Andy 93, 155, 173, 208
Harvard Graduate School of Education 182, 233
Hattie, John A. C. 46, 48, 195
Hawke, Bob 198
Hays, Gavin 85
Hendry, Adam 85
Hesperia School 156
Higher School Certificate (HSC) 86, 140, 183, 189, 191, 192
Highly Accomplished and Lead certification 165
high-quality schooling 59
Hobbs, Linda 90
Hogan, Anna 19
Hogarth, Melitta 107
holistic learning 236
Holland, D. 11
holodeck 226, 230n2
Holper, Paul 222–223
HSC *see* Higher School Certificate (HSC)
HSIE *see* Human Society and Its Environment (HSIE)
human capital 49, 82
humanity, development of 74–76
Human Society and Its Environment (HSIE) 89–91
hyper-accountability 163, 166, 242

ILSAs *see* International Large-Scale Assessments (ILSAs)
Imagining the Future (Torok and Holper) 222
Independent Review into Regional, Rural and Remote Education 215
Independent Schools Council of Australia 40
Independent Schools Victoria 234
Indigenous and Aboriginal community engagement: benefits of 127–129; overview 124–126; purpose 126–127; questions and strategies 129–130
Indigenous Critical Discourse Analysis 107
Indigenous cultural learning programmes 133–136, 234–235, 237–238
individual development, and LLtM 238–239
individualised learning 156
Ingvarson, Lawrence 101
innovation *see* networks, and innovation
instructional leadership 195
International Large-Scale Assessments (ILSAs): Australia *vs.* Kazakhstan 55–56; description 59; PISA 57–59; validity 59–62
International Summit on the Teaching Profession (2018) 95

Jantzi, Doris 216
Jerrim, J. 62

Kazakhstan, education in 55–56
Kennedy, Aileen 176–177
Kenny, John 90
Key Learning Area 91
K-12 Innovation Partnership 66
Klein, Naomi 48
Kneyber, René 3, 5
'Knights of Knowledge' program 226
Korthagen, Fred 168
Kriedemann, Brett 173

Ladson-Billings, Gloria 45
Ladwig, James G. 192
Lampert, Magdalene 180
landownership 234
Langer, Jessica 228
Langworthy, Maria 48
Lasic, Tomaz 145
LAST *see* Looking at Students' Thinking (LAST)

Index 257

leadership: crisis 214; instructional 195; practices to engender culture of trust 209–212; women's, in rural schools 216–218; *see also* flipped school leadership
Leading Learning that Matters (LLtM): at Beaconhills College 234–235; collaborative structures of 237–238; and individual development 238–239; key leadership practices 235–240; overview 233–234; shared vision of 236; sustaining progress 239–240
learnification 35, 43
learning: collaborative, by design 67–69; digital 229; holistic 236; Indigenous cultural, programmes for 133–136, 234–235, 237–238; individualised 156; project-based (PjBL) 85, 87; teaching and 195; *see also* professional learning
Learning Community 225, 228
Learning Frontiers 70–71
'Learning Frontiers Program' 223, 227
'Learning Symposiums' 228
Lefstein, Adam 62
Leithwood, Kenneth 216
Lesson Study protocols 99
Lewis, Ben 133
Lewis, Stephan 224
Lingard, Bob 19
Linsley, Jan 175
listening, active/empathic 210
LLtM *see* Leading Learning that Matters (LLtM)
Lofthouse, Rachel 172
Looking at Students' Thinking (LAST) 184
Loveless, Tom 62
Lowe, Kevin 124

Malcher, Cameron 39
McGinley, Stephen 236
McKinsey 44
MADALAH Indigenous Youth Leadership Program Scholarship 135
Maddock, Sam 237–239
mainstream schooling: *vs.* alternative education 143–144
Makaton 175
Makerspace 145–148
managerial professionalism 175
Māori students, achievement of 47, 49, 125–126
Marr, David 189, 191

Marzano, Robert 45–46
Masada College 182, 185
Masters, Geoff 223, 224
MATSITI *see* More Aboriginal and Torres Strait Islander Teachers Initiative (MATSITI)
Maxton, James 198
May, Josephine 119
mechanistic improvement: *vs.* ecological growth 168–170
Meijer, Paulien 11
Melbourne Declaration on Educational Goals for Young Australians 1, 59, 158
Mesman, Jessica 45–46
Metamorphosis *178*, 179
Midnight Oil 102
Milne, Anne 47, 49
mindless compliance 164
mining boom 206
Mockler, Nicole 12, 165
Moorditj Mob 133–134
Moore, Alex 164
More Aboriginal and Torres Strait Islander Teachers Initiative (MATSITI) 110
Munro, Chris 163
MySchool 206, 223–224

NAIDOC *see* National Aborigines and Islanders Day Observance Committee (NAIDOC)
Nakata, Martin 124
Nanus, B. 207
NAPLAN *see* National Assessment Program in Literacy and Numeracy (NAPLAN)
National Aboriginal and Torres Strait Islander Education Strategy 2015 109–111
National Aborigines and Islanders Day Observance Committee (NAIDOC) 134
National Assessment Program in Literacy and Numeracy (NAPLAN) 2, 10, 24, 86, 95–97, 99, 150, 152, 155, 189, 191–193, 206, 208, 223–224
National Council for Measurement in Education (NCME) 60
National Curriculum Framework 151
National Excellence in School Leadership Initiative (NESLI) 218
National Partnership for Improving Teacher Quality 10

National Policy for the Education of Girls (1987) 120
National Professional Standards for Teachers and Principals 10
NCME *see* National Council for Measurement in Education (NCME)
neoliberal 3, 4, 10, 11, 40, 43, 44, 49, 108, 121; neoliberalism xi, 48, 49, 119
NESLI *see* National Excellence in School Leadership Initiative (NESLI)
Netolicky, Deborah M. 1, 9, 242
networks, and innovation: British Columbia 65–67; Campbelltown Performing Arts High School 67–69; creative reimagining 71–72; ELEVATE community 69–70; Learning Frontiers 70–71; trust and agency 64–65
new education paradigm: implementation of 225–230; overview 222; principles of 225; purpose 222–224
'New Pedagogies for Deep Learning' 227
New South Wales (NSW) 86, 116, 118, 120, 133; Board of Studies 129; Department of Education 138, 142; out of field teaching 90; professional learning in 39–41; working class women in 115
New South Wales Teachers Federation (NSWTF) 21
New York Times 71
Niesche, Richard 10
Noongar people 146, 148n1
Nova Scotia, government of 93
NSW *see* New South Wales (NSW)
NSW Board of Studies 129
NSWTF *see* New South Wales Teachers Federation (NSWTF)

Oakeshott, Michael 190
O'Connor, Michael T. 93, 98, 102n1
OECD *see* Organisation for Economic Co-operation and Development (OECD)
OECD PISA study 151
Ontario Teachers' Federation 78
Organisational Trust Inventory (OTI) 209
Organisation for Economic Co-operation and Development (OECD) 57–58, 61, 96, 149, 153, 157–158, 205, 207, 224
organising activities 191, 193–195
OTI *see* Organisational Trust Inventory (OTI)

Outdoor Education programme 235, 237
out of field teaching 89–92
over-scaffolding corporate programs 91

parents, power of 32–33
Parramatta Marist High School 85–87
Pasifika students 47, 49
PAT *see* Progressive Achievement Tests (PAT)
Paterson, Cameron 1, 64, 242
PBL *see* problem-based learning (PBL)
pedagogies: culturally sustaining 45–47; signature 90
peer-coaching 87
performance slippage 153
performativity 4, 138; and coaching for agency 163–164; and CPD 173–175
Perkins, David N. 64, 232
PERMA theory 199
Perso, Thelma 125
Personalising Student Learning 226
Piccoli, Adrian 41
Pink, Daniel 140
Pink Floyd 145
PISA *see* Program for International Student Achievement (PISA)
PjBL *see* project-based learning (PjBL)
Policy and Program Memorandum (PPM) 80
policy discourses 109–110
political discourses 108–109
Porter, Theodore 47
positive discrimination policy 157
PPM *see* Policy and Program Memorandum (PPM)
Prep Professors Program 228
preschoolers, learning to use Blackwood leaves as soap *232*
Priestley, Mark 163, 167
problem-based learning (PBL) 85
Proctor, Helen 119
professional capital 66, 82
professional development 166
professional identities: overview 9–10; and performative drivers 10–12; vulnerable voices 15–16
professional identity formation 219
professional intent 175–177
professionalism 173–175
professional learning 152, 218–219; in Canada 75–77; celebration and reflection 184; culture of thinking 185; evolving process 184–185; in NSW

39–41; overview 182; puzzle of practice 183; Study Groups 182–184
Professional Practice Mentor 91, 3, 10, 164–166, 169
professional standards 10, 164–166
Program for International Student Achievement (PISA) 2–3, 41, 56–62, 74, 153, *154*
Progressive Achievement Tests (PAT) 24
project-based learning (PjBL) 85, 87
Project Zero 182, 233
public education 78–79
pupils, power of 33–34
Puttnam, Lord David 224
The Puzzle of Motivation (TED Talk) 140
puzzle of practice 183, 184–185
Pygmalion effect/Rosenthal effect 230n1

Queensland Curriculum and Assessment Authority (QCAA) 129
Queensland University of Technology 208
'Questions Sorts' 183

Realm of Concern/Realm of Influence protocol 184
Record of School Achievement 139–140
recruitment 194–195
Redfern Statement 107, 109, 112
#RedforEd movement 93
Reggio Emilia 225
Registered Training Organisation (RTO) 139
relatedness/belonging 142–143
relational approach 189, 194
Republic Polytechnic 85
research-based teaching methods 82
Research in Australian Educational Leadership 214
Restorative Practices 142–143
Review of Funding for Schooling 154
RHHS Creative Inquiry Cycle 90
Rickards, Field 101
Riley, Chris 139
risk, and vulnerability: culturally sustaining pedagogy 45–47; description 44–45; overview 43–44; technological disappointment and sacrifice zones 47–49
Ritchhart Ron 182
Robinson, Sarah 163, 167
Robinson, Sir Ken 223
Robinson, Viviane M. J. 195

Rolling Stones 33
Rooty Hill High School (RHHS) 89, 92
Rosenthal effect/Pygmalion effect 230n1
RTO *see* Registered Training Organisation (RTO)
rural schools: context 215; professional identity formation in 219; professional learning in 218–219; women's leadership in 216–218
Rutkowski, David 55
Ryan, Mary 25
Ryan, Richard 140
Rycroft-Smith, Lucy 169, 173

Sachs, Judyth 165, 175
sacrifice zones 47–49
Sahlberg, Pasi 149, 205, 223
sample-based educational evaluation systems 151
Savage, Catherine 125
Savage, Glen 224
Schleicher, Andreas 48, 72
Schneider, Benjamin 169, 207
school-based curriculums 151–152, 155–156
school choice 157–158
school performance 152–153
Schwandt, Thomas A. 59
SDT *see* Self Determination Theory (SDT)
Self Determination Theory (SDT): autonomy 142; belonging/relatedness 142–143; competence 141–142; overview 140
self-efficaciousness 86–87
self-inspection 150
Seligman, Martin E. 199
Sellar, Sam 55
Selvakumaran, Yasodai 89
SEND *see* Special Educational Needs and/or Disability (SEND)
Sergiovanni, Thomas 207–208
Service Learning 143
SES *see* socioeconomic status (SES)
shared vision, of LLtM 193, 236
Sharing the Learning Summit 78
Sheumack, Tony 234–240
signature pedagogies 90
Silicon Valley approach 43
Simkins, Tim 216
Six Key Pillars 235, 236
Smyth, John 191
social capital 82

social constructivism 177
social justice arguments 31
socioeconomic status (SES) 22
solidarity, and specificity: of teachers 98–99
spatio-temporal conditions 191, 193, 195
Special Educational Needs and/or Disability (SEND) 175
special education system 156
staff visibility 211
Stake, R. E. 59
standardised teaching 156
Standards for Educational and Psychological Testing 60
state-led curriculum practice 155–156
The State of Educators Professional Learning in Canada 75
STEAM Centre 229
Steinbach, Rosanne 216
Stiegelbauer, Suzanne 166
Stockholm syndrome 72
'Strategic Corporal' 72
strategy *see* National Aboriginal and Torres Strait Islander Education Strategy 2015
Student Bank 229
Student Parliament 228
students: academic achievement, and strength of socioeconomic gradient *151*; autonomy of 142; competence in 141–142; 'disengaged' 139–140; Māāori, achievement of 47, 49, 125–126; Pasifika 47, 49; vulnerable 94–95; *see also* Aboriginal and Torres Strait Islander students
Study Groups 182–184
'Supporting Women in their Leadership Journey' 218
system restructuring 20–21

TALIS *see* Teaching and Learning International Survey (TALIS)
teacher-led educational improvement: and collaborative professionalism 79–81; de-privatisation of professional practices 78–79; evidence-informed professional judgement 76–77; humanity development 74–76; overview 74; TLLP 78–79
Teacher Professional Learning business model 39–40
teachers: deprofessionalisation of 25–27; identities 90; power 34–36; professionalism 20–21

Teachers' Education Review Podcast: description 41–42; overview 39; professional learning in NSW 39–41
teachers' wellbeing: assessments 95–96, 101; caring cost 94; collaborating with competitors 99–100; collective autonomy 98; enhancing 98–101; expectations 95; external support and partnership 100–101; individualised solutions 96–97; initiatives 95; overview 93–94; six threats to 94–97; solidarity and specificity 98–99; vulnerable students 94–95
teaching: and learning 195; out of field 89–92; research-based methods 82; standardised 156
Teaching and Learning International Survey (TALIS) 75
Teaching School 175–177
technological disappointment 47–49
Te kotahitanga program 125
Tell Them From Me survey 138, 142
test-based accountability 152–153
Tewahangarakhen, Honyery 47
Thomson, Greg 55
Thomson, Pat 10, 190, 216
Thornburg, David 226
Through Growth to Achievement 74
Thrupp, Martin 25
TIMSS *see* Trends in Mathematics and Science Study (TIMSS)
TLLP 78–79
TLM *see* Transformational Leadership Measurement (TLM)
Torok, Simon 222–223
Towards a New End: New Pedagogies for Deep Learning (NPDL) 48
Transformational Leadership Measurement (TLM) 209
Trends in Mathematics and Science Study (TIMSS) 2, 55–56
Trotter, Ray 222
trust, and agency 64–65
Trust Barometer 207
Trust in Schools (Bryk and Schneider) 207
Tuning 184
Turnbull, Malcolm 107, 108, 113
Twitter 172
Uluru Statement from the Heart 109, 112–113
UNDRIP *see* The United Nations Declaration on the Rights of Indigenous Peoples (UNDRIP)

The United Nations Declaration on the Rights of Indigenous Peoples (UNDRIP) 112

'Usable Knowledge' 228

van Nieuwerburgh, Christian 166
Vass, Greg 125
Ventilla, Max 48
Verloop, Nico 11
Vickers, Margaret 120
Victorian Education Department 222
Vietnam War 64
Vine, Jennie 226, 228
Visible Thinking 183
vulnerability *see* risk, and vulnerability

Wallace, Jim 211
Washington, Shaneé 93, 102n1
Watterston, Barbara 214, 216, 218
Wesley College 133–135

'what works' approach, to leadership development 3, 10, 47, 49, 214, 216, 220
Wiliam, Dylan 3, 141
Wilson, Daniel G. 232
Wilson, Viv 174
women leading rural schools: description 216–218; flipping the system for 220; overview 214–215; and professional identity formation 219; and professional learning 218–219; rural context 215
Wooranna Park Primary School 222, *227*, 228–229
working class girls, school lives of 115–118, 120–122
Working with Aboriginal Communities 129
World Economic Forum 43
Wright, Nigel 189

Youth Off The Streets 137, 139–144

Zak, Paul 209

For Product Safety Concerns and Information please contact our EU
representative GPSR@taylorandfrancis.com
Taylor & Francis Verlag GmbH, Kaufingerstraße 24, 80331 München, Germany

www.ingramcontent.com/pod-product-compliance
Lightning Source LLC
Chambersburg PA
CBHW051538230426
43669CB00015B/2637